John Bennnluis
Guillaume Budé
Paris, 1997

# Sophistical Rhetoric
# in Classical Greece

Studies in Rhetoric/Communication
Thomas W. Benson, General Editor

# Sophistical Rhetoric in Classical Greece

John Poulakos

University of South Carolina Press

The author acknowledges the following sources for their permission to use previously published material in this book: From "Terms for Sophistical Rhetoric" in *Rethinking the History of Rhetoric*, edited by Takis Poulakos, copyright 1993; by permission of Westview Press, Boulder, Colo. From "Toward a Sophistical Definition of Rhetoric," *Philosophy and Rhetoric* 16, no. 1 (1983): 35–48, copyright 1983 by Pennsyvania State University; by permission of Penn State Press, University Park, Penn. From "Early Changes in Rhetorical Practice and Understanding: From the Sophists to Isocrates," *Texte: Revue de Critique et Théorie Littéraire* 8–9 (1989): 307–24; by permission of Les Editions Paratexte Ltees, Toronto. From "Rhetoric, the Sophists, and the Possible," *Communication Monographs* 51, no. 3 (1984): 215–26; by permission of Speech Communication Association, Annandale, Va. From "The Possibility of Rhetoric's Early Beginnings," in *The Van Zelst Lecture in Communication*, copyright 1991; by permission of Northwestern University, Evanston, Ill.

Published in Columbia, South Carolina, by the University of South Carolina Press

Manufactured in the United States of America

Library of Congress Cataloging-in-Publication Data

Poulakos, John, 1948–
    Sophistical rhetoric in classical Greece / John Poulakos.
        p.    cm. — (Studies in rhetoric/communication)
    Includes bibliographical references and index.
    Contents: Sophistical rhetoric and its circumstances — Terms for sophistical rhetoric — Plato's reception of the sophists — Isocrates' reception of the sophists — Aristotle's reception of the sophists.
    ISBN 0–87249–899–9
    1. Rhetoric, Ancient. 2. Sophists (Greek philosophy) I. Title. II. Series.
PA3265.P68  1994
808'.0481—dc20                                                94–18680

*To Dionysius, a master of opportunities*
*To Anastasia, a servant of proprieties*
*To Valy, a visionary of possibilities*

# Contents

# A Note on Translations and Editions Used

When citing material from or about the sophists in English, I am using the translations found in Rosamond K. Sprague, ed., *The Older Sophists* (Columbia: University of South Carolina Press, 1972). I am also using her system of reference. Thus, in the citation "Gorgias (82B.8)," "82" refers to Gorgias; "B" refers to the section entitled Fragments; and "8" refers to a fragment attributed to Gorgias by Clement. When citing in Greek, I am using Hermann Diels, *Die Fragmente der Vorsokratiker*, 2nd ed. (Berlin: Weidmannsche Buchhandlung, 1922).

When citing from Plato in English, I am using the translations in Edith Hamilton and Huntington Cairns, eds., *The Collected Dialogues of Plato* (Princeton: Princeton University Press, 1973), or those in the Loeb texts. In some cases, I am using a combination of the two.

When citing in Greek, I am using the Loeb texts for Plato. Unless otherwise noted, I am also using the Loeb texts in the case of Isocrates, Aristotle, Aristophanes, Thucydides, and the other ancient authors.

No author I know of has found a satisfactory solution to the problem of using the personal or possessive pronouns (third person singular) so that, when their reference is a gender-free noun (i.e., person, politician), they treat the masculine and feminine genders equally. This problem has been especially acute while writing this book, which includes close readings and exact translations of passages in Greek, a language whose nouns are masculine, feminine, or neuter. As the reader will notice, my use of the aforementioned pronouns in this book is not uniform throughout. When discussing matters reflecting the Hellenic culture of the fifth and fourth centuries B.C., or when explicating a particular Greek passage, I have used "he" and "his" to refer to a masculine noun. But when I generalize and my comments apply to modernity, I have used "(s)he" and "his/her" to refer to a gender-free noun.

It is noteworthy that the Greeks, too, had concerns, although different from ours, about the gender of particular nouns and pronouns. See, for example Aristophanes' *Clouds* (685 ff.) and Aristotle's *Sophistical Refutations* (chap. 14).

# Orientation

Broadly speaking, this book is about our capacity for and susceptibility to rhetoric, two characteristics that for many centuries have been construed mostly as liabilities and once in a great while as endowments. Since the time of the pre-Socratics, people have been schooled to think of their capacity for most words as a proclivity to error, excess, or indulgence. Moreover, they have been trained to believe that their susceptibility to the charming words of others constitutes a weakness to be overcome by means of such fortifying agents as approved versions of reason, dialectical know-how, and objectivity. The logic of this kind of inculcation rests on the axiom that most human beings are deficient by nature, and the corollary that they need to be improved. According to self-righteous church figures, shrewd tyrants, and unwise thinkers, improvement consists of espousing their moralistic blueprints, following their political manifestos, and adopting their hyperlogical schemata respectively. In their minds, betterment demands that one become increasingly knowing, rational, and moral; at the same time it requires that one overcome ignorance, irrationality, and evil in its linguistic manifestations. In its simplest form, this directive amounts to the approval of some words and the disapproval of others. That this is so becomes apparent when one notes that the lessons of the improvers of humankind have generally sought justification in appeals to destiny, divine revelation, or clear and distinct ideas; and it also becomes apparent when one discovers that most improvers have consistently warned against any language that allows for human passions, inexplicable desires, or efforts to constitute one's life the best way one can. Linking such language to the devil term sophistry, they have propagated a pervasive logophobia, the fear that untamed utterances spell calamity and that uninspected discourses can lead to yet another Fall. In conjunction with this fear, they have also issued time and again this warning about the human capacity to listen: it must discriminate between various voices and turn itself obediently only to the one voice that really knows; the one that speaks with the authority of the hidden secrets of the universe. Between the injunction for muffled, endlessly qualified, or silent speech on the one hand, and the directive for exclusive attentiveness to the authentic voice of the Logos on the other, rhetoric has always had to reassert itself and demonstrate its necessity.

In contrast to their logophobic schooling, people have been reassured from time to time that their capacity for rhetoric distinguishes them from animals and accounts for human civilization. Whether this reassurance ever made anyone feel affirmed as a human being is very doubtful. Equally doubtful is the notion that the belief in our mastery over animals or our genius for civilization suffices to render the worth of our being unquestionable. One need not go very far to see that much of what we are is animal; and human civilization is far from a marvelous accomplishment in which we can all delight self-contentedly, without shame. Therefore, when one wishes to have influence on others, being assured of one's domination over animals can only serve as a meaningless form of consolation; and when one wonders about one's place in the world, being reminded of the progress of civilization can only fuel self-doubts and intensify one's alienation from others.

Someone once said that if you tell people for a hundred years that they are dogs, they will start barking. In the same spirit we can say that if you tell people for centuries that their desire to speak borders on transgression, they will fall silent. Once they do, adding insult to injury, you can assure them that their freedom of speech is constitutionally protected. In this way, you will be able to control them twice over: first because they will refrain from persuasive speaking, and second because they will mistrust even, or especially, the few eloquent transgressors of silence. In effect, you will have them convinced that they ought to be worthy servants of the Word (of the Church) and faithful followers of the Words (of the State). Over time, however, learned mistrust turns into apathy, while imposed servitude fosters the most daring dreams of freedom. Eventually, there comes a moment when even officially sanctioned Words fall on deaf ears. Depending on how one reads our present predicament, we may be living out this very moment.

The other side of the hypothetical scenario of barking people covers the occasional reminders of the greatness of humans vis-à-vis their infinite faculties, including the one for rhetoric. That side says that if you tell people once in a while that they are magnificent creatures, they might breathe momentary sighs of relief and, like Narcissus, stand amazed at the sight of their own image. But temporary relief often functions as appeasement designed to maintain the peace. Alternatively, living out the illusion of one's magnificence usually means looking not at the ways one affects and is affected by language but at language itself or at oneself in itself. To do so, however, is to commit the same error Narcissus did. He spent too much time looking at the mirrored likeness of himself and, in the process, he not only failed to realize where he was, but he also forgot all about Echo and the other nymphs.

Insofar as all writing is directed against some other writing, I am writing here against the false promise of pure discourse, discourse cleansed of its rhetorical impurities. Accordingly, I am attempting to rid rhetorical practice of various and sundry "isms," especially those that have so many convinced that the cosmos is already charted ideationally, and all that remains for us is to discover and follow its paths and byways. Likewise, I am writing against those who claim to have transcended language and to be dealing in such languageless entities as concepts, ideas, and truths. At the same time, I am writing against the platitudes of those who celebrate, always prematurely, the abstraction of humankind and who have retreated all too soon to the simplistic adage that everything is rhetoric. Drawn into the game of those who claim a monopoly on the truth, the fans of humankind fail to see, just like their opponents, that rhetoric is not an all or nothing proposition but rather a proposition of countless discursive attempts with uncertain outcomes. In so doing, they, too, stand in the way of rhetoric.

But writing against something is always easier than writing for something. Critics with a sharp eye for imperfection always abound as writing for something never comes flawless. Even so, there is something to be said about this kind of writing, all along acknowledging one's shortcomings, and not hiding behind the excuse of waiting for the inspiration from the muses, or for the completion of an instance of flawlessness. Accordingly, I am writing for the love of rhetoric, the games language plays, the fascination with naming and turning phrases. I am also writing for the unceasing effort to reach others and the desire to be reached by them, the wish to have impact on and be persuaded by them, to secure their assent and invite their cooperation. Further, I am writing for the resolve to tell what is kept from being told, to retell what needs to be retold, to find the arguments that will win a crucial case or carry a day that matters. And I am writing for the courage to talk back, to voice dissent, to register objections, to expose the untruths of the Truth. Most of all, I am writing for the will to create symbolic worlds more becoming of and more inhabitable by human beings, the search for discourses that utter the hitherto unuttered, discourses that create attractive spaces inviting us to occupy them.

Clearly, I do not side with those who view the world of words as the peculiar province of petty academicians, or with those who seek to control and regulate it by means of supposedly extralinguistic postulates and geometrical models—unfortunately for them, getting outside language is not a viable option, and measuring the earth does not tell us how to address others. At the same time, I do not side with those who are prepared to celebrate everything equally so long as it is based on language; this readiness amounts to a blind spot that keeps away from their view the shameful results of discourse. Rather, I side with those who see language as a powerful instrument through which we shape and are shaped from the moment we become aware of it to the moment we exit from the world. Like all powerful instruments, language can be used to produce admirable as well as frightening results. It all depends on how we use it and whether we are conscious of the uses to which we and others put it.

In a narrow sense, this book is addressed to those who have been studying rhetoric, its countless uses, its long history, and its various theories—much of what I have to say comes from their contributions to the field, and aspires to return the favor. In a wider sense, it is addressed to less-known others whose intellectual tastes and disciplinary sensibilities I barely know—all I have dared assume here is that some of them might be interested in what is being written about rhetoric these days. In a still wider sense, it is addressed to no particular audience. Instead, it is attempting to create one. In all three senses, I hope to please my readers' fancy and to stimulate their thinking.

# Sophistical Rhetoric
# in Classical Greece

# Introduction

During the last twenty-four centuries, the story of the Greek sophists has been told many times over by historians, philosophers, philologists, and others. Today, the narrative repertoire on Hellas' early rhetoricians includes stories about a suspect epistemological and moral doctrine (Plato), a necessary moment in the history of philosophy (Hegel), a unique cultural phenomenon (Nietzsche), and a profound intellectual movement (Jaeger, Kerferd). From the outset, one is struck by the story's variations, variations that can be attributed to the personal preoccupations and intellectual orientations of their authors or the peculiar concerns of the epochs in which the authors and their readers lived. But the most remarkable feature of the story is its persisting appeal despite several kinds of adversity, including the loss of original texts, hostile reviews by unsympathetic commentators, and the scholarly excesses of literal-mindedness on the one hand and overinterpretation on the other.

Even though each version of the story highlights some things while shading others, all versions converge on one point — the story is important enough to be taken into account. Regardless of the interests each version serves, the sophists of the fifth century B.C. have proved time and again provocative enough to have attracted both detractors and defenders. At present, they are enjoying considerable popularity as their defenders seem to outnumber their detractors. This was not always so. But the scholarship of the last one hundred and fifty years seems to have restored the sophists' tainted reputation of intellectual dishonesty and moral indecency. For example, Plato's questionable tactics of dismissing them all too easily have been exposed repeatedly (Havelock, Irwin, Vickers), while some sophistical fragments have been shown to be intellectually meritorious (Untersteiner, Guthrie, Kerferd). As a result of this studied emancipation, the sophists are being read more receptively today than in the past. So much so, in fact,

1

that sophistry is in danger of becoming the new orthodoxy in the study of Hellenic and other rhetorics.

Although sympathetic to the sophists, I am not interested in rehabilitating them once more. Hegel, Grote, Nietzsche, and others in the nineteenth century did that, and there is no sense in repeating their admirable work. Nor am I interested in crying foul in the face of the pre-nineteenth-century unflattering portrayals of the sophists. Plato and his disciples said what they had to say. If, as a result, the sophists and their rhetoric were slighted, the injury has been identified and redressed. The fact is that the sophists are no longer dismissed or ignored in the histories of Western thought; and this fact must be the starting point of any contemporary study about them. But if this is so, there is little to be gained by arguing, once again, that Plato was wrong or unfair when it came to the sophists. There is even less profit in the reactionary argument that the only kind of rhetoric is the sophistical. The first argument suffers from "the conservative safety of language without history"[1] while the second suffers from the reverse. If we are to make some sense out of the sophists today, we need to ask why their rhetoric turned out the way it did, not whether Plato was right or fair. Perhaps this question could not have been asked before some of Plato's awesome power had been challenged; but today it can. As I pointed out earlier, the sophists are presently being read more sympathetically than ever before.

Even so, recent readings vindicating them share a remarkably similar set of assumptions with earlier readings vilifying them. Like their predecessors, many modern commentators assume that the discourses attributed to the sophists are stable objects of investigation; objects, that is, that can be explored disinterestedly, examined closely, and possessed epistemologically. Second, they assume that we, the present interpreters, can indeed recover and have access to the past-as-it-was and can disregard, untroubled, the distance separating our times, our society, and our culture from that of the ancients. Third, they assume that human understanding remains constant from one period of history to another, and, therefore, some aspects of the past inform parallel aspects of the present. Fourth, they assume that knowledge of something from the past is good either in itself or because it can enable us to imitate the splendid achievements of our ancient predecessors and avoid their errors. On the basis of these assumptions, most commentators have sought to inform us about the sophists and their doctrines, to offer us access to what is inaccessible to the untrained eye and thus enlarge our learnedness and deepen our appreciation on a matter whose significance is presumed by virtue of its location in the very distant past.

Perhaps these assumptions were useful during the nineteenth century, a time during which the pioneers of classical philology organized and codified the materials of antiquity. But in the light of recent developments in historical and literary studies, these assumptions are at least questionable. In particular, historians are no longer regarded as disinterested observers who simply describe how things were, but rather as interested parties who, consciously or unconsciously, affect the shape of their investigations. Similarly, the notion that human understanding remains unaltered from one historical moment to another and from one society to another has in more recent times been superseded by the notion of time- and place-dependent understandings. Third, the view that the past is recoverable as it really was has yielded to the view that any discussion of the past constitutes an interpretive construction from a particular perspective of the present. Fourth, the idea of timeless history has been replaced by that of present histories (historical statements are always made from and are influenced by one's life in the present).

My own biases as a commentator are informed by these latter preferences. Accordingly, I treat past texts not as fixed monuments to be consumed cognitively but as elusive documents that can stimulate readers to rethink the constitution of their own lives and to entertain possibilities for their reconstitution. As I discuss the sophists and their early receptions, I seek neither to add to an already crowded store of detailed scholarship about their doctrines nor to deepen our sufficiently deep appreciation of Hellas' first intellectuals. Approaching sophistical rhetoric as a fertile field of study, I attempt to cultivate perspectives on such interrelated issues as the cultural situatedness of rhetoric, the production of belief, the meaning of authority, the linguistic empowerment or enfeeblement of the individual, the structure of sociopolitical relations, and the complexities of human communication. As I do so, I assume that one studies the past not in order to become familiar with it, and thus learned, but in order to make sense out of and come to terms with some of the irresolutions of the present. At the same time, I assume that one looks at the past futuristically, so as to go beyond it, to forget it even temporarily, to work against its burdens, and thus to become able to express the hitherto unexpressed. This is not to say that one can appropriate the past as one pleases; nor that the past can be imported intact into the present. Rather, it is to say that a given look into the past is motivated by considerations grounded in the present. At the same time, such a look constitutes an attempt to encounter what opposes and problematizes one's motives and understandings. In short, the past provides neither ready-made solutions to the problems of the present nor hard-won understandings that can be twisted at will. If it is true that the past offers assistance and comfort, it is also true that it offers resistance and discomfort. In view of these considerations, past works are valuable not in themselves but because they can prompt subsequent readers to see themselves doubly: first, as vulnerable subjects susceptible to the forces of the world before them and around them, and second, as active agents capable of influencing the shape and direction of their own worlds.

On these terms, a thorough discussion of sophistical rhetoric requires that we consider the sophists' cultural predicament, their fragmentary texts (Diels and Kranz), and representative instances of the history of their early reception. The purpose of such a project, however, is not to correct prior views on the sophists and offer truer interpretations, nor is it to resolve conflicts between competing interpretations. As I have said, my intention is to treat the rhetoric of the sophists so as to stimulate some new thinking on our own rhetorics. But because the sophists' discourses are generally recounted by nonsophists, sophistical rhetoric can only be the result of derivation and extrapolation.

This book situates the sophists in the cultural environment of the latter half of the fifth century B.C., and argues that their rhetoric was shaped by the logic of circumstances, the ethic of competition, and the aesthetic of exhibition. Second, it examines the preserved textual materials of and about the sophists, and derives a rhetoric that can be called sophistical. Third, it considers three major receptions of sophistical rhetoric: the Platonic, which sought to eliminate it by exposing its disregard for ethical and epistemological criteria; the Isocratean, which tried to harness its energy by putting it in the service of pan-Hellenism; and the Aristotelian, which attempted to temper its excesses by correcting its errors in reasoning and readjusting its direction and purposes in the name of theory. Insofar as echoes of these three receptions can still be heard, I argue that the Platonic, Isocratean, and Aristotelian receptions are not simply three isolated individualistic reactions, but three typical responses to sophistical rhetoric.

During the time between the fifth century B.C. and the present, many a commentator of Hellenic antiquity has touched upon the sophists. But as I have indicated, contemporary understanding is not simply a function of an exhaustive list of prior works on a given subject—representative receptions do suffice. The conceptual lines I have drawn, then, provide primarily a background against which I put forth my views of sophistical rhetoric. As I discuss the three fourth-century receptions and the three corresponding understandings to which they point, I show that sophistical rhetoric opposes regulative practices, resists appropriation, and frustrates corrective schemes. So conceived, the perspective I am proposing helps explain why previous scholarship has, with few exceptions, sought to discredit sophistical rhetoric, or deny it the role of shaping human agency and affecting the public sphere.

Since the sophists' own texts have not survived, and since all we have are second-hand accounts and critical commentaries about them, reception theory provides a convenient theoretical framework for the available material. A particular reception tells us not only how a given commentator has construed the sophists but also under which version of rhetoric the commentator was toiling, what questions (s)he was trying to answer, and what specific tasks (s)he was attempting to accomplish. Moreover, a given set of receptions indicates how sophistical rhetoric fared in a given epoch and invites us to explain why it was treated in a particular manner during a particular historical moment. Finally, the various receptions at our disposal not only present us with several historical vantage points from which to see sophistical rhetoric; they also demand that we take them into account as we formulate our own reception. Thus, it would not be unfair to say that this book constitutes a reception of receptions.

As first advanced by Hans Robert Jauss,[2] reception theory sought to provide an alternative to the two most dominant approaches to literary studies during the late 1960s—Marxism and Formalism. Jauss argued that while Marxism focuses on how a work was produced and Formalism on how a work is represented, neither approach pays adequate attention to the way the work was received by its initial as well as its subsequent audiences. Asserting that literature's impact is a significant part of its social function, Jauss noted that "the historical life of a literary work is unthinkable without the active participation of its addressees." In so doing, he linked the historical study of literature to the rhetorical tradition, a tradition whose principal concern has always been the influence of an address on its audience.

Objecting to the notion of objectivity in history, Jauss rejects attempts to ground the history of literature on a collection and classification of past literary data. His rationale is that a literary work is not an object in itself but something that acquires an eventful character every time it is read by a reader who realizes its uniqueness when comparing it to other works (s)he has read. In his words, a literary work is "more like an orchestration that strikes ever new resonances among its readers and that frees the text from the material of the words and brings it to contemporary existence." Still, a work's impact will fade with the passage of time unless future readers rediscover and respond to it or unless future authors undertake "to imitate, outdo, or refute it."

Jauss points out that the reception of a literary work takes place not in a vacuum but within a system of expectations determined in part by the reader's pre-understanding of the work's genre and his/her understanding of "the forms and themes of already familiar works." Through implicit or explicit allusions, overt or covert signals, and hints or announcements, the work evokes the reader's horizon of expectations and then proceeds to vary, correct, alter, or reproduce it. To the extent that a work is received in ways that meet the audience's horizon of expectations, it can be said to perpetuate the prevailing aesthetic norms, to reinforce familiar literary practices, and to fulfill the need for their confirmation and reproduction. But insofar as it is received in ways that deny, negate, frustrate, or surpass the audience's expectations, it can be said to call into question familiar experiences, to demand the apprehension of yet unthought thoughts, and to create a distance between itself and the existing horizon of expectations. In either case, the worth of a work and the status of the horizon of expectations at a given time and place are determined by the ways in which a work is received both by its earliest as well as its later audiences.

Attempting to specify how a work is understood, Jauss discounts the idea that a work possesses a timeless objective meaning that can be discovered by its readers "through mere absorption in the text." At the same time, he dismisses the notion that a work can be understood from the perspective of the past, or that of the present, or that of the "verdict of the ages." Because a past work was produced within one system of expectations and because a present interpreter exists within another, the proper understanding of a text always entails a fusion of the two horizons. In this way, reception theory argues for "placing oneself within a process of tradition in which past and present are constantly mediated." In doing so, it avoids the extremes of classical philology, which claims to interpret ancient texts objectively, and modernist criticism, which often disregards their historical character.

It is quite possible that a work may not be understood properly by its first readers, even if they realize the need for a fusion of the horizons of the past and the present. Once in a while, a work deviates from the horizon of expectations of its time so greatly that its first audience cannot grasp its virtual significance. In such cases, the work either recedes into oblivion or reemerges at a later time, when the horizon of expectations has been constituted so as to accommodate now what it previously could not. As Jauss puts it: "The distance between the actual first perception of a work and its virtual significance . . . can be so great that it requires a long process of reception to gather in that which was unexpected and unusable within the first horizon." Insisting that the new must be treated not only as an aesthetic but also as a historical category, reception theory analyzes literature diachronically and seeks to find how a given work was first received, during which period was its newness first realized, or under what preunderstandings it was made to reemerge from the past.

A strictly diachronic analysis of a literary work, however, runs the risk of ignoring the fact that every work always exists in the present, alongside other works from other areas (i.e., art, law, economics, science, politics). On the other hand, a strictly synchronic analysis runs the risk of treating works whose understanding has been conditioned by a long history of reception as if they were products of the present. Dismissing the notion that "everything that happens contemporaneously is equally informed by the significance of this moment," Jauss argues that "the historicity of literature comes to light at the intersections of diachrony and synchrony." Endorsing Kracauer's notion of "the non-contemporaneity of the contemporaneous," Jauss theorizes that the horizon of expectations in a given historical moment can be conceived as "that synchronic system in relation to which literature that appears contemporaneously could be received diachronically in relations of noncontemporaneity, and the work could be received as current or not, as modish, outdated, or perennial, premature or belated."

Jauss concludes his theory by returning to the rhetoricity of literature, its capacity to affect its readers by modifying their horizon of expectations and, consequently, their actions. Convinced that the imitative presuppositions of traditional literary sociology and of contemporary structuralism miss the "socially *formative* function of literature," he posits that reception theory emphasizes that very function by considering the difference between the literary and the historical horizons of expectation. The historical horizon is mainly determined by and seeks to preserve actual experiences, while the literary goes beyond this preservation as it "also anticipates unrealized possibility, broadens the limited space of social behavior for new desires, claims, and goals, and thereby opens paths of future experience."

This brief account of Jauss' theory of reception is not meant as a preview of a mold within which all that follows in this book is made to fit. Rather, it is meant as an announcement of my understanding of and approach to the task before me. As will become evident, however, Jauss' theory is helpful only part of the time.

Although I do not wish to advance a lengthy critique of reception theory, I nevertheless must point out that my gravest reservation about Jauss' formulation regards his conceptualization of reading. Reading is far from a disinterested activity. Because human perception is highly selective and active in constructing meaning, because we as readers are taught to read in certain ways, and because we exist within a sociopolitical milieu, we read guided not only by a particular horizon of literary expectations; we also read with specific interests in mind. This means that the impact of a given work is not simply received or felt by its readers — it is also made by them. That is at least one reason why the readings of a work, both within a period and across periods, are often less uniform than conservative methodologists would like.

With this reservation in mind, I want to touch on some areas of Jauss' theory that do not fit my subject matter exactly. To begin with, it seems that a proper discussion of sophistical rhetoric would require access both to the sophists' works themselves and to the receptions of these works. But while we have access to a great many receptions, we have only a few, secondhand specimens of sophistical texts. To complicate things further, we do not know what of the sophists' writings their commentators from antiquity had read. Therefore, we can only go by the commentators' accounts of what the sophists said, even if those accounts may be the result of reputation, hearsay, or memory rather than close readings. In this book, then, sophistical work refers not to an autonomous text written by one sophist or another but to a title of a work, a phrase, a statement, or a speech whose authorship is attributed to a particular sophist. The problem, however, is not so much one of authenticity as one of response—I am concerned less with verification and more with critical reception. Accordingly, I do not intend to discern whether the sophists did in fact say what is attributed to them; rather, I intend to examine the responses the so-called sophistical materials drew. In this regard, I pay more attention to those who undertook "to imitate, outdo, or refute" the sophists (Plato, Isocrates, Aristotle), and less attention to those who sought to chronicle their lives and report their doctrines (Xenophon, Philostratus, Diogenes Laertius).

Second, the horizon of expectations within which a particular reception of sophistical rhetoric was produced is not especially easy to reconstruct. If, as Jauss argues, a critical response is shaped in part by the reader's pre-understanding of, and familiarity with, certain genres or the forms and themes of other works, it would seem that a given reception requires that we have some idea of its author's acquaintance of other works. However, it is virtually impossible to know with any degree of certainty what other works a particular author had read before writing a reception of the sophists. And even if we did know, it would be equally impossible to establish how those other works colored the author's reading of sophistical rhetoric. Thus we are faced with a difficult methodological issue: Can we realistically reconstruct the horizon of expectations within which an author's reception was shaped by becoming familiar with all the author might have read before writing a particular reception? And even if we were to grant that we might be able to in the case of a single author, the problem seems insurmountable when many authors are involved. On the assumption that we write not only in response to what we read but also in response to our own circumstances, the reception of each author discussed in this book will be treated as a response to both his view of the sophists' discursive practices and to the prevalent issues of his time. What these issues were will be construed from the author's own allusions to them and from historians' commentaries on the period under study.

Third, whether we are looking at a past work or its past reception, the perspective of the present is unavoidable. And even though we may not disregard the historical character of the work or its reception, our understanding of either can only be from the perspective of the present. What follows in this book is the result not so much of a perfectly controlled fusion of different horizons as of a present reception informed by three receptions from the past—Plato's, Isocrates' and Aristotle's. If I seem to privilege the present, I do so out of necessity, not out of presumption. I do not believe that the most recent interpretation of a work is also necessarily the best. In other words, I do not claim to understand sophistical rhetoric more correctly or better than my predecessors. I only claim that, insofar as my reception is the beneficiary of their labors, it covers more ground than theirs. I also claim that to the extent that my reception is conditioned by some of the concerns of our modernity, it may prove more useful to my contemporaries. When another period dawns, this reception, too, will have to make room for others.

### Notes

1. Edward W. Said, *Beginnings* (Baltimore: Johns Hopkins University Press, 1975), 13.
2. All quoted material in the following discussion is from Hans Robert Jauss, *Toward an Aesthetic of Reception* (Minneapolis: University of Minnesota Press, 1982), 19–41.

# Chapter 1

# Sophistical Rhetoric
# and Its Circumstances

The first generation of sophists burst on the scene of the Hellenic culture some time in the middle of the fifth century B.C. and exited some time during the early part of the fourth, leaving behind an ambiguous legacy, many disciples, and a host of thorny questions. On account of their moment in history, the sophists can be said to have been both the beneficiaries and benefactors of an age of cultural exuberance, political expansion, economic growth, intellectual experimentation, and robust artistic expression. By most standards of historical judgment, the fifth century was a remarkably exciting age, and it was the sophists' good fortune to have been part of it. Still, some scholars of Hellenic antiquity insist on studying the sophists apart from the culture, focusing simply on their brief biographies, essential doctrines, or unique contributions to the edifice of Western thought. In so doing, these scholars inevitably assign the sophists doctrines that, in themselves, make little or no sense unless they are forced to fit the design of such trans-historical frameworks as the history of philosophy, the history of literature, the history of education, or, more recently, the history of rhetoric. While such a compromise may be necessary when we cut across many centuries and thinkers, it is, nevertheless, a compromise that lacks the texture and the color afforded by a focus on the specific cultural setting of a particular group of thinkers. If we are to go beyond the limits of a set of sketchy biographies, essentialized doctrines, or contested contributions to posterity, we need to follow the sophists' trails in Hellenic antiquity. More specifically, we need to look for their starts and stops, instances of convergence with and divergence from others, the overall pattern of their movement, as well as their collective predicament within the cultural terrain in which they lived and achieved notoriety.[1]

Still, studying a group of intellectuals exclusively in the light of

11

their age has its limitations. Although an age is more than the sum of the events and notions that can be said to have made it an age, it is still mainly an abstraction that leaves its makers out of account. But if this is so, the point is to favor neither an age nor its makers as individuals. Rather, the point is to show a reciprocal influence between the two, to ask, that is, how the age shaped the makers and how they, in turn, helped shaped it. Only then can we advance a sensible understanding of either.

Prior scholarship on the sophistic movement has sought to explain its emergence by account of the favorable intellectual climate in Periclean Athens, the Hellenic cultural center to which most celebrated sophists were drawn.[2] Although plausible, this explanation is too general and as such can account for the emergence of virtually everything (i.e., sculpture, drama, philosophy, architecture, science) in the Athenian culture. More importantly, such an explanation overlooks three crucial points. First, intellectual movements are born not *in vacuo*, but in the midst of a set of cultural givens of practice and thought already in motion. Second, they spring up not simply as a result of a conducive climate but in order to address particular circumstances and to fulfill certain societal needs. Third, they inadvertently grow alongside some established cultural practices and against others, producing innovative results despite the resistance of the tradition or the potential risks of criticisms that may eliminate them.

To understand sophistical rhetoric, then, means to specify the circumstances in which it occurred, to know the needs it sought to satisfy, to link it to prevalent cultural practices that helped shape its character, and to articulate the reactions it drew from subsequent thinkers. When situated culturally, the Greek sophists can be shown to have been not only products but also catalysts of their age, an age that facilitated their emergence, adopted many of their views and practices, and eventually initiated their denigration for centuries to come. In the same way, the sophists' rhetoric can be shown to have constituted not just an isolated activity by a class of talented individuals out of step with the tenor of their times, but rather a vital symbolic practice in the very culture that encouraged, produced, and critiqued it.

During the period of the sophists' emergence, the Hellenic culture was undergoing several changes, two of which are of special note. The first was from aristocracy to democracy. Initially introduced in Athens by Cleisthenes' constitutional revisions early in the fifth century, and later consolidated by the political reforms of Ephialtes and Pericles in the 460s, this change was not limited to the structural features of a political system of governance but involved other social, intellectual, and cultural arrangements as well. Specifically, the aristocracy of the nobility was yielding to a democracy of citizens;[3] the aristocracy of the myths was losing its authority to a democracy of public arguments;[4] the aristocracy of the oracles was receding before a democracy of human laws;[5] and the aristocracy of poetry was relinquishing its glory to a democracy of prosaic discourses.[6] In short, this was a change from the few to the many or, to put it in Aristotelian terms, from the extremities to the middle.[7] It was a change, however, that was far from total—much of what assumed a democratic character did preserve some aristocratic features. For example, excellence in citizenship was still measured in terms of such deeds as victories in athletic competitions or generous gifts to one's city; laws preserved the oracular quality of prophesying the very human behaviors they were seeking to regulate; public arguments often derived their efficacy from the power of the myths they invoked; and prosaic discourses did not escape entirely from poetry as public audiences expected to hear in the speeches of their contemporary orators a good measure of the familiar poeticisms of their past poets.[8]

Caught in the midst of this pervasive change, the sophists responded neither as passive observers nor as active resisters but as energetic catalysts, accelerating its rate and enlarging its scope. By offering rhetorical instruction to those who could pay for lessons, they increased the number of the beneficiaries of learning without reducing the number of privileged aristocrats. Moreover, their rhetorical prose was one of the earliest efforts to break away from the cultural dominance of poetry; but it was a prose relying on the use of the poetical techniques of past poets.[9] As Aristotle points out in his *Rhetoric* (3.1.8–9), the sophists were among the first to borrow the techniques of the poets on matters of style and delivery. Furthermore, their use of familiar mythical figures in their speeches helped preserve the legendary names whose character and deeds had shaped the culture's earlier system of values. Even so, the portrayal of those same figures in a new light challenged traditional notions of morality and reflected the rise of a new political and civic consciousness. Prodicus' Heracles, for example, was not the Heracles of incredible accomplishments requiring raw physical strength but a reflective character facing a dilemma between virtue and vice, pondering which path to choose. Similarly, Gorgias' Helen was no longer a woman of loose morals but a victim of circumstances and forces beyond her control; and his Palamedes was no longer simply a victim of Odysseus' ploys but an inventor of things useful to civilized life. In the same vein, Protagoras' gods, Zeus, Prometheus, and Hermes, were no longer concentrating exclusively on the enlargement and security of their respective spheres of responsibility; rather, they put their own preoccupations aside in order to attend to the survival of humankind. Finally, the sophists' discourses, initially affected by poetical techniques, began leaving poetry's metric limitations behind, and turned to the prose that the common people were speaking in the agora, the courts, and the Assembly. Such a turn must have led to the awareness that several established discursive practices and the culture's mythology were subject to change.

In a culture gradually placing its fortunes in the hands of the many rather than the few, sophistical rhetoric proved indispensable. Claiming to empower its possessors, it presented itself as a valuable commodity, an instrument that both the lingering aristocracy and the emerging democracy could use profitably. Caught in the whirlwinds of democracy, the aristocrats had interests to protect. Therefore, it was in their best interest to learn persuasive tactics in order to influence large juries and legislative assemblies of commoners to vote the right way. On the other hand, common citizens had a chance for the first time to make their voices heard and their wills done when it came to the legal and political affairs of their city. Therefore, it behooved them to learn how to articulate their positions eloquently and express their arguments persuasively. In their pedagogical capacity, then, the sophists did not only seek to mold effective citizens for the city-state but also furnish interested individuals with the rhetorical sophistication necessary to survive the new changes. Contrary to what some of their critics have said, the sophists' motto was not the survival of the fittest but fitting as many as possible for survival. In this sense, the sophists can be said to have helped strengthen the recently instituted democracy by forging a mentality aware of the centrality of persuasion in the coordination of sociopolitical action and the resolution of human conflicts. At the very least, this mentality was consistent with the partial empowerment of the traditionally weak and the partial disempowerment of the hitherto powerful. Insofar as the sophists enabled more people to enter the contests and spectacles of public life, the rhetoric they taught created at least two new possibilities: first, the possibility of the weaker challenging the stronger; and second, the possibility of revitalizing calcified discursive practices. Together, these two possibilities created a new world, simultaneously contesting the one already in place.

In addition to its democratizing function, however, sophistical rhetoric inaugurated a new aristocracy, crowning "logos" the new master of the polis—a master whom all had to serve but whom only few could serve with distinction.[10] Inasmuch as the sophists regarded virtually all people capable of and subject to rhetorical persuasion, they can be said to have viewed rhetoric as a universal capacity. But insofar as they realized that only few could excel in eloquence, they can be said to have regarded rhetoric as a supreme art.[11] In both cases, however, their message underscored neither the primacy of the world nor the primacy of human beings; rather, it emphasized the primacy of logos as the medium circulating between human beings and constituting both human beings and the world. In this sense, they can be said to have instituted a new regime whose sympathies and character were neither aristocratic nor democratic but logocratic.

The second noteworthy change, during the age of the sophists, involved the growth of the middle class, a class defined by newly acquired wealth and occupying the mid-point between the land-owning nobility and the serfs.[12] As early as the latter part of the sixth century B.C. the elegist Theognis had identified the beginnings of this change in these words:

> In our rams, asses and horses we endeavour to preserve a noble breed, and we like to mate them with a good stock. Yet the nobleman does not scruple to marry a low-born wife, so long as she brings him money, nor does a woman refuse the hand of a low-born suitor, preferring riches to nobility. What they honour is money. The nobleman marries into a family of base birth, the base-born into a noble family. Wealth has blended breed. So do not wonder that the breed of the citizens is dying out; for noble is being blended with base.[13]

Theognis' sentiments aside, the advent of the middle class in the fifth century B.C. was a consequence of such phenomena as a growing population, increased commercial activity, higher demand for trade labor, and newly instituted political arrangements offering the common citizen new political powers. Unlike Theognis or some of their contemporaries, the sophists did not see this development as a turn for the worse. On the contrary, they capitalized on its reality and intensity by undertaking to teach, in addition to the sons of the noble, the sons of well-to-do merchants, artisans, and tradespeople. Being of middle-class origin themselves, the sophists were part of a greater change, a change they were instrumental in turning into a permanent feature of the Hellenic social and political landscape of the fifth and fourth centuries B.C.[14]

A variation of the growth of the middle class included the appearance of resident aliens as a class at the center of two polar classes—citizens and noncitizens. Also members of this new middle, the sophists managed to achieve prominence in the Hellenic world, in effect demonstrating that neither nobility nor citizenship were necessary requirements for worldly success and fame. If the sophists' example had any force, it must have been that the potential for success was tied to the cultivation of the capacity for rhetoric.

The sophists are generally known not so much for their accomplishments in their own home communities as for their travels from city to city, seeking to persuade youths to study under them the new arts of language (rhetoric and disputation). Apparently successful in this endeavor, they were thought by their near contemporaries to have made fortunes. But neither their teaching profession nor their financial success in it nor their impact on the world of thought proved sufficiently strong to win them an unambiguously positive standing in the Hellenic world of their time or in that of posterity. There are at least three reasons why this is so.

First was their social and legal status. Wherever we meet the sophists in our readings, they are typically resident aliens.[15] Neither citizens nor noncitizens, aliens were welcome in some city-states and unwelcome in others. Sparta, for example, occasionally expelled them from its territory through the legal mechanism of alien acts (ξενηλασίαι). By contrast, Athens treated them more generously, offering them personal freedoms, access to employment, and protection under its laws.[16] If we can believe Thucydides' Pericles, Athens was a city confident of the efficacy of its institutions, committed to the freedom of thought, hospitable to aliens, and dedicated to the cultivation and intellectual enrichment of its citizens.[17] Accordingly, the Athenians opened their gates to the sophists as important thinkers from whom they could profit. At the same time, the Athenians viewed them as worthy intellectuals who could contribute meaningfully to the cultural exuberance of the city.[18] In so doing, Athens could satisfy the mental curiosity of its young, and offer its citizens opportunities to hear stories of other societal and political arrangements.[19] The bet in both cases was that the Athenians would perceive the differences between their city and others, and conclude that, compared to their near or distant neighbors, they were better off.

During the fifth century B.C., aliens became an integral part of Athenian society; so much so, that some historians have noted that non-Athenian visitors "supplied Athens with many of her outstanding men—painters, sculptors, musicians, doctors, philosophers, poets and orators."[20] Still, these outstanding men were under some restrictions—they could not acquire real property, participate in official political activities, or serve in the courts or the Assembly. Moreover, they were required to pay a special alien tax, serve in the military, and be sponsored by a citizen.[21] Finally, the resident aliens as a class occasionally found themselves in conflict with the class of citizens, whose political status was unquestionably higher.[22]

The second reason for the sophists' negative standing was their cosmopolitanism.[23] By virtue of their many travels, the sophists acquired cosmopolitan outlooks. These outlooks were free from the provincialism characteristic of a self-centered community that, insulated from other communities, considers itself sufficiently accomplished in all its forms of organized life. Insofar as a cosmopolitan outlook consists of many different views gathered from various local mentalities, it can be said to be sensitive to differences, to entertain a variety of logics, and to have the advantages of comparison and choice over a single-minded, parochial perspective. Comparison and choice, however, are not always advantages, especially in the minds of highly conservative communities. In such communities, the cosmopolitan visitor is usually a foreigner whose stay and activities are often viewed with suspicion, the fear being that the foreigner may smuggle into the host community an impure mixture of ideas, a mixture incompatible with the local traditions, customs, and culture. Thus to tell Hellenic audiences that "the Messagetes cut up their [dead] parents and eat them and they think that to be buried in their children is the most beautiful grave imaginable"[24] or that "the Persians think . . . that men should have intercourse with their daughters, mothers, and sisters"[25] was to shatter the belief in the universality of laws, to shake people's confidence in the propriety of Greek laws, and to leave the door open to practices regarded illegal and disgraceful in Hellas.[26]

The third reason for the sophists' poor reputation was their intellectualism. Although each sophist was learned in a variety of subjects of knowledge (arithmetic, astronomy, geometry, music, argumentation, linguistic research, history), they all taught rhetoric. But as aliens, they could teach mainly a general rhetoric, which the students could later adapt to the peculiarities of their circumstances. The sophists' itinerant predicament did not permit them to teach rhetorics born out of and tied to local traditions. Such rhetorics would have required a thorough understanding of the unique features of each city-state in which they taught. But, if it is granted that a visitor seldom knows and can hardly be expected to be familiar with the nuances of the life of his/her hosts, this requirement of understanding could hardly be met. This explains, at least in part, the sophists' reputed use of model speeches composed with a set of commonplaces (*topoi*) in mind.[27]

But despite its necessarily general character, the sophists' rhetoric could not avoid entirely the perception of being potentially subversive. Because it lacked specificity, it was thought to be fraught with deliberate ambiguity, and, as such, subject to multiple interpretations and uses or abuses. If some of the sophists' students, then, put the rhetoric they had just learned to uses the larger community regarded improper, it is not hard to see how local citizens, already suspicious of traveling foreigners, would arrive at the conclusion that responsibility for such uses lay with the teachers.[28]

But the sophists did not confine themselves to teaching a general rhetoric. They also practiced particular rhetorics as they put some of their intellectual energies to the service of logography for politicians or for litigants and defendants in court cases.[29] In this capacity, they had real occasions in which to make good on their intriguing but controversial promise to have the weaker argument prevail over the stronger. Depending on how a particular case was argued, reactionary citizens in the audience could detect, behind a set of unusually stretched or twisted arguments, an alien logographer frustrating the local understandings of power and justice.[30] Plato's proposed law to deal with alien logographers, although authored well after the sophists' heyday, provides a hint of the kind of reaction they probably drew from people sharing the Platonic mindset:

> If anyone be held to be trying to reverse the course of just pleas in the minds of the judges, or to be multiplying suits unduly or aiding others to do so, whoso wishes shall indict him for perverse proce-

dure, and he shall be tried before the court of select judges; and if he be convicted, the court shall determine whether he seems to be acting from avarice or from ambition; and if from the latter, the court shall determine for how long a period such an one shall be precluded from bringing an action against anyone, or aiding anyone to do so; while if avarice be his motive, *if he be an alien he shall be sent out of the country and forbidden to return on pain of death,* but if he be a citizen he shall be put to death because of his unscrupulous devotion to the pursuit of gain. And anyone who has twice been pronounced guilty of committing such an act from ambition shall be put to death. (*Laws,* 11.938a–c; emphasis added)

We will return to Plato when we examine his reception of the sophists more closely. For now the point remains, alien logographers had not blended perfectly into the society of their hosts.

Aristophanes is less severe than Plato in his assessment of the sophists' intellectualism. Even so, they seem to have elicited from him the kind of reaction that greets novel ideas and practices with skepticism, and reasserts with renewed zeal the authority and value of the tradition. In the *Clouds,* for example, he satirizes the sophists by exposing their lessons as teaching the students how to "speak and conquer, right or wrong" (99), "to talk unjustly and—prevail" (114), to engage in the "hair-splittings of subtle Logic" (130). Accordingly, he suggests that those who wish to study under them are interested in learning "the knack of reasoning down all Justice" (885) and escaping "the clutches of law" (434). In effect, the sophists' typical student aspires to be:

> Bold, hasty, and wise, a concocter of lies,
> A rattler to speak, a dodger, a sneak,
> A regular claw at the tables of law,
> A shuffler complete, well worn in deceit,
> A supple, unprincipled, troublesome cheat;
> A hang-dog accurst, a bore with the worst,
> In the tricks of the jury-courts thoroughly versed.
> (445–51)

Aristophanes does not stop with the suggestion that the sophists were undermining the ethical infrastructure of the society. In the famous exchange between the Just Argument and the Unjust Argument, he goes on to portray the clash between the time-tested tradition of raising youth in pre-sophistical times and the questionable novelties of contemporary rhetorical education. Midway in the play, the Just Argument, trying to persuade the young Pheidippides of the superiority of the tradition, speaks of the good old days:

> When Honour and Truth were in fashion with youth
>     and Sobriety bloomed on our shore;
> First of all the old rule was preserved in our school
>     that "boys should be seen and not heard:"
> And then to the home of the Harpist would come
>     decorous in action and word
> All the lads of one town, though the snow peppered down,
>     in spite of all wind and all weather:
> And they sang an old song as they paced it along,
>     not shambling with thighs glued together:
> "O the dread shout of War how it peals from afar,"
>     or "Pallas the Stormer adore,"
> To some manly old air all simple and bare
>     which their fathers had chanted before.
> And should anyone dare the tune to impair
>     and with intricate twistings to fill,
> Such as Phrynis is fain, and his long-winded train,
>     perversely to quaver and trill,
> Many stripes would he feel in return for his zeal,
>     as to genuine Music a foe.
> And everyone's thigh was forward and high
>     as they sat to be drilled in a row,
> So that nothing the while indecent or vile
>     the eye of a stranger might meet;
> And then with their hand they would smooth down the sand
>     whenever they rose from their seat,
> To leave not a trace of themselves in the place
>     for a vigilant lover to view.
> They never would soil their persons with oil
>     but were inartificial and true.
> Nor tempered their throat to a soft mincing note
>     and sighs to their lovers addressed:
> Nor laid themselves out, as they strutted about,
>     to the wanton desires of the rest:
> Nor would anyone dare such stimulant fare
>     as the head of the radish to wish:
> Nor to make over bold with the food of the old,
>     the anise, and parsley, and fish:
> Nor dainties to quaff, nor giggle and laugh,
>     nor foot within foot to enfold.

When the Unjust Argument interrupts here and remarks that this is an antiquated line of thought, the Just Argument responds:

> Yet these are the precepts which taught
> The heroes of old to be hardy and bold,
>     and the men who at Marathon fought!
> But now must the lad from his boyhood be clad
>     in a Man's all-enveloping cloak:
> So that, oft as the Panathenaea returns,
>     I feel myself ready to choke
> When the dancers go by with their shields to their thigh,
>     not caring for Pallas a jot.
> You therefore, young man, choose me while you can;
>     cast in with my Method your lot;
> And then you shall learn the forum to spurn,
>     and from dissolute baths to abstain,
> And fashions impure and shameful abjure,
>     and scorners repel with disdain:
> And rise from your chair if an elder be there,
>     and respectfully give him your place,
> And with love and with fear your parents revere,
>     and shrink from the brand of Disgrace,
> And deep in your breast be the Image impressed
>     of Modesty, simple and true,
> Nor resort any more to a dancing girl's door
>     nor glance at the harlotry crew,
> Lest at length by the blow of the Apple they throw
>     from the hopes of your Manhood you fall.
> Nor dare to reply when your Father is nigh,
>     nor "musty old Japhet" to call
> In your malice and rage that Sacred Old Age
>     which lovingly cherished your youth.

At this point, the Unjust Argument tells Pheidippides that if he follows the advice of the Just Argument he will be called a booby, a dunce. The Just Argument retorts:

> But then you'll excel in the games you love well,
>     all blooming, athletic and fair:
> Not learning to prate as your idlers debate
>     with marvelous prickly dispute,
> Nor dragged into Court day by day to make sport
>     in some small disagreeable suit:
> But you will below to the Academy go,
>     and under the olives contend

With your chaplet of reed, in a contest of speed
  with some excellent rival and friend:
All fragrant with woodbine and peaceful content,
  and the leaf which the lime blossoms fling,
When the plane whispers love to the elm in the grove
  in the beautiful season of Spring.

If then you'll obey and do what I say,
And follow with me the more excellent way,
Your chest shall be white, your skin shall be bright,
Your arms shall be tight, your tongue shall be slight,
And everything else shall be proper and right.
But if you pursue what men nowadays do,
You will have, to begin, a cold pallid skin,
Arms small and chest weak, tongue practiced to speak,
Special laws very long, and the symptoms all strong,
Which show that your life is licentious and wrong.
And your mind he'll prepare so that foul to be fair
And fair to be foul you shall always declare;
And you'll find yourself soon, if you listen to him,
With the filth of Antimachus filled to the brim!
(962–1023)

If Aristophanes' remarks are at all representative of widely shared reactions against the new rhetorical intellectualism of the age, it is clear that the sophists and their lessons were met with considerable resistance from the conservative quarters of the culture; and as one might expect, this resistance eventually began influencing the attitude of the masses, a traditional stronghold of anti-intellectualism. The attitude of the masses was complicated as it combined admiration with envy, hospitality with xenophobia, trust with suspicion, and gratitude with resentment. The negative aspects of this attitude stemmed partly from the perception that the sophists were affecting adversely the life of the towns they were visiting by attracting the young away from their local communities, and by challenging the traditional legacies of the home front.[31] To the extent that the sophists were considered responsible for the physical or intellectual departure of young men from their homes or tradition, they were regarded as vandals who came into a city and destabilized it by pitting young against old and by depleting its human resources. In this regard, the typical sophist was, in the eyes of the lay public, a charming foreign guest who, like Paris, on the strength of inflated promises, had persuaded Helen to abandon her home in search of greener pastures. Naturally, such a perception turned a traveling sophist into an object of suspicion. Protagoras' explanation of the professional hazards of being a sophist tells the story of an ambiguous occupation and a dubious reception:

> When one goes as a stranger (ξένον ἄνδρα) into great cities, and there tries to persuade the best of the young men to drop their other connexions, either with their own folk or with foreigners, both old and young, and to join one's own circle, with the promise of improving him by this connexion with oneself, such a proceeding requires great caution; since very considerable jealousies are apt to ensue, and numerous enmities and intrigues. (*Protagoras*, 316c–d)

Clearly, being a sophist, even where welcome, was not always safe. But if this was so, what were the sophists to do in the face of such risks? Plato's *Protagoras* points out that the most frequent course of action wise men before him had taken was to disguise the true character of their profession. As he tells Socrates:

> sophistry is an ancient art, and those men of ancient times who practiced it, fearing the odium it involved, disguised it in a decent dress, sometimes of poetry, as in the case of Homer, Hesiod, and Simonides; sometimes of mystic rites and soothsayings, as did Orpheus, Musaeus and their sects; and sometimes too, I have observed, of athletics, as with Iccus of Tarentum and another still living—as great a sophist as any—Herodicus of Selymbria, originally of Megara; and music was the disguise employed by your own Agathocles, a great sophist, Pythocleides of Ceos, and many others. (*Protagoras*, 316d–e)

It would be unwarranted, however, to think that the sophists met hostility and rejection everywhere they went. Their considerable popularity and financial success militate against such a conclusion. It would also be unwarranted to infer from the above passage that they were forced to practice their rhetorical *techne* covertly. Protagoras himself is made to disapprove of his predecessors' practice of disguising their profession. For one thing, it had not worked; for another, he believed, open admission is a better policy than denial. Accordingly, he declares: "I admit that I am a sophist and that I educate men" (*Pro-*

*tagoras,* 316b). Although Protagoras is being ironic in claiming these early poets as disguised sophists, his claim suggests that the Hellenic culture of his time was fertile enough to allow an unapologetic sophistic to grow on its soil. And as the historical record indicates, sophistic not only grew, it eventually became a powerful force—a force that could not be ignored.

The above discussion should make clear that the sophists were both outsiders and insiders. Having come from the outside of the cities in which they taught, they were working inside them temporarily. This geographical ambiguity means that their home was at once nowhere and everywhere. When in Athens, they were carrying along ideas from Abdera or Leontini; and when in Sparta, Elis or Ceos were not entirely out of mind. But whether in Athens or Sparta, they must have been quite aware that they were not citizens. Surrounded by institutions that may have differed from those of their native land, the sophists nevertheless had to tolerate these institutions without feeling the kind of loyalty towards them that the indigenous population had been taught to feel. Subject to laws that may have seemed strange to them, they had to observe the laws just the same, without necessarily being convinced of their efficacy or fairness. Even so, the sophists had one advantage over ordinary citizens—they could always escape institutions and laws either from within (by contesting their meaning) or from without (by leaving the territory of their operation and enforcement and going to yet another city).[32] As transients, they must have had no stakes in the political structure or direction of the particular city of their temporary residence. Their principal interest must have been in that city's continued willingness to accommodate them for a while—as long as the city allowed them to teach their craft, they must have been content. For their part, all the sophists had to do was show some respect for the sensibilities of their hosts, and try not to offend them explicitly.

But just as the sophists traveled from location to location, so too they traveled from idea to idea.[33] And just as they did not settle in any one city, so too they did not inhabit any one intellectual domain permanently. Thus when Gorgias revisited Parmenides' idea of Being, he wrote a discourse on nonbeing; when Protagoras encountered the doctrine of the unity of logos, he countered with *dissoi logoi;* and when Antiphon witnessed discord among the Hellenes, he wrote about and praised concord. This does not mean, as some scholars have argued, that the sophists were philosophers interested in articulating doctrines on such matters as the nature of the negative, the essence of difference, or the substance of political harmony respectively. It simply means that from the sophists' point of view certain already formulated ideas did not seem necessarily so. Hence their alternative and oppositional responses. Had they encountered different circumstances and ideas, it is not inconceivable that they might have responded differently. Inasmuch as the sophists' purpose was to demonstrate that the world could always be recreated linguistically, restated in other words, and thus understood otherwise, the search for their essential doctrines is in vain. What they have left behind is not what they really believed. Their works represent only sketchy illustrations of what can be done with language.

Clearly, the sophists' geographical and intellectual itinerary suggests that they often thought both about where they were and where they were not, who they were and who they were not, which doctrines were dominant in the stations of their trails and which had yet to be expressed. In short, they thought in doubles. And herein lies the profound ambiguity of their ways of being in the world.[34] Faithful to no singular perspective, loyal to no given institution, and committed to no specific political system, they can be said to have lived and worked more according to the circumstances they encountered and less according to established custom or principle. The sociopolitical changes which they found themselves in the midst of, their extensive travels, and their rhetorical lessons dictated that the sophists adapt to ever-changing situations, capitalize on opportunities, steer clear of risks, adjust themselves to different laws and institutions, accommodate a variety of students, and tailor their messages to suit the sensibilities and tastes of their diverse audiences. In all of these ways, the sophists call to mind two contemporary sophist-like figures— Deleuze's nomad and de Certeau's *bricoleur*.[35]

Deleuze explains that nomads neither participate in the administrative and ideological system of the communities in which they reside nor operate at the center of "the despot's bureaucratic machine."[36] Rather, they live and operate at the periphery, where they can decodify existing social and institutional codes, and where they themselves cannot be overcodified by the despotic apparatus. This state of affairs leads to an ongoing opposition between the despot and the nomads. While the despot's purpose is to integrate the nomads into the existing system, theirs is to create new means of preserving their nomadic ways, ways that elude or evade the system's integrative capacities. If the despot is to integrate them, (s)he must internalize their ways of thinking, that is, think nomadically. From the other side, if the nomads are to escape the despot's grasp, they must anticipate that person's purpose and think despotically. Insofar as this mutual adoption of the other's thinking is carried out by both sides, the opposition between despot and nomads can get "to the point where they become confused with one another."[37] At that exact point, the nomads can be said to have succeeded, at least in part—having blurred distinctions vital to the despot's authority, they send him/her after a new version of clarity in the wilderness of ambiguity.[38]

On a parallel vein, Deleuze suggests that nomadic thought differs fundamentally from its philosophical counterpart in at least two ways. First, it "pretends to express its dynamism within the compass of laws (while rejecting them) . . . and of institutions (while ridiculing them)."[39] By contrast, philosophical thought is almost always "essentially related to law [and] institutions." Specifying this point historically, Deleuze notes that "within the Greek city-state, philosophic discourse remained in a strict relation with the despot (or at least within the shadow of despotism)."[40] The second difference between nomadic and philosophic thought is that the former is both stimulated by and directed to what is exterior to it, whereas the latter subjects what comes to it from the exterior to a hyperanalytical interiority in such a way and to such an extent that the distinction between exterior and interior is dissolved in favor of interiority. In Deleuze's words, "to hang thought on the outside is what philosophers have literally never done, even when they spoke about, for example, politics; even when they treated such subjects as walking or fresh air."[41]

Deleuze's discussion of the relationship between nomads and despot underscores some of the points of our earlier discussion. First, it points out that geographically as well as intellectually the sophists were nonstationary. As such they could not easily be identified or located (a difficulty made apparent in Plato's Sophist, to which we will return). In and through their elusive moves on the periphery of traditionally accepted beliefs and practices, some sophists were able to decodify the dogmatism of past conceptualizations of law while others called into question such commonly accepted institutions as slavery.[42] For example, Antiphon, Hippias, Critias, and Callicles, without referring to any specific law, rejected the notion that human laws are natural, arguing instead that they are tyrannical because they compel people to do things against their nature.[43] On another vein, sophists

like Alcidamas denounced the institution of slavery, pointing out that
it was based on human conventions, not on the natural state of
things.[44]

Second, Deleuze's distinction of nomads and despot along the continuum of exteriority and interiority, emphasizes a parallel distinction
between sophists and philosophers along the continuum of the active
and the contemplative life. Here it should be recalled that the sophists
were public people making their livelihood by preparing others to
address political, legal, and social issues effectively. In short, their focus was on the affairs of the polis, not the affairs of the mind. This
focus explains why they often took leads from their audiences, and
designed their discourses with those exact audiences in mind.[45] By
contrast, philosophers proved themselves to be men of extreme introspection, more attentive to the integrity of their ideas than to the
dispositions of large audiences. Consider how Socrates describes philosophers in the *Theaetetus*:

> The leaders [of philosophy], in the first place, from their youth up,
> remain ignorant of the way to the agora, do not even know where
> the court-room is, or the senate-house, or any other public place of
> assembly; as for laws and decrees, they neither hear the debates
> upon them nor see them when they are published; and the striv-
> ings of political clubs after public offices, and meetings and ban-
> quets, and revellings with chorus girls—it never occurs to them
> even in their dreams to indulge in such things. And whether any-
> one in the city is of high or low birth, or what evil has been inher-
> ited by anyone from his ancestors, male or female, are matters to
> which they pay no more attention than to the number of pints in
> the sea, as the saying is. And all these things the philosopher does
> not even know that he does not know; for he does not keep aloof
> from them for the sake of gaining reputation, but really it is only
> his body that has its place and home in the city; his mind, consid-
> ering all these things petty and of no account, disdains them and is
> borne in all directions, as Pindar says, "both below the earth," and
> measuring the surface of the earth, and "above the sky," studying
> the stars, and investigating the universal nature of everything that
> is, each in its entirety, never lowering itself to anything close at
> hand. (173c–74a)

The sophistical response to Socrates' hyperinteriorization of the life people live in the exterior, best expressed by Callicles, highlights the crucial difference between a rhetorically and a philosophically in-formed life:

> If a man is exceptionally gifted and yet pursues philosophy far on in life, he must prove entirely unacquainted with all the accom-plishments requisite for a gentleman and a man of distinction. Such men know nothing of the laws of their cities, or of the lan-guage they should use in their business associations both public and private with other men, or of human pleasures and appetites, and in a word they are completely without experience of men's characters. And so when they enter upon any activity public or pri-vate they appear ridiculous. (*Gorgias*, 484c–d)

Going one step further, Callicles points out why he thinks Socrates, the philosopher, is worthless: "You neglect, Socrates, what you most ought to care for . . . and you could neither contribute a useful word in the councils of justice nor seize upon what is plausible and con-vincing, nor offer any brilliant advice on another's behalf" (*Gorgias*, 485e–86a).

No matter how peripheral, mundane, inconsistent, and self-contra-dictory, the sophists' decodifying pronouncements proved suffi-ciently provocative to draw the attention of the intellectual despots of the fourth century. As we will see later on, Plato, Aristotle, and to a lesser extent Isocrates took it upon themselves to clarify what the sophists had obscured. In so doing, they set before them the tasks of diffusing the impact of sophistical rhetoric on the Hellenic culture and of rearticulating the importance of the stability that comes from ob-serving the state's laws and upholding its established institutions.[46] Whether the intellectuals of the fourth century succeeded is an open question. What is more certain is that the sophists have yet to be in-tegrated into any despotic system of thought.

As we have seen, the sophists' nomadic ways dictated that they make do with the cultural resources available to them at any given time and in any given place. Making do as an everyday practice has recently been discussed by de Certeau vis-à-vis the *bricoleur*, a clever and crafty character who puts the materials (especially of language) (s)he can find into new forms and to new uses in order to adapt them to his/her own interests and purposes. The bricoleur's linguistic ac-tions depend on myriads of combinations of *trajectories*, instances of discursivity produced within a larger linguistic system but obeying their own logic, not that of the system in which they belong and from which they emerge. Although de Certeau provides no examples of trajectories, he explains that they "trace out the ruses of other interests and desires that are neither determined nor captured by the systems in which they develop." Moreover, he points out that while the larger system of language may discern the elements of the trajectories inside itself, it cannot grasp their form. In his words, the system "determines the elements used but not the 'phrasing' produced by the bricolage (the artisan-like inventiveness) and the discursiveness that combine these elements."[47]

We have already referred to a few sophistical trajectories (laws are tyrannical, slavery is a human-made institution, nonbeing is on equal footing with being, every issue has two or more opposing sides, cooperation is the other side of competition). We could easily supplement our discussion by adding Protagoras' human-measure dictum as well as his religious agnosticism,[48] Gorgias' radical distinction between empirical and symbolic reality,[49] Critias' sociological view of religion,[50] Lycophron's nominalistic explanation of nobility of good birth,[51] and Thrasymachus' notion of justice as nothing but the interest of the stronger.[52] But by far the most common trajectory attributed to the sophists is that of turning the weaker argument into a stronger one.[53] At a strictly intellectual level, such a claim must have sounded exciting if only because it was novel and daring. But at the practical level, the implication must have been quite clear—if it could succeed, it could disrupt the known order of things by turning it upside down. Judging from the accusation against Socrates,[54] the mere possibility of empowering the hitherto weak and disempowering the traditionally strong must have caused alarm especially among those who had customarily commanded the stronger arguments and, therefore, had had the upper hand in determining intellectual, political, legal, and economic matters. By contrast, it must have inspired some hope among the "lesser," that is, the poor, the common, and the marginalized. Ironically, the weaker-stronger trajectory fell, on a few occasions, in the hands of clever students, who turned it on their sophistic teachers when it came time to pay (*Gorgias*, 519c–d).

De Certeau's bricoleur lives and operates, like those around him/her, within a vast field of speaking and other linguistic practices.[55] But whereas many of those around him/her use language strategically, the bricoleur employs it tactically. Explaining the difference between these two kinds of practice, de Certeau likens strategy to a calculus of power-relations that requires "a subject of will and power (a proprietor, an enterprise, a city, a scientific institution) [that] can be isolated from [its surrounding] 'environment.'" De Certeau goes on to explain that "A strategy assumes a place that can be circumscribed as proper (*propre*) and thus serve as the basis for generating relations with an exterior distinct from it (competitors, adversaries, 'clienteles,' 'targets,' or 'objects' of research)."[56] In contrast to a strategy, de Certeau notes, a tactic constitutes:

> a calculus which cannot count on a "proper" (a spatial or institutional localization). . . . A tactic insinuates itself into the other's place, fragmentarily, without taking it over in its entirety, without being able to keep it at a distance. It has at its disposal no base where it can capitalize on its advantages, prepare its expansions, and secure independence with respect to circumstances. *The "proper" is a victory of space over time* [emphasis added]. On the contrary, because it does not have a place, a tactic depends on time—it is always on the watch for opportunities that must be seized "on the wing." Whatever it wins, it does not keep. It must constantly manipulate events in order to turn them into opportunities. The weak must continually turn to their own ends forces alien to them. This is achieved in the propitious moments when they are able to combine heterogeneous elements.[57]

In sum, these "two ways of acting (strategically or tactically) can be distinguished according to whether they bet on place or time." More specifically, "strategies pin their hopes on the resistance that the establishment of a place offers to the erosion of time; tactics on the clever utilization of time, of the opportunities it presents and also of the play that it introduces into the foundations of power."[58]

The connections between sophist and tactician on the one hand and between philosopher and strategist on the other are unmistakable. De Certeau himself, referring to the former connection, observes that:

> in the enormous rhetorical corpus devoted to the art of speaking . . . the Sophists have a privileged place, from the point of view of tactics. Their principle was . . . to make the weaker position seem the stronger, and they claimed to have the power of turning the tables on the powerful by the way in which they made use of the opportunities offered by the particular situation.[59]

On account of their travels, which precluded a permanent place of operations; their resident-alien status, which prevented them from participating fully in the political sphere; and their practice of reversing stronger and weaker arguments, which denied them access to established positions of power, the sophists depended on the resources of the cities they visited, worked as conditions permitted, and lived according to the circumstances they encountered. For them, place represented not a territory in which one settles, but a point through which one passes, only to go on. In other words, the sophists did not *move into* but *passed through* certain places. As we have already seen, they usually arrived on the scene from elsewhere, entered intellectual contests, performed rhetorical displays, and went on to other places to do more of the same. But if this is so, they must be viewed not as settlers of clearly defined ideational territories, but as restless importers and exporters of intellectual goods whose consumption by the local consumers unsettled communities of thought accustomed to the goods of the local economy.

According to de Certeau's vocabulary, the sophists were not strategists but tacticians who had to make do by relying on "a clever utilization of time." Naturally, such a reliance, played a determining role in the kind of rhetoric they practiced and taught. We have already noted that their itinerant ways gave their rhetoric a general character (model speeches utilizing commonplaces), while their logographic practices resulted in a rhetoric of particulars (political or forensic speeches for specific issues and occasions). But there was yet another aspect to their rhetoric. Often the result of improvisation (αὐτοσχεδιάζειν) or an unrehearsed utterance on the spur of the moment, their rhetoric sought to emphasize the importance of spontaneity in the production of oral discourse.[60] In all three cases, however, their rhetoric consisted of existing materials put into new forms, now by combining heterogeneous elements, now by separating homogeneous ones. Examples of the former practice include: combining justice with power (*Thrasymachus*, 85B.6a) and religion with social control (*Critias*, 88B.25). Examples of the latter practice include: the separation of logos from substances and existing things (ὑποκείμενα καὶ ὄντα) (*Gorgias*, 82B.3.84) and the differentiation of debate (ἀμφισβητεῖν) from dispute (ἐρίζειν) and satisfaction (εὐφρένεσθαι) from pleasure (ἥδεσθαι) (Prodicus, 84A.13).

Unlike the sophists, the philosophers of the fourth century can be viewed as strategists in command of a place of operations (Isocrates' school of rhetoric, Plato's Academy, and Aristotle's Lyceum). In de Certeau's language, all three were cognitive proprietors, intellectual entrepreneurs, and mentors of research programs. Operating from their circumscribed institutional locations, they produced discourses that turned the sophists into adversaries, competitors, and objects of research. These discourses sought to make proper the practices of the sophists by means of critique, appropriation, and correction. In and through their discourses, the philosophers attributed to the sophists certain positions, in effect relocating them in the less reputable domains of thought, domains in which they were destined to remain for many centuries to come. Precisely how this happened will be seen when we examine the receptions of sophistical rhetoric by Plato, Isocrates, and Aristotle. For now, we need only point out that insofar as the philosophers' places of operation survived them, they can be said to have triumphed, until recently at any rate, over the sophists, and to have secured the independence of their doctrines from the vagaries of circumstances and the irregularities of time. In a word, the doctrines of the philosophers maintain their appeal to this day despite the passage of time and the changes in circumstances.

Thus far we have seen that the rhetoric of the sophists was in part shaped by their predicament, which was largely determined by the sociopolitical needs and circumstances of the Hellenic culture of their time. We have also seen that the culture was sufficiently spacious to entertain and accommodate the sophists once they surfaced in its midst. For their part, the sophists capitalized on the opportunities that presented themselves, and created more opportunities by combining the resources of tradition with those of innovation. In effect the sophists became instrumental in opening wider the gates of the culture, and challenging what was already there. In the rest of this chapter, we will focus on two specific cultural practices, contests and spectacles, showing how they shaped sophistical rhetoric and how it shaped them.

## Competition and Sophistical Rhetoric

The starting point of this section is that sophistical rhetoric emerged in a culture of competition. Normalized and internalized through the organization of the Olympic Games, this institutionalized form of cultural activity shaped sophistical rhetoric in its image, making public discourse a matter of competition. In turn, sophistical rhetoric pushed

competition beyond the boundaries of the stadium and into the rhetorical forums of the court and the Assembly. In so doing, it helped
produce the awareness that words do more than announce the world
in the manner of pre-sophistical poetry—they also question it, challenge it, attack it, defend it, or maintain it. In other words, words enable one to compete with and challenge what is already uttered and
already in currency.

Writing on the prevalence of competition in early Hellenic life,
Nietzsche asserts that behind the idea of contest one can find the desire for a second genius as a preventative measure against genius. In
Hellas the way to the highest point of any human endeavor was filled
with contests, struggles, and battles. But the arrival at the highest
point signaled neither the elimination of all opposition nor the recognition of one's achievement for all time. Once at the top, a genius
could expect to be challenged by a second genius. Whether in education, athletics, or art, what drove individuals and institutions was
competition:

> To the Ancients . . . the aim of the agonistic education was the wel-
> fare of the whole, of the civic society. Every Athenian . . . was to
> cultivate his Ego in contest, so far as it should be of the highest ser-
> vice to Athens and should do the least harm. . . . [T]he youth
> thought of the welfare of his native town when he vied with others
> in running, throwing, or singing; it was her glory that he wanted to
> increase with his own; it was to his town's gods that he dedicated
> the wreaths which the umpires as a mark of honour set upon his
> head. . . . But as the youths . . . were brought up struggling
> against one another, so their educators were in turn in emulation
> amongst themselves. Distrustfully jealous, the great musical mas-
> ters, Pindar and Simonides, stepped side by side; in rivalry the
> sophist . . . meets his fellow sophist; even the most universal kind
> of instruction, through the drama, was imparted to the people only
> under the form of an enormous wrestling of the great musical and
> dramatic artists.[61]

In a more prosaic fashion, Richard Garner has recently affirmed
Nietzsche's view by pointing out that competition was "embedded
early in the culture . . . and . . . spread to all areas of human activity," from war to the hunt, and from the debates of the Assembly to
the words within a sentence.[62] In the same vein, Garner observes that

"Greek culture and social organization were replete with figures of competition and combat. In general, this was as true of the form of poetic figures of speech as of athletic and military struggle."[63]

If we accept competition as one of the cultural givens in the Hellenic world of the sophists, and if we assume a reciprocal influence between rhetoric and the culture in which it is uttered, symbolic contests in a highly competitive environment are to be expected. That the sophists were grafting aspects of the competitive ethic to their rhetoric becomes apparent if we view them as the heirs of the poetical tradition, as the recipients, that is, of the words of poets like Pindar, whose victory odes had elevated the athlete to the highest status among humans:

> By poets wise that man is held happy, and is a theme for their song, whosoever, by being victorious with his hands or with the prowess of his feet, gaineth the greatest prizes by courage or by strength, and who, while still living, seeth his youthful son happily win two Pythian crowns. The brazen heaven he cannot climb; but as for all the bright achievements which we mortals attain, he reacheth the utmost limit of that voyage.[64]

The sophists, however, went beyond their poetic heritage in at least two ways. Unlike many poets before them, they were not content to stand at the sidelines of athletic or bellicose contests exalting the victors and praising heroic deeds and ideals.[65] Instead, they themselves, like athletes, musicians, rhapsodes, and dramatists in their era, entered contests.[66] Second, they pushed the competitive ethic into new vistas by construing public discursive practices as instances of an ongoing agonistic enterprise. That this is so is evident from several sources. Gorgias, for example, is reputed to have remarked that a rhetorical contest "requires two kinds of excellence, daring and skill; daring . . . to withstand danger, and skill to understand how to trip the opponent. For surely speech, like the summons at the Olympic games, calls him who will, but crowns him who can" (82B.8). In the same vein, the epigram found in 1876 in Olympia suggests that Gorgias thought of rhetoric as a competitive proposition:

> No one of mortals before discovered a finer art
> Than Gorgias to arm the soul for contests of excellence.
> (82A.8)

Like Gorgias, Protagoras seems to have made a connection between verbal disputation and wrestling and to have written handbooks on both (*Sophist* 232d–e). As such, it is no wonder that he should have thought diplologically, in terms of two arguments (*dissoi logoi*) in contest with one another, rather than monologically, in terms of a single, uncontested logos. As we have seen, the link between sophistical rhetoric and competition is hinted at in the *Protagoras*, where Protagoras says that sophistry before his time was often disguised in various forms, athletics being one of them (316d–e). In the same dialogue, Protagoras refers to himself as a veteran competitor of rhetorical combats when he discloses that he has undertaken in his life-time many contests of speech (πολλοῖς ἤδη εἰς ἀγῶνα λόγων ἀφικόμην) (335a). Accordingly, Socrates likens Protagoras to a fighter, and after hearing his comments on poetry, he says, "I felt as though I had been struck by a skillful boxer, and was quite blind and dizzy with the effect of his words" (339e). In a later passage, Socrates uses the same language of athletic contest when discussing the way in which Simonides the poet set out to overthrow Pittacus' saying that it is hard to be good (343c). These Socratic remarks are consistent with one of Protagoras' preserved titles, *On Truth or Refutations* (the Greek for refutations being (καταβάλλοντες)—literally, knock-down arguments). The sophists' affinity for verbal competition is further attested in the *Euthydemus*, where Plato tells us of Euthydemus' and Dionysodorus' love for eristic disputation, their use of words as weapons (272a), their interest in beating their interlocutors in debate, and their pursuit of victory at all costs. In the same dialogue (305b), Plato also refers to an orator as someone who excels in the contests of the courts (τῶν ἀγωνίσασθαι δεινῶν ἐν τοῖς δικαστηρίοις); and in the *Hippias Minor*, he portrays Hippias as a competitor in intellectual contests at the Olympic Games (363c–64a).

When pieced together, the evidence suggests a connection between some forms of sophistical rhetoric and competition, basically implying that the language of athletic events supplied a rich vocabulary for the discourses of and about rhetoric. Moreover, it suggests that the sophists were thought to have turned rhetoric into a competitive enterprise, thus upholding the agonistic tradition they had stepped into, and, at the same time, shifting the emphasis from events outside of language to language itself. Accordingly, they seem to have reasoned that if one athlete could outdistance, outlast, or outplay another, a given discourse could outwit, outmaneuver, or outdazzle another.[67] Finally, our evidence intimates that the sophists expanded the field of competition from the stadium and its athletic contests to the courtroom and its legal battles, and to the Assembly and its political struggles. They accomplished this by combining two heterogeneous elements—athletics and discourse. In effect they created a new amalgam which Aristotle would later call forensic rhetoric.

If there is one place where the drama of rhetorical competition was most intense, it was the courtroom. While in the stadia onlookers could witness well-trained bodies competing for an olive branch and fame, in the courts audiences could hear well-crafted arguments competing for large monetary sums or verdicts of life or death. In both arenas, however, the common goal was victory. In his analysis of the pleasure of victory in the *Rhetoric* (1.11.14–15), Aristotle links courtroom battles to athletic competition:

> "Victory," he says, "is pleasant; not only to those who love to conquer but to all; for there is an idea of superiority, which all [people] with more or less eagerness desire. And since victory is pleasant, combative sports and intellectual contests are pleasant. . . . [W]here there is competition there is victory. That is why courtroom battles and debating contests are pleasant to those who are accustomed to them and capable [of competing in them]."

One of the more interesting features of this Aristotelian account is that it places physical contests (μαχητικὰς) and competitions in disputation or controversy (ἐριστικάς) in the same category—games or amusements (παιδιὰς). Such a classification suggests that intellectual competition in Aristotle's time was regarded as an acceptable form of pastime. However, Aristotle also explains that victory is pleasant because the victor usually becomes the recipient of both honor and good reputation (καὶ τιμὴ καὶ εὐδοξία), two of the most pleasant things, especially when they are conferred by neighbors, fellow citizens, contemporaries, or the public in general. If we accept this Aristotelian account, it is not hard to see that the motive for victory and the quest for honor and good reputation were so strong in the Hellenic culture that they often overshadowed the wish for justice in the courts. As Garner has shown, the agonistic orientation in Athens was so all-encompassing that "the language of the democratic courts . . . at times placed competitive ideals above justice."[68]

Like Aristotle, Plato acknowledges the competitive character of rhetoric as it was practiced in the legal domain. As we have seen, his conception of an orator is that of an accomplished contestant in the courts of law (*Euthydemus* 305b). Consistent with this conceptualization, Plato likens legal trials (ἀγῶνες) to time-bound competitive events in which the race (δρόμος) is often for the defendant's life (*Theaetetus*, 172e). Throughout his works, Plato uses the term *agon* to refer to a trial (*Apology*, 34c; *Crito*, 45e; *Theaetetus*, 172e), or a lawsuit (*Republic*, 362b; *Apology*, 24c). He also uses the term to refer to a contest or a competition in general (*Phaedo*, 90b). Finally, he uses it in conjunction with other terms (i.e., μάχη, ἄμιλλα) denoting competition, fight, battle, or contest, symbolic or otherwise.

Plato's understanding of the link between rhetoric and competition goes beyond its manifestation in the courts. For him orator (ῥήτωρ) and contestant (ἀγωνιστής) are virtual synonyms. Accordingly, he has Socrates tell Phaedrus that becoming a perfect orator—that is to say, an accomplished contestant (ἀγωνιστὴν τέλεον γενέσθαι) requires talent, knowledge, and extensive practice (*Phaedrus*, 269d). In the *Gorgias* (456b), Plato has Gorgias predict that in a rhetorical contest (λόγῳ διαγωνίζεσθαι) between an orator and a doctor the discourse of the orator would prevail. Gorgias admits later that both rhetoric and athletic contests (like boxing, wrestling, and fighting) must be used fairly (δικαίως καὶ τῇ ῥητορικῇ χρῆσθαι, ὥσπερ καὶ τῇ ἀγωνίᾳ) (*Gorgias*, 457b).

Much of Plato's language about sophists and their use of discourse reveals an intimate connection between sophistical rhetoric and athletic competition. In the *Sophist* (231d–e) for instance, he refers to the typical sophist as an athlete of words (περὶ λόγους ἦν τις ἀθλητής). In the *Theaetetus* (164c–d), Socrates critiques part of his exchange with Theodorus on the grounds that it is overly competitive and insufficiently cooperative or reflective, "We seem to be acting like professional debaters . . . and we do not see that we, who claim to be not contestants for a prize but lovers of wisdom (οὐ φάσκοντες ἀγωνισταὶ ἀλλὰ φιλόσοφοι), are doing just what those ingenious persons do." Later on in the same dialogue, Plato has Socrates distinguish the competitive sophist (ἀγωνιζόμενος) from the dialectical philosopher (διαλεγόμενος):

> it is unfair in discussion when a man makes no distinction between merely trying to make points and carrying on a real argument. In the former he may jest and try to trip up his opponent as much as

he can, but in real argument he must be in earnest and must set his interlocutor on his feet, pointing out to him those slips only which are due to himself and his previous associations. (167d–ff)

Finally, Plato makes another, this time more curious distinction between those who love competition and those who obey the laws. Echoing Xenophanes' earlier sentiment that "the state would not . . . be any the more law-abiding even if there should be a good boxer among the folk, or a champion in the pentathlon, or in wrestling, or in swiftness of foot, which is the most honored exhibition of strength among all the contests of men in games"[69] Plato says, "That man is by far the best who, in preference to victory at Olympia or in any other contests (ἀγώνων) of war and peace would choose to have a victorious reputation for service to his native laws, as being the one man above all others who has served them with distinction throughout his life" (*Laws*, 729d). For all his criticisms and condemnation of the sophists' rhetorical athleticism, Plato is not very far from the sophists—when he has Socrates enter into dialectical combat with them, he too seeks to win, to have his argument prevail.

This section points out that, for the sophists, being an orator meant both accepting and issuing symbolic dares. It also meant engaging in the challenge of established rhetorical practices, in the sort of verbal combat in which no point of view can remain unopposed and no argument can stay unassailed for too long. Lastly, it meant acknowledging that a prevalent argument was prevalent, not by virtue of its historical status or its logical validity, but because it had been tested by and had withstood the attack(s) of the opposing side(s). But if this is so, the well-known account of the sophists as teaching how to make the weaker argument appear the stronger seems perfectly justified. They not only taught their students verbal skills to win arguments but they themselves entered public contests seeking to achieve victories by overcoming other contestants, dislodging opponents, and overpowering adversaries. That they should have done so is not, as Plato would later insist, a sign of moral perversion, misguided effort, or intellectual inferiority; rather, it is a mark of their adoption and transformation of the widespread cultural practice of competition. As we have seen, Plato too discusses rhetoric in terms of athletic competition; and by the time we get to the opening lines of Aristotle's *Rhetoric*, we see that it is the terminology of civic contest, defense and

accusation (ἀπολογεῖσθαι καὶ κατηγορεῖν), that specifies the boundaries of the discussion on rhetoric and dialectic.

## Spectacles and Sophistical Rhetoric

The culture in which sophistical rhetoric emerged was not only a
culture of competition, it was also one of spectacles. When the sophists converged on Athens, the most accomplished form of spectacle
was the drama of the theater. As in the case of competition, this institutionalized form of cultural activity shaped sophistical rhetoric in
its image, making public discourse a matter of performance and exhibition. In turn, sophistical rhetoric took exhibition outside the boundaries of the theater and into the forums of legal and political speaking.
In so doing, it helped create the awareness that words do more than
call forth the world the way poetry had done; they also create it, display it, and exaggerate some of its features and understate others. In
other words, words are not only instruments of representation or ve-
hicles of meaning but also actions performed on stages of their own
making.

Whether in the form of gymnastic games, theatrical performances,
state festivals, or public debates, spectacles were a big part of everyday life in the Hellenic culture, a culture that celebrated itself in many
and elaborate ways.[70] This is another way of saying that Nietzsche's
observation, that even the spectacle of drama was performed only after keen competition among dramatic artists, has another side—the
keenest of athletic competitions took the form of public spectacles.
But if this is so, it should come as no surprise that the sophists' rhetorical practices adopted the cultural aesthetic of exhibition. Largely
an outdoors people, the Hellenes of the fifth century B.C. produced
their discourses (rhetorical, poetical, or philosophical) for the outside;
they literally spoke them "out there,"[71] for the world to see and hear.

Insofar as the outside is the world of appearances, it is natural that
the sophists should have concerned themselves with the form and
performance of public rhetoric. The conceptualization of discourse as
content is largely a post-sophistical development made possible by
the outbreak of the silent revolution of writing.[72] Addressing the Hellenic affinity for form and semblances, William Archer Butler wrote:

> In religion, the Greek delighted in the temple and the procession
> more than in the god; in poetry, his joys, his sorrows, his medita-

tions, were moulded in a form essentially picturesque, — such as the eye could contemplate; in the ideal beauty of statuary, his taste inclined to precision of outline even more than to depth of expression; in history . . . he inclined to the perfection of style more than the perfection of veracity; in national policy, wealth and power themselves were scarcely valued in comparison to the floating phantom of "glory" which is their shadow.[73]

Making his comments specific to rhetoric, Butler went on to say that "the Athenian listener preferred (not merely the semblance without the reality, to the reality without the semblance of reason — but even preferred) the semblance without, to the semblance with the reality of truth. The brilliant falsehood, which defied . . . logical detection, was the very triumph of form and colour over weight and solidity . . . it was . . . the very perfection of imitation."[74]

Drama was a cultural phenomenon that provided many opportunities for the diversion and entertainment that comes from hearing and seeing the conflicts of the human condition performed on the make-believe world of the stage. The significance of drama in the Hellenic culture has been addressed by George Grote, who wrote, "The reception of such pleasures through the eye and the ear, as well as amidst a sympathizing crowd, was a fact of no small importance in the mental history of the people. It contributed to exalt their imagination, like the grand edifices and ornaments added during the same period to their acropolis."[75] On a parallel note, Nietzsche asserted a connection between theatrical performances and rhetorical displays when he declared that "the Athenian went to the theater *in order to hear beautiful speeches.*"[76] Taking this connection to reflect a culture of appearances, he exclaimed, "Oh, those Greeks! they knew how to live. What is required for that is to stop courageously at the surface, the fold, the skin, to adore appearance, to believe in forms, tones, words, in the whole Olympus of appearance. Those Greeks were superficial — *out of profundity.*"[77]

If Butler, Grote, and Nietzsche do have a point, it is no wonder that the tradition depicts the sophists as virtuosos of extravagant linguistic displays who amazed their audiences with brilliant styles, colorful appearances, and flamboyant personalities (80A.23; 82A.1.2–3, 1a, 2, 4.2.–4; 84B.2.34; 85A.13; 86A.2.7; 87B.44a; 88A.1). Nor is it any wonder that they made exaggerated claims to prospective students (*Sophist*, 233e; *Euthydemus*, 274a), and used figures and tropes excessively.

After all, early tragedy was designed to honor Dionysus, the god of appearances and excess. Even when it came to charging admission fees for a performance, the sophists seem to have followed the example of drama. In this regard, we might recall here Socrates' complaint that he is too poor to attend Prodicus' fifty-drachmai lecture and can only afford the one-drachma one (*Cratylus*, 384b). We might also recall that Plato portrays the sophists as imitators, and as producers of images who are preoccupied with appearances and rhetorical exhibitions (*Gorgias*, 447c). Finally, we might recall that he represents them as undisciplined quasi-artists whose main concern is the pleasure of their audience (*Gorgias*, 502a–d), whose art (really a knack) is an art of deception (*Sophist*, 240d), and whose real business is entertainment (*Sophist*, 235a).

Show, appearance, art, deception, imitation, illusion, and entertainment are terms that would seem to describe the theater, not rhetorical discourse. But with Plato, these terms describe both; and well they should. As Aristotle was to point out later, the resemblance between a theatrical and a rhetorical performance is unmistakable. For one thing, both rely on delivery for their enactment: "It is plain that delivery has just as much to do with oratory as with poetry" (*Rhetoric*, 3.1.3). For another, at least one kind of rhetoric, epideictic, aims mostly at the same thing drama does, ἐπίδειξις (show, exhibition). Without precluding the possibility that forensic and deliberative rhetoric do likewise, Aristotle specifies that the audience of epideictic, the most spectacular type of rhetoric, is similar to that of drama: it consists of θεωροί (spectators) (*Rhetoric*, 1.3.2) for whose pleasure and assessment it is produced (2.18.1). Further, both theatrical and rhetorical performances require dramatic ability (τὸ ὑποκριτικόν). That is why Aristotle predicts that "when the principles of delivery [in rhetoric] have been worked out, they will produce the same effect as on the stage" and informs us that Thrasymachus had been one of very few people to have done work on those very principles (*Rhetoric*, 3.1.7). Finally, Aristotle alludes to the efficacy of dramatic (or rhetorical) delivery when he observes that performers do well not only on the theatrical stage but also on the public arena, "just as in drama the actors now count for more than the poets, so it is in the contests of public life" (*Rhetoric*, 3.1.4). As Aristotle saw it, orators like Gorgias had relied heavily on the arts of recitation and acting to render their oratorical performances impressive. They also borrowed freely from the language of the poets in order to win the fame and popularity the poets had won.

The connection between sophistical rhetoric and dramatic spectacles is further supported by the traditions that Antiphon was writing tragedies before turning to rhetoric (87A.5.7); that Critias may have written as many as four dramas (88.introduction); and that Gorgias was interested in tragedy, especially that of Aeschylus.[78] Although we cannot be certain about these traditions, the force of drama in shaping the sophists' rhetoric seems undeniable.

In the case of drama, what brought protagonist and chorus together on the stage was a certain irresolution demanding action on the part of the protagonist. Under the direction of the playwright, the protagonist often found him/herself at odds with the chorus and torn between the divine and the human worlds. In the case of rhetoric, what brought orator and audience together was an issue demanding a rhetorical choice, a choice, that is, between competing and conflicting discourses. The spectators of a theatrical event heard the protagonist speak his/her mind out-loud in an effort to resolve split loyalties or clear internal doubts. They also heard the chorus warning and reminding the protagonist that any course of action designed to settle the issue at hand would have grave consequences. The listeners of a rhetorical event saw the orator display his words in full public view, conjuring up linguistic images that created virtual experiences, in effect focusing their sight onto his discourse and away from the discourses of others. Thus if it is true that, as Nietzsche points out, the Hellenes went to the theater in order to hear beautiful speeches, it is also true that they attended rhetorical events in order to see spectacular theatrical performances.

Precisely what did the Hellenes see when attending the sophists' rhetorical performances? In Gorgias' rhetoric, they could see a Helen subjected to divine (fate or Eros) and human (violence or persuasion) forces greater than herself—a variation of what they had seen in Euripides' *Helen* and *Trojan Women*. In Prodicus' rhetoric they could see a Heracles pondering which of the two paths to follow (vice or virtue)—a version of the *Heracles* of Sophocles. And in Antiphon's court speeches they could see varieties of conspiracy, murder, revenge, and conflicting forms of justice reminiscent of Aeschylean drama; while in his tetralogical compositions they could see discourses taking turns repudiating one another, the very kinds of exchanges they had seen between the Just Logos and the Unjust Logos in Aristophanes' *Clouds*.

In more general terms, the spectators of sophistical performances saw the orators wear the masks of logos, masks concealing the true identity of the speaker's thoughts in the same way that theatrical masks kept the identity of the actor hidden. As in the case of dramatic spectacles, rhetorical performances often served as forms of diversion. But since diversion does not preclude instruction, rhetorical spectacles, especially panegyrics or *epitaphioi*, often functioned as means of social critique and the articulation of new visions of order.[79] Even so, the one message that can be said to have overshadowed all others in any rhetorical ἐπίδειξις was the message that language could not be delivered from its fundamental ambiguity. Thus to engage in rhetoric, too, was to admit, if only implicitly, an otherness to one's own discourse. In drama, the otherness of the human world was represented by the world of the gods with the protagonist caught hopelessly in the middle. In rhetoric, and under the pressures of social and political life, action required that one assert the apparent superiority of a given discourse and treat its otherness as inferior.

The above discussion points to a certain link between some forms of sophistical rhetoric and dramatic spectacles. Insofar as the sophists turned rhetoric itself into a spectacular enterprise, they can be said to have relied on—indeed, imitated—aspects of the dramatic tradition they had encountered. But insofar as they expanded the field of the spectacular from the theater to the courtroom, the Assembly, or other places of public gathering, they can be said to have theatricalized rhetorical discourse, thus giving it a new face. Thus, by combining two heterogeneous elements, spectacles and discourse, the sophists in effect created a new amalgam—the amalgam that Aristotle would later call epideictic rhetoric.

As in the case of rhetoric and contests, Plato recognized the connection between sophistical rhetoric and theatrical spectacles. That this is so is apparent in the *Theaetetus* where he has Socrates distinguish between philosophers on the one hand and orators and poets on the other, "we who belong to this band [the philosophers] are not the servants of our arguments, but the arguments are, as it were, our servants, and each of them must await our pleasure to be finished; for we have neither judge, nor . . . any spectator (οὔτε γὰρ δικαστὴς οὔτε θεατὴς) set over us to censure and rule us" (173c). In the *Republic*, Plato makes another distinction, this time between philosophers on the one hand and lovers of spectacles, the arts, and action (φιλοθεάμονάς τε καὶ φιλοτέχνους καὶ πρακτικούς) on the other: "The lovers of sounds and sights delight in beautiful tones and colors and shapes and everything that art fashions out of these, but their thought is incapable of apprehending and taking delight in the nature of the beautiful itself" (476b).

Focusing more sharply on the lovers of sounds (φιλήκοοι), Plato argues that "you couldn't induce them to attend a serious debate or any such entertainment, but as if they had farmed out their ears to listen to every chorus in the land they run about all the Dionysiac festivals, never missing one." (*Republic,* 475d). In contrast to these spectacle-loving simpletons, philosophers are enamored of the spectacle of the truth (τοὺς τῆς ἀληθείας . . . φιλοθεάμονας) (475e). Conceiving of public diversion as a means of public improvement, Plato argues in the *Laws* that:

> rightly speaking, the judge [should] sit not as a pupil but as a teacher of the spectators, being ready to oppose those who offer them pleasure in a way that is unseemly or wrong; and that is what the present law in Italy and Sicily actually does; by entrusting the decision to the spectators, who award the prize by a show of hands, not only has it corrupted the poets . . . but it has corrupted also the pleasures of the audience; for whereas they ought to be improving their standard of pleasure by listening to characters superior to their own, what they now do has just the opposite effect. (659a–c)

As one might expect, one of Plato's greatest objections to the rhetoric of display was that it had spread outside the theater and had turned legal trials into matters of sights and sounds, as if they were theatrical shows and nothing more (*Laws,* 767e). In the *Laws* (876b) he observes that the courts have become like theaters—both are filled with the tumult of the spectators, who are roaring out with their praise or blame of each speaker. So much so, Plato thought, that the whole State was faced with a difficult situation. In effect, Plato objected to the theatricalization of legal procedures, or to what he calls "the spirit of lawlessness" brought about by poets and orators. By making the spectators believe that they are able judges of theatrical or oratorical performances, reciters and declaimers have installed a theatrocracy of taste in the place of an aristocracy of intelligence (*Laws,* 701a–b).

In effect, Plato was voicing the same dismay Thucydides' Cleon had expressed when addressing the Assembly during the Mytilenean debate. Scolding his listeners for their inordinate love of rhetorical spectacles, Cleon is reported to have said the following:

It is your wont to be spectators of words and hearers of deeds (θεαταὶ μὲν τῶν λόγων γίγνεσθαι, ἀκροαταὶ δὲ τῶν ἔργων). . . . You are adepts not only at being deceived by novel proposals but also at refusing to follow approved advice, slaves as you are of each new paradox and scorners of what is familiar. Each of you wishes above all to be an orator himself, or, failing that, to vie with those dealers of paradox by seeming not to lag behind them in wit but to applaud a smart saying before it is out of the speaker's mouth; you are as quick to forestall what is said as you are to foresee what will come of it. You seek, one might say, a world quite unlike that in which we live, but give too little heed to that which is at hand. In a word, you are in thrall to the pleasures of the ear and are more like men who sit as *spectators at exhibitions of sophists* than men who take counsel for the welfare of the state (ἁπλῶς τε ἀκοῆς ἡδονῇ ἡσσώμενοι καὶ σοφιστῶν θεαταῖς ἐοικότες καθημένοις μᾶλλον ἢ περὶ πόλεως βουλευομένοις) (3.38.4–7; my emphasis)

Judging from the comments of Thucydides, Plato, and Aristotle, sophistical rhetoric was understood not only as a matter of competition, but also as a matter of exhibition. Accordingly, for the sophists being an orator meant treating audiences to discursive spectacles, staging the word, and making the oration appear beautiful, thus endowing it with irresistible power. At the same time, it meant understanding that no set of arguments could expect to be successful without taking into account the pleasure of its viewing audience.[80] Lastly, to be an orator meant to recognize that discourse was well-received not only on account of its superior strength but also on account of its higher aesthetic appeal.[81] Thus the familiar depiction of the sophists as teachers of poeticized prose and performative skill seems warranted. Indeed, they did not claim that the weaker argument *is* the stronger argument; only that they could make the weaker argument *appear* stronger. That they should have done so is not a sign of questionable designs on unsuspecting audiences, but a mark of the well-defined motivation to deceive—a motivation tied to the pleasure of speaking. As Gorgias is said to have noted in reference to tragedy, "the deceiver is more justly esteemed than the non-deceiver and the deceived is wiser than the undeceived"; and as Plutarch explains further, "The deceiver is more justly esteemed because he succeeds in what he intends, and the deceived is wiser, for a man who is not imperceptive is easily affected by the pleasure of words" (82B.23).

This chapter has situated the sophists and their rhetorical discourses in a cultural milieu marked by the logic of circumstances, the ethic of competition, and the aesthetic of exhibition. In so doing, it has attempted to explain why sophistical rhetoric assumed the character it did, not why the fourth-century intellectuals denounced it (the latter question will be entertained in later chapters). The next chapter seeks to articulate in some detail sophistical rhetoric as a practice by exploring the notions of opportunity, playfulness, and possibility as constitutive functions of circumstances, competition, and exhibition respectively.

## Notes

1. While one may discern differences among the individual sophists we know of, the rhetorical movement they are said to have launched cannot be apprehended by attending to those differences. Nor can it be apprehended by resorting to the additive principle of understanding. Sophistical rhetoric is something greater than the sum of all we can say about each sophist.
2. See, for example, George B. Kerferd, *The Sophistic Movement* (Cambridge: Cambridge University Press, 1981).
3. See K. E. Wilkerson, "From Hero to Citizen: Persuasion in Early Greece," *Philosophy and Rhetoric* 15, 2 (Spring, 1972): 104–25.
4. Wilhelm Nestle, *Vom Mythos zum Logos* (Aalen: Scientia Verlag, 1966).
5. See Jean-Pierre Vernant and Pierre Vidal-Naquet, *Myth and Tragedy in Ancient Greece*, trans. Janet Lloyd (New York: Zone Books, 1990), 305–24; Robert Parker, "Greek States and Greek Oracles" in P. A. Cartledge and F. D. Harvey, eds., *CRUX: Essays in Greek History Presented to G. E. M. de Ste. Croix* (London: Duckworth and Co., 1985), 298–326.
6. See Eric A. Havelock, *Preface to Plato* (Cambridge, Mass.: Harvard University Press, 1982); Thomas Cole, *The Origins of Rhetoric in Ancient Greece* (Baltimore: Johns Hopkins University Press, 1991), 33–112.
7. See Aristotle, *Politics*, 4.9.8.
8. As late as 370 B.C. (the accepted date of Isocrates' *Helen*), Isocrates relies on the myths of Helen, Theseus, and Heracles in order to advance his pan-Hellenic program. And despite his eighty-two years in 353 B.C. (the date of his *Antidosis*), he still praises discourses that are "akin to works composed in

rhythm and set to music." These discourses, he observes, "set forth facts in a style more imaginative and more ornate . . . and they use throughout figures of speech in greater number and of more striking character. All men take as much pleasure in listening to this kind of prose as in listening to poetry." (*Antidosis*, 47).

9. For Gorgias' reliance on the poetical language of the playwrights, see Octave Navarre, *Essai sur la Rhétorique Grecque avant Aristote* (Paris: Librairie Hachette et Cie, 1900), 92–119; W. Vollgraff, *L' Oraison Funèbre de Gorgias* (Leiden: E. J. Brill, 1952). On the shift from poetry to rhetorical prose see Cole's account: "For a crucial series of decades in the course of the fifth and fourth centuries a host of Sophists, scientists, physicians, polymaths, logographers, orators, statesmen, dramatists, and exegetes disputed among themselves the position left vacant by the collapse of poetry's undisputed claims to be the moral and intellectual mentor of Greece. Victory went ultimately to the group of combatants best able to develop . . . a new form of discourse (artistic — that is, rhetorical — prose) capable of rivaling poetic performances in its power to satisfy the curiosity, engage the sympathies, and fire the imagination of an audience, whether hearers or readers." Cole, *The Origins of Rhetoric in Ancient Greece*, 28–29.

10. Consider, for example, Gorgias' reputed remark that "speech, like the summons at the Olympic Games, calls him who will, but crowns him who can" (82B.8).

11. See *Philebus* (58a), where Gorgias is said to have held that "the art of rhetoric surpasses all others . . . makes all things subject to itself, not by force, but by their free will, and is by far the best of all arts."

12. See Aristotle, *Politics*, 4.9.3.

13. Cited in George Thomson, *Aeschylus and Athens: A Study in the Social Origins of Drama* (London: Lawrence & Wishart, 1980), 201–2.

14. See Victor Ehrenberg, *From Solon to Socrates: Greek History and Civilization during the sixth and fifth centuries B.C.* (London: Methuen & Co., 1970), 330–32.

15. For a detailed discussion of the legal status of aliens, see Douglas M. MacDowell, *The Law in Classical Athens* (Ithaca, N.Y.: Cornell University Press, 1986), 75–79.

16. Of course, there were exceptions, as in the case of Aristotle, who wrote that "in Athens things which are considered proper for a citizen are not permitted to an alien, and it is dangerous to live in Athens." Cited in Frank L. Vatai, *Intellectuals in Politics in the Greek World* (London: Croom Helm, 1984), 95. Aristotle's testimony, however, may reflect only his own reaction to the treatment he received by Athenians on account of his suspected pro-Macedonian sympathies.

17. As Pericles is made to say in his *Funeral Oration*, "We throw our city open to all the world, and we never by alien acts debar anyone from learning or

seeing anything which an enemy might profit by observing if it were not kept from his sight" (Thucydides, 2.39.1).

18. See Isocrates' *On the Peace* (21).

19. Consider, for example the arrangements reported by the author of the second section of *Dissoi Logoi* (Concerning the Seemly and the Disgraceful) (90.2.1–28).

20. J. B. Bury, S. A. Cook, F. E. Adcock, eds., *The Cambridge Ancient History*, vol. 5 (New York: Macmillan and Co., 1927), 6.

21. In addition to these constraints, there was a curious legal procedure observed in Athens every sixth prytany according to which three citizens and/or three metics were tried annually as sycophants. See *The Constitution of Athens* (43.5) in J. M. Moore, *Aristotle and Xenophon on Democracy and Oligarchy* (Berkeley: University of California Press, 1975). For commentary on this practice, see Richard Garner, *Law and Society in Classical Athens* (London: Croom Helm, 1987), 97, 70.

22. See Jean-Pierre Vernant, *Myth and Society in Ancient Greece*, trans. Janet Lloyd (New York: Zone Books, 1988), 21–22.

23. A cosmopolitan is a person whose city (*polis*) is not any one known city but the whole world (*kosmos*).

24. *Dissoi Logoi*, 2.14.

25. Ibid., 2.15.

26. Ibid., 2.14, 15.

27. Consider, for example, Antiphon's *Tetralogies*, Gorgias' *Helen* and *Palamedes*, or Prodicus' *Choice of Heracles*.

28. This is the tacit understanding against which Gorgias defends himself in the *Gorgias* (456b–57c).

29. Antiphon, for example, is said to have been the first to compose speeches for suits in the lawcourts (87A.3.5, 4.10, 6.7).

30. According to Philostratus, "Comedy lampooned Antiphon for his cleverness in pleading suits and for selling at a high price, particularly to those who stood in jeopardy, speeches composed to frustrate the course of justice" (87A.6.7).

31. See Plato's *Apology*, 19e–20a.

32. This is precisely what Aristotle, who was not an Athenian citizen, did when he moved to Chalcis rather than face charges of impiety in Athens.

33. The assumption here is that intellectual domains and cities resemble each other in at least three senses: (a) both can be defined by precise coordinates, (b) both require some familiarity on the part of the settler, and (c) both are in competition with other domains or cities.

34. Aristotle alludes to this ambiguity when he says in the *Politics* (1.1.9) that an ἄπολις (one without a city) is either φαῦλος (low in the scale of humanity) or κρείττων ἢ ἄνθρωπος (above humanity, more powerful than man). Further on, he observes that whoever is so self-sufficient that he has no need to enter

into partnership with a city-state must be either θηρίον (beast, animal) or θεός (god) (1.1.12).

35. See Gilles Deleuze, "Nomad Thought" in David B. Allison, *The New Nietzsche: Contemporary Styles of Interpretation* (Cambridge, Mass.: MIT Press, 1988), 142–49; and Michel de Certeau, *The Practice of Everyday Life*, trans. Steven F. Rendall (Berkeley: University of California Press, 1984).

36. Deleuze, 148. By "despot" I understand ruler or master in a broad sense, a sense that includes such rulers or masters as law or society at large.

37. Deleuze, 148. If we follow Deleuze's logic, we are in a position to understand the difficulties the Eleatic Stranger and Theaetetus face in the *Sophist* as they try to distinguish between the sophist and the philosopher. Their difficulties are due to the fact that the differences between the identities of sophist and philosopher are not immediately apparent; on the contrary, the two identities are often confused with one another. By following Deleuze, we can also understand Plato's proposed law to deal with the sophist's legal meddlesomeness (*Laws*, 938a–c) as an expression of the frustration a despot feels when trying to normalize the nomads.

38. See Aristotle's *Sophistical Refutations*, 166a.7–21, 177a.9–177b.34.

39. Deleuze, 143.

40. Ibid., 148. That this is so is evident in Plato's efforts to educate Dionysius philosophically, Aristotle's overseeing the education of Alexander the Great, and Isocrates' political advice to the Kings of Cyprus and Macedon.

41. Ibid., 145.

42. On the question of the sophists' views on law, see W. K. C. Guthrie, *The Sophists* (Cambridge: Cambridge University Press, 1971), 55–134; George B. Kerferd, *The Sophistic Movement* (Cambridge: Cambridge University Press, 1981), 111–30. On the question of slavery, see Guthrie, 155–60; Kerferd, 156–60; Augoustos Bayonas, "'Η 'Αρχαία Σοφιστική καὶ ὁ Θεσμός τῆς Δουλείας," *Athena* 68 (1965): 115–68.

43. See 86C.1, 87.2.90.fragment A, 88B.25; *Gorgias*, 483a–86d.

44. Guthrie, 155–60.

45. Plato makes this point in the *Gorgias* (481d–82a) by having Socrates critique Callicles for catering to fickle Athenian audiences, a practice that results in an inconsistent rhetoric.

46. Consider, for example, Plato's *Laws* and *Republic*, Aristotle's *Politics* and *Sophistical Refutations*, and Isocrates' *Antidosis* and *Against the Sophists* as works designed to repudiate sophistical claims and practices, and trying to remap the social, political, and intellectual terrain of their times.

47. De Certeau, xviii.

48. See 80B.1 and 4.

49. See 82B.3.84 and 11a.35.

50. See 88B.25.

51. Lycophron's reported utterance reads as follows: "Now the nobility of good birth is obscure, and its grandeur a matter of words" (83.4).

52. See 85B.6a.

53. See Alexander Sesonske, "To Make the Weaker Argument Defeat the Stronger," *Journal of the Philosophy of History* 6, no. 3 (July 1968): 217–32.

54. "Socrates is a criminal and a busybody, investigating the things beneath the earth and in the heavens and *making the weaker argument stronger* and teaching others these same things" (*Apology*, 19b; my emphasis).

55. Grounding his discussion of the bricoleur's operations on his discursive practices, de Certeau explains that "speaking operates within the field of a linguistic system; it effects an appropriation, or reappropriation, of language by its speakers; it establishes a *present* relative to a time and place; and it posits a *contract with the other* (the interlocutor) in a network of places and relations. . . . [U]sers make (*bricolent*) innumerable and infinitesimal transformations of and within the dominant cultural economy in order to adapt it to their own interests and their own rules" (xiii–xiv).

56. De Certeau, xix. For further discussion on the notion of strategy, see 35–36.

57. Ibid., xix. For further discussion on the notion of tactic, see 36–37.

58. Ibid., 38–39.

59. Ibid., xx.

60. In this regard, the doxographic tradition reports that Protagoras expounded on the importance of the opportune moment (καιροῦ δύναμιν ἐξέθετο) (80A.1.52) and Gorgias improvised easily (ῥᾶστα ἀπεσχεδίαζεν) (82A.1.3), trusting to the moment (τῷ καιρῷ) to speak on any subject (82A.1a).

61. See Friedrich Nietzsche, "Homer's Contest," in *Early Greek Philosophy and Other Essays*, trans. Maximillian A. Mugge (New York: Gordon Press, 1974), 58–59.

62. Garner, 60.

63. Ibid., 58. On the same issue, H. C. Baldry notes: "Most aspects of Greek life were strongly influenced by the idea of competition—not for profit, but for prestige, repute, glory. The rivalry between the heroes in the *Iliad* sets a pattern which is reflected later in peacetime activities as well as war: not only athletic contests at the Games, but contests between 'rhapsodes' in the recitation of Homer, between playwrights and between actors in the theatre." H. C. Baldry, *The Greek Tragic Theatre* (New York: W. W. Norton & Co., 1971), 19.

64. Cited in Rachel Sargent Robinson, *Sources for the History of Greek Athletics* (Chicago: Ares Publishers, 1955), 96.

65. See Werner Jaeger, *Paideia: The Ideals of Greek Culture*, vol. 1, trans. Gilbert Highet (New York: Oxford University Press, 1970), 303–10; Henri I. Marrou, *A History of Education in Antiquity*, trans. George Lamb (New York: Sheed and Ward, 1956), 10–47.

66. See, for example, Plato's portrayal of Hippias and Protagoras as contestants in the *Hippias Minor* (363c–64a) and the *Protagoras* (335a), respectively.
67. So Lysias in his *Funeral Oration*, 2: "while my speech is about these men, my contest (ἀγών) is not with their deeds, but with the speakers who have preceded me in praising them." In her analysis of the genre of *epitaphios* (funeral oration), Loreaux observes that orators chosen to eulogize the dead were competing with one another: "Each epitaphios is engaged in an agon with all the others; and well beyond the gymnastic, hippic, and musical competitions included in the official program of the funerals, there continues from one celebration to another an endless agon epitaphios. . . . In that neverending competition no winner is declared, but no orator forgets to measure himself against his predecessors." Nicole Loreaux, *The Invention of Athens: The Funeral Oration in the Classical City*, trans. Alan Sheridan (Cambridge, Mass.: Harvard University Press, 1986), 241.
68. Garner, 3.
69. Robinson, 91.
70. For a description of Athens as a city of festivals and other spectacles, see Isocrates' *Panegyricus*, 43–46.
    Focusing on the prevalence of drama in Athenian life, Baldry observes that drama was "not the favourite pastime of the few, but a great civic and religious occasion for the community as a whole, rich in pomp and ceremony, financed from the public treasury and from private wealth, involving hundreds of participants, attended by many thousands; a central event in the year, which not even the stresses of war and defeat could stop." H. C. Baldry, *The Greek Tragic Theatre* (New York: W. W. Norton & Co., 1971), 35.
71. As Baldry (16–17) observes, "What mattered [in the life of Periclean Athens] was the spoken word, the use of the human voice as a means of communication or persuasion or entertainment; and in this . . . the ancient Athenians had the advantage over the comparatively inarticulate creature that is modern man. Brilliant utilisation of the spoken word, mostly in the open air, was the central feature both of their vivid but erratic politics and of what we now misleadingly call their 'literature.' Most of the 'literary' genres which the Greeks created sprang from types of occasion involving speech or song: epic, for example, from recital before feating nobles or festival crowds; oratory, from political debate in the assembly or from the law courts; the philosophic dialogue, from conversation in the market-place or the wrestling school; drama, from the festivals of Dionysus in the open-air theatre."
    On the same point, reference can also be made to Randall's remark that "fifth-century Athenian life was born of the city, of the market place, the gymnasium or exercising field, the theater, and the common table." From this kind of life "one gets the impression that the Athenians never went home. They lived in the open . . . and engaged in talk, talk, talk." See John

Herman Randall, Jr., *Plato: Dramatist of the Life of Reason* (New York: Columbia University Press, 1970), 81–82.

72. Havelock, *Preface to Plato*, 41.

73. William Archer Butler, *Lectures on the History of Ancient Philosophy* (London: MacMillan and Co., 1874), 227.

74. Ibid., 228.

75. George Grote, *A History of Greece*, vol. 7 (London: John Murray, 1888), 6.

76. Friedrich Nietzsche, *The Gay Science*, trans. Walter Kaufmann (New York: Random House, 1974), #80.

77. Friedrich Nietzsche, "Nietzsche Contra Wagner," in *The Portable Nietzsche*, trans. Walter Kaufmann (New York: Viking Press, 1971), 683.

78. See Thomas G. Rosenmeyer, "Gorgias, Aeschylus, and *Apate*," *American Journal of Philology* 76 (1955): 225–60.

79. For a comprehensive treatment of the role of the funeral oration in public life, see Nicole Loraux, (n. 67).

80. As Segal has shown in the case of Gorgias, πίστις (belief) can most easily be achieved by an orator if it is founded on τέρψις (aesthetic delight). See Charles P. Segal, "Gorgias and the Psychology of the Logos," *Harvard Studies in Classical Philology* 66 (1962): 99–155.

81. The doxographic tradition portrays the sophists as masterful stylists. See, for example, 82A.1.2, 84B.2.34, 85A.13, 86A.2.7, 88A.1.

# Chapter 2

# Terms for
# Sophistical Rhetoric

In the last chapter, the sophists were situated in the midst of two important changes: the replacement of the few by the many, and the rise of the middle class. Discussed both as subjects to and catalysts of these changes, they were shown to have responded to their circumstances by making do with the cultural resources at their disposal. Their tactical uses of language and their clever utilization of time were presented as two ways of decodifying strategic moves of the established order. By virtue of these practices, the sophists were depicted as explorers and exploiters of opportunities of their own or others' making. Further, their rhetoric was discussed in terms of the ethic of competition and the aesthetic of spectacles. As a competitive enterprise, sophistical rhetoric attacked some discourses and defended others. In the same capacity, it also provided its students with the discursive means needed to play the roles of verbal attacker or defender as the circumstances of a particular contest dictated. As an aesthetic undertaking, it offered its spectators linguistic images of possible worlds, worlds hitherto unuttered. In the same capacity, it offered its pupils examples of staging words depicting worlds that had yet to be. Having thus situated the sophists, we are now in a position to take a closer look at some of their remaining texts.

This chapter reviews two common ways of reading the sophists and proposes a third which attends to both the cultural dynamics discussed in the previous chapter, and to some sophistical texts produced under the influence of these dynamics. In what follows, I argue that sophistical rhetoric revolves around the notions of opportunity, playfulness, and possibility. After explaining how this is so, I illustrate each notion with a rhetorical piece attributed to a particular sophist.

The fragmentariness and disparity of the sophists' surviving texts make any discussion of their rhetoric difficult. How can these materials be read profitably today? What is a reader to do with hundreds of pieces of discourse and several more or less complete rhetorical compositions (speeches) attributed to an unspecified number of authors? Reading each fragment or speech individually, in itself, may produce as many isolated understandings as there are fragments and speeches, but it cannot provide a common thread that would weave them all into an intelligible whole. On the other hand, reading all of the pieces as a totality may yield a sensible gestalt, but it will be a gestalt marked by gaps, breaks, inconsistencies, and contradictions. How, then, can readers resist the temptation of fidelity to the pieces of the reconstructed textual evidence and at the same time produce a telling story out of them? Conversely, how can they guard against the tendency to force into a tightly woven discursive pattern textual pieces that do not fit and at the same time avoid risking an unintelligible or incoherent rhetoric?

Addressing the issue of reading the sophists' materials, Havelock argues that "the task of piecing them together to make a coherent picture requires philological discipline, a good deal of finesse, and also an exercise of over-all judgment which must be content to leave some things unsettled."[1] For Havelock, these requirements might produce interesting results but only if the commentator is aware that the sophists were men of "intellectual status and prestige," and only if (s)he decides to treat what they taught "seriously or not at all."[2] Finally, the crucial importance of the reader's perspective cannot be ignored— what a reader looks for determines in large measure what (s)he will or will not find.[3]

Addressing the same issue with greater specificity, R. F. Holland rejects the formulation of some classical philologists that, "a fragment . . . is like a code message which it is the task of the scholar to decipher."[4] The goal for him is not decipherment but understanding; and understanding can be accomplished neither by considering "the history and etymology of the words" of a particular fragment nor by assigning exact meanings to each of them, but by entertaining various "uses to which the statement may be put" or by ascertaining the functions the fragment was meant to serve according to its author.[5] Holland insists that a fragment from antiquity cannot be treated as a cryptogram whose decoding requires the discovery of the correct linguistic key. This is so because what a fragment says depends less on the verbal clarification of each of its terms and more on the circumstances of its utterance. Therefore, the reader has to reconstruct those circumstances, search for the fragment's "context of argument," and make reference to the kinds of discussions in which it could have been included.[6]

Havelock's and Holland's methodological insights are well taken. Even so, Holland is helpful only where a single fragment is concerned. His minimalist approach offers no guidance on how to move from fragment to fragment or from fragment to speech, or how to arrange them intelligibly. On the other hand, Havelock does not specify what constitutes finesse or, for that matter, how or when one knows that one has a good deal of it. Nor does he caution about the limitations and pitfalls of the strict use of philological discipline. Despite his warning that any story about the sophists will necessarily be incomplete, he does not instruct readers, save by way of his own example, on how to read the available textual pieces. Clearly, Havelock's and Holland's suggestions offer two problematic ways of reading the sophists' textual materials. Havelock would have us piece them together without expecting to achieve closure. On the other hand, Holland would have us situate each piece of discourse into a reconstructed historico-linguistic context without venturing beyond a single piece or inquiring into the relationship of any two or more pieces. But if we grant that the wish to make sense of sophistical rhetoric can be satisfied neither by a hopelessly incomplete narrative (Havelock) nor by a myriad of isolated understandings (Holland), we are faced with a methodological dilemma. How can we, on the one hand, avoid a scattered rhetoric, a rhetoric without a general view of the whole, and, on the other hand, escape a totalized rhetoric, one that ignores the peculiarities of the parts of our fragmentary record?

One way out of this dilemma is to read the sophists' materials in the light of a constellation of singular terms derived from their rhetorical compositions and reported practices. Addressing the efficacy of this approach, Weaver points out that "a single term is an incipient proposition, awaiting only the necessary coupling with another term." Defining a term as "a name capable of entering into a proposition," he argues that single names are provocative not in themselves but because they "set up expectancies of propositional embodiment."[7] Although Weaver was searching for terms offering "a descriptive account"[8] of the prevailing rhetoric of his culture, the same procedure can be followed when trying to interpret a corpus of texts from another culture or another time.[9] Proceeding synecdochically, this procedure attempts to illuminate the whole (sophistical rhetoric) with the light of some of its parts (singular terms). As applied to the texts of the sophists, this procedure does not privilege the conceptual parameters of any one fragment or speech as it happens to have been copied, recopied, canonized, or handed down; nor does it favor the construction of a perfectly self-enclosed narrative that would incorporate all the fragments and speeches. Rather, it focuses on a set of three terms out of thousands, and argues that most sophistical discourses issue from and point to these terms. In effect, this procedure advances plausible narratives that despite their inconclusiveness and partiality can, if considered together, help us make some sense out of the sophists' fragmentary remains. Of course, much of the understanding gained by the execution of this procedure depends on the terms chosen and on their contemporary relevance. As will become apparent, the terms I have chosen (opportunity, playfulness, possibility) find warrant by virtue of their relation to the three aspects of the sophists' cultural situation as it was discussed in the previous chapter. Thus opportunity corresponds to the logic of circumstances, playfulness to the ethic of competition, and possibility to the aesthetic of exhibition.

A set of terms-in-themselves, however, rarely furnishes understandings free from the dangers of nominalism. Strictly speaking, terms inherited from classical antiquity are found in and taken from specific texts and it is to those texts that they must be returned for their meaning, illustration, and justification. By extension, texts containing the terms mentioned were produced within a cultural horizon of discourses, and it is in the light of that horizon (as reconstructed today) that they must be seen. Accordingly, the following discussion of sophistical rhetoric features the aforementioned three terms by situating them culturally and illustrating them textually.

However, no set of terms, no set of illustrative texts, and no reconstructed cultural horizon can exhaust the sophists' rhetoric. This is so because their rhetoric is not an object to be uncovered and brought to the light of its own truth; nor is it a project to be completed once and for all. Rather, it is an enterprise in which to be engaged again and again. To follow Dodds, historical judgment is "for ever in the making because the present is for ever in the making and we cannot see the past except by the light of the present."[10] As long as there are readers of sophistical rhetoric, their attempts to make sense out of it will always be guided and influenced by their own circumstances on the one hand, and by its relevance on the other. In short, sophistical rhetoric constitutes an open-ended proposition, a proposition demanding to be rearticulated, rewritten, and rethought every now and then according to the preoccupations of its readers and commentators.

The Greek terms I am using in this chapter are καιρός (opportune moment, right time, opportunity), παίγνιον (game, play, diversion, playfulness), and τὸ δυνατόν (that which can be done, the possible, possibility). Each term appears in some form of propositional embodiment somewhere in the fragments; precisely where and how many times are not interesting questions.[11] And as suggested earlier, the same holds true when it comes to the etymology, the exact meaning, or the verbal clarification of each term. Although the beneficiary of much philological research, this is not a philological study. As such, the terms I highlight are significant not because the sophists used them, or because they appear in the sophists' texts more frequently than other terms, or because they hold some privileged meaning. Rather, these terms are significant because they can help explain common features or tendencies of the available sophistical texts and because they can render the rhetorical practices of the sophists meaningful.

Beyond its particular propositional embodiments, each term makes sense not in itself but as an alternative to a particular binary opposition: καιρός to the opposition of the proper and the improper (τὸ πρέπον and τὸ ἀπρεπές); παίγνιον to the opposition of the stronger and the weaker (τό κρεῖττον and τὸ ἧττον); and τὸ δυνατόν to the opposition of the actual and the ideal (τὸ ἐνεργόν and τὸ ἰδανικόν).[12] Linked to one another in a particular way, all nine terms provide a culturally and terminologically sound perspective from which to approach and understand sophistical rhetoric. Put another way, these terms specify what sophistical rhetoric does and how it differs from other rhetorics, including those of the fourth century B.C.

Diagramatically, the relations of the terms I have mentioned look as follows:

| Culture | Oppositions | Sophistical Rhetoric |
|---|---|---|
| circumstances | proper-improper | opportunity |
| competition | stronger-weaker | playfulness |
| exhibition | actual-ideal | possibility |

Before I discuss each of the above oppositions separately, it should be noted that all three are informed by Protagoras' notion of *dissoi lo-*

*goi*, the notion that on every issue there are two arguments opposing each other (80A.1.51). Asserting that human language manifests itself in at least two opposite ways at any given time, Protagoras' insight suggests a twofold symbolic world consisting of contrary discourses, and counsels against attempts to fuse them into one unified entity. In a Protagorean world, universal agreement on any one matter is not possible. Everything that gets said can only be understood in terms of something other, something different, and, more specifically, something opposite. Even the notion of *dissoi logoi* makes sense only if opposing and opposed by the notion of εἷς λόγος (one argument, one view, one position). Likewise, the well-known Protagorean dictum, of all things man is the measure, is meaningful only insofar as it counters and is countered by the view that of all things god is the measure.[13] In a univocal world, every single utterance would have its place unquestionably, and there would be no need for debate or persuasion—everyone would be listening to and speaking the same logos. But in the polyvocal world we inhabit, the status of all things is questionable; and this is why people often find themselves at odds with one another, disagreeing, differing, and seeking to resolve their differences symbolically. This state of affairs accounts for the pervasive presence of rhetorical persuasion in human communities. Because every issue admits of at least two contrary *logoi,* and because the imperative to action generally permits only one of the two to prevail in a given instance, rhetoric affords people a means through which they can persuade one another to favor, at a given moment, one logos over all others.

Clearly, Protagoras' notion of *dissoi logoi* provides a worldview with rhetoric at its center. Stressing a particular kind of difference (opposition) rather than identity, this worldview demands of the human subject a multiple awareness, an awareness at once cognizant of its own position and of those positions opposing it. In fact, Protagoras' idea goes as far as to posit that a position cannot even be articulated except against the background of an opposition. This means that any one discourse is oppositional and, as such, always directed against other discourses. Moreover, it means that in order to understand an issue, one must be prepared to listen to at least two contrary sides; and in order to decide how to act, one must espouse one of the two sides or come up with a third.

Since we have no Protagorean discourse that illustrates the notion of *dissoi logoi,* I turn to Prodicus' story of *Heracles at the Crossroads*

(84B.2), which does.[14] Unlike the heroes of epic poetry, whose fates are often determined by the Olympian gods and whose actions are prescribed by a rigidly defined system of rules and roles, Prodicus' hero, Heracles, finds himself torn between two equipotent tendencies—one toward vice and the other toward virtue. Uncertain of which path to follow, he goes to ponder the matter in seclusion. There, he is met by two women, Vice and Virtue, both of whom are aware of his ambivalence. Vice approaches him first and urges him to take her path to happiness, a path promising to her followers carefree living, sensuous pleasures, enjoyment of the fruits of others' labor, and full satisfaction of their appetites. Then Heracles is approached by Virtue, who promotes her own path, a path whose rewards (divine favors, human love, community honors, national admiration, material gains, and bodily vigor) require service to the gods, to friends, and to community and country, and hard work and the subjection of the body to the mind. There ensues before Heracles a heated exchange between Vice and Virtue during which each argues for the superiority of her own way to happiness as well as the inferiority of the way of her competitor. The story ends with no sign of decision on the part of Heracles.

This story has been read in various ways, now as a "masterpiece of stylistic elegance," now as an ethical treatise attesting to the sophists' interest in ethics.[15] One of the more interesting readings is Biesecker's.[16] Contrasting the epical to the rhetorical consciousness, she argues that Prodicus' story articulates a subject position inhabited by opposing tendencies from which a person is expected to choose one. For Biesecker, when the difference between at least two alternatives is great, choice is relatively easy; but when the alternatives are equivalent, choice is often difficult, if not impossible. A perfectly rational assessment of such alternatives always leads to a point of balance, a dilemma, which entails a standstill. But since the imperative to action demands that an impasse be overcome and that a choice be made, the human subject must in some way disturb the balance of perfectly opposed alternatives. This means that in the final analysis one must prefer one option over all others. Such preference can be brought about through rhetorical persuasion, which consists of comparing available options and eventually giving more weight to one over all the rest. In specific terms, Heracles, whom Prodicus portrays as "ἀποροῦντα ποτέραν τῶν ὁδῶν τράπηται" (pondering which of the paths to follow) (21), will have to break out of his aporetic state and choose either the way of Vice or that of Virtue on account of the persuasive force of one appeal over the other. Put differently, Heracles will, sooner or later, have to choose, if he is to act, and follow the path of the more persuasive advocate. The fact that he does not make a choice in the preserved version of the story need not concern us here. For the purposes of this discussion, the important point is that Heracles has been addressed not by a single logos but by *dissoi logoi.*

With Protagoras' notion of *dissoi logoi* in mind, let us turn to the discussion of the three oppositions that inform sophistical rhetoric and to the three corresponding alternatives around which it revolves. First, the *prepon-aprepes* pair. Springing from one's sense of placing a particular thing in a particular place, and the will to repeat, *to prepon* (the appropriate, the proper) alludes to the realization that speech exists in space and is uttered both as a learned response to and a habitual linguistic imposition on a situation reminiscent of the past.[17] According to this realization, occasions for speech are finite in number (i.e., funerals, festivals, trials), and have a way of reappearing from time to time. Thus any one encounter in and with the world of discourse constitutes a variation of a previously experienced situation and calls for a more or less predictable restatement of what has already been said. In this regard, *to prepon* represents a conventional principle according to which the production of meanings in language is historically determined; at the same time, it posits that, in most respects, the present resembles, and therefore must be understood in terms provided by the past.

*To prepon* is the result of general agreements on how to address recurring topics and occasions properly. As we grow within a set of parameters of rhetorical practice, we learn that on certain occasions and before certain audiences only certain utterances are appropriate. In this regard, we also learn that speaking in public is highly regulated according to established norms of appropriateness that we are expected, more or less, to observe. Over time, these norms tend to harden and become highly specific types of rhetoric (i.e., the apology, the eulogy, the encomium). When this happens, most orators tend to address typical situations in typical ways. In other words, they tend to speak following predictable rhetorical forms and searching for predictable responses from their audiences.

The rhetor who operates mainly from the sense afforded by *to prepon*, relies on normative standards of speech, and speaks in terms of familiar *topoi* (known categories, commonplaces), which address a situation in its typicality, its resemblance to prior and similar situations. In so doing, the rhetor serves as a reminder of previous utterances, as a voice endorsing the way things have traditionally been addressed. At the same time, (s)he suggests, by virtue of his/her practice, that the unfamiliar should be understood in terms of the familiar.

*To prepon* opposes and is opposed by *to aprepes* (the inappropriate, the improper). Like the appropriate, the inappropriate is largely the outcome of a set of discursive practices that derive their weight and justification from past agreements. In other words, the inappropriate, too, is a category learned historically and sustained by the force of certain accepted prohibitions against specific utterances. What is improper is so by virtue of its deviation from or disregard of standard rhetorical practices within a community of orators and listeners.[18] Insofar as the appropriate-inappropriate opposition concerns itself with already settled discursive territories, it disregards the uniqueness of a given situation, and in so doing leaves out of account unsettled linguistic regions. These regions can begin to be settled when one creates and capitalizes on opportune rhetorical moments (*kairoi*).[19]

Springing from one's sense of timing and the will to invent, *kairos* alludes to the realization that speech exists in time and is uttered both as a spontaneous formulation of and a barely constituted response to a new situation unfolding in the immediate present. According to this realization, time is understood as "a succession of discontinuous occasions rather than as duration or historical continuity" while the present is conceived not "as continuous with a causally related sequence of events" but as "unprecedented, as a moment of decision, a moment of crisis." In this regard, *kairos* represents "a radical principle of occasionality" that views "the production of meaning in language as a process of continuous adjustment to and creation of the present occasion."[20]

The rhetor who operates mainly with the awareness of *kairos* responds spontaneously to the fleeting situation at hand, speaks on the spur of the moment, and addresses each occasion in its particularity, its singularity, its uniqueness. In this sense, (s)he is both a hunter and a maker of unique opportunities, always ready to address improvisationally and confer meaning on new and emerging situations.

Because what gets said kairotically is unprecedented, without precedent, it has no ready-made audience. As such, it can startle its listeners; and once the moment of its utterance has passed, it can well be forgotten or remembered for its impropriety. But if what gets said on the spur of the moment happens to fall on receptive ears and make unexpected sense, it will eventually find its place in the audience's standard linguistic currency, and thus become part of their store-house of appropriate responses, ready to be recalled at some future occasion. In other words, what is spoken in and through the aware-ness of *kairos* can, in time, turn into one of the categories of *to prepon*. The reverse does not obtain. Because what gets said from the vantage of *to prepon* is decided historically, it seeks to perpetuate or strengthen the density it has acquired over time. As such, a proper utterance rec-ommends itself as a criterion of the traditionally acceptable and resists innovation, except insofar as innovation constitutes a natural exten-sion of the tradition. Because it reinforces what listeners already know and because it reassures them of the continuing value of their discursive sensibilities, an appropriate expression can usually count on an already well-disposed audience.

By contrast, what gets said kairotically strives to expand the fron-tiers of language and invite an audience to settle them. In so doing, it ignores the appropriate-inappropriate opposition and underscores the crucial roles occasionality and temporality play in the practices of rhetoric. In effect, *kairos* demands the awareness that one's sense of appropriate and inappropriate speech is not especially useful at the precise moment of a given utterance. Further, it insists that some-thing is not appropriate or inappropriate at all times and in all situa-tions. What is said at any one time and in any one situation can be construed as appropriate or inappropriate regardless of prior constru-als; but how it will be construed depends not only on one's reading of the occasion of its utterance but also on its persuasiveness.

That *kairos* can overturn the tradition-bound categories of *to prepon* or *to aprepes* and reverse their status does not mean that anything goes — before anything can go, a great deal must be in place. Rather, it means that what is generally regarded as appropriate or inappropri-ate has no necessary bearing on a discourse uttered in a specific temporal, occasional, or situational context. What is believed to be ap-propriate or inappropriate is based only on past agreements on the proper boundaries of discourse. However, by virtue of their nonne-cessity, these agreements are vulnerable to the force of new linguistic creations produced at the moment when an utterance disturbs silence or precedent. Thus whether certain versions of propriety or impropri-ety will be acknowledged and invoked at any given time is indeter-minate; and whether they will remain unchanged in the future is an open-ended question. In the domain of rhetoric, every agreement is subject to review and dissolution whenever spontaneity manages to outweigh memory and habit. Further, the capacity of *kairos* to challenge a particular form of *to prepon* means that what is considered appropriate today has not always been so; there was a time when that form, too, was first introduced either in addition to or at the expense of other notions of propriety. The authority or presence of *to prepon* at any given moment signifies only that it continues to be useful, or that the opportune moment that would reverse or displace it has yet to arrive.

To illustrate the proper-improper opposition and opportunity as a third alternative, I turn to Alcidamas' discourse *Peri ton Sophiston*.[21] Composed at a time when written rhetorical compositions had just started to gain popularity in a predominately oral culture, this speech argues for the superiority of the spoken over the written word. Although Alcidamas shows himself to be cognizant of the paradox he is engaging in by *writing* about extemporaneous speaking (29–33), he nevertheless argues that it is only in and through this kind of speaking that orators can meet the situational demands of public, forensic, and private discourses. Likewise, he proposes that it is only during a rhetorical performance that orators can speak on the spur of the moment and address effectively unexpected crises that may arise. By contrast, written discourses are distant from the immediate circumstances of the present and are thus unable to capitalize on or make evident an opportune moment (9). In other words, written compositions are always too late to save the day, and tend to fail at the critical moment (10). Attention to *kairos* demands full presence and the readiness to speak on whatever arises during a rhetorical event.

Likening speeches to living human bodies, Alcidamas hints at the difference between the fluidity of spoken words and the rigidity of their written copies: "And, just as the living human body has far less comeliness than a beautiful statue, yet manifold practical service, so also the speech which comes directly from the mind, on the spur of the moment, is full of life and action, and keeps pace with the events like the real person, while the written discourse, a mere semblance of the living speech, is devoid of all efficacy" (28). But even as he declares his preference for the oral over the written mode of rhetoric, Alcidamas gets caught in the non-*kairotic* character of his own discourse. Arguing for the primacy of the occasionality and situationality of all oral discourse, he nevertheless finds himself outside the very practice he advocates. In other words, he comes very near to saying that the appropriate thing for an orator to do is speak, not write, his orations with an ear to their creation of and response to specific opportunities. But in saying so, Alcidamas seems to be attempting the impossible—to make *kairos* a subset of *to prepon*. Addressing the dilemma that Alcidamas, or anyone who seeks to formalize *kairos*, faces, White writes:

> no treatise on the occasional nature of utterance could be itself exempt from occasionality, or the inevitability of its own supersession. If every occasion presents a unique challenge to the situational, context-oriented consciousness of the sophist, then the sophist's interpretive ingenuity will nowhere find itself resumed in a definitive statement.[22]

To White's observation we can add that knowledge of *kairos* is a contradiction of terms forcing us to attend more to the eventfulness of the phenomenon of speaking and less to its written description or explanation.

The second opposition that informs sophistical rhetoric is that between *to hetton* and *to kreitton*. *To hetton* denotes that which is weaker, inferior, lesser than something else. In rhetoric, *to hetton* refers to that argument or position which commands less power because the majority shuns it or is not persuaded by it. By contrast, *to kreitton* denotes that which is stronger, superior, greater than something else. In rhetoric, *to kreitton* refers to that argument or position which is dominant because the majority has found it more persuasive than other alternatives. When advocating something *hetton*, the orator relies on the resources of language and its surrounding circumstances to move what is regarded as weaker to a position of strength. At the same time, and in a similar manner, the orator attempts to show how *to kreitton*, despite its dominance, is defective, ineffective, or harmful—that is, how *to kreitton* is weaker than generally thought. To be successful in this endeavor means to reverse in some measure the established hierarchy of things. By contrast, the orator who speaks about a *kreitton* argument depends on the audience's familiarity with discourses that have already won their approval and seeks to have them reendorse that of which they are already persuaded. At the same time, the orator attempts to point out that *to hetton* belongs precisely where it is: under the rule of *to kreitton*. To be successful here means to reaffirm established structures of symbolic strength and weakness and thus to secure the perpetuation of some aspect of the present state of affairs.

An argument or position is not *hetton* or *kreitton* in itself but in relation to another argument and as a result of one or more rhetorical contests. Put differently, *to hetton* and *to kreitton* allude to a past verdict that pronounced a winner and a loser at the conclusion of a competitive event. According to this agonistic view of rhetoric, an argument acquires or loses power in use, and no argument is victorious or vanquished once and for all. Because the circumstances calling for arguments change, any one argument can lose its strength or overcome its weakness in some future contest. This is another way of saying that the status or position of an argument is always situationally determined. Therefore, today's loser may be tomorrow's winner and vice versa. Because people often seek to resolve their differences symbolically, and because differences can be settled only temporarily, the *hetton-kreitton* opposition turns rhetoric into symbolic combat carried on by willing contestants seeking the laurels of victory. By extension, it turns the orator into a contestant who competes against others to win. Finally, it turns words into instruments or maneuvers used to defeat an opponent.

A contest requires at least two contestants. Often many contestants enter a round of rhetorical competition; but in the end, there are generally many losers and only one winner. Of the many discourses competing for victory in a given contest, one pattern of discourse finally emerges victorious. Once a particular contest is over, *to kreitton* concerns itself with how to avoid losing future contests, while *to hetton* becomes preoccupied with how to win in the days ahead. An argument that has lost a contest may never reappear to fight another round of symbolic competition; or it may reappear reworded and reformulated, ready to challenge the winner of the past. By contrast, an argument that has won a contest may in time have to defend itself in future contests. In rhetoric, competition between arguments never ceases.

To enter arenas of symbolic competition means to be willing to play, win, or lose. Whether entering as a challenger or challenged, one, by virtue of one's entry, helps perpetuate competition as a practice. In doing so, one not only agrees to play a particular game but also endorses the tacit understandings that have made the game possible. By extension, one plays not only for a victory but also for the pleasure inherent in playing. In rhetoric, one plays both specific games, as in the case of a legal battle or a political race, and the broader game of language. In the former instance, one generally seeks to win, which means to bring the game to a particular end. In the latter, one seeks pleasure, which requires that one prolong the game as long as possible. Within a specific rhetorical game, a contestant wins not by having the stronger argument but by playing the game more skillfully than his/her opponent; conversely, a contestant loses not by having the weaker argument but by playing the game less skillfully than his/her opponent. In other words, it is skill in language that determines rhetorical strength or weakness in a specific game. But within the broader game of language, there are no winners or losers—only players; therefore, it does not matter whether an argument is judged stronger or weaker. What does matter is the continuation of the game.[23]

To illustrate the weaker-stronger opposition and playfulness as a third alternative, let us turn to Gorgias' *Encomium of Helen* (82B.11).[24] This oration apparently seeks to refute Helen's detractors, that is, those who believe that she was responsible for the Trojan War and all the ills that befell the Hellenes as a result. It also seemingly attempts to restore Helen's reputation by removing the blame attached to her name. Toying with language and with his readers throughout the speech, Gorgias offers a splendid demonstration of the way in which a widely held opinion (*kreitton*) can be shown to be groundless (*hetton*). Working against the generally accepted argument of the mythopoetic tradition (Helen is blameworthy for eloping with Paris) by exposing its logical weaknesses, Gorgias suggests an alternative argument (Helen is innocent of the charges against her).

His approach is as simple as it is ingenious. Helen did what she did because the gods so willed, or she was physically overpowered by her abductor, or she was persuaded by words, or she fell in love. In all four cases, she cannot be blamed because the gods, a man, persuasion, and love are much stronger than a woman. The details of each argument aside, Gorgias' case is held together by the notion that "it is the nature of things, not for the strong to be hindered by the weak, but for the weaker to be ruled and drawn by the stronger, and for the stronger to lead and the weaker to follow" (6). However, Gorgias undermines this very notion as he takes a weaker claim (Helen is praiseworthy) and tries to make it stronger than the already dominant view (Helen is blameworthy). What allows him to do this is a shift from the natural to the social domain as well as the awareness of the power and instability of language. As he explains in the middle part of the speech (8–14), logos manifests itself in various ways (poetry, incantations, argument), all of which can affect the human psyche powerfully (in the same way certain drugs can affect the human body). As evidence of the instability of logos, Gorgias points out that if one were to study scientific discussions, public debates, and philosophical disputes, one would easily see that over time one opinion is always displaced by another. No opinion can prevail forever.

For the purposes of our discussion, whether Helen is blameworthy or praiseworthy is not the point. Rather, the point is that no argument or position, no matter how entrenched, can dominate the mental world of an audience once and for all. In and through the interplay of language use, any one argument can be overthrown and replaced by another. This is so because, as Gorgias points out, opinion, which most people take "as counselor to their soul . . . is slippery and insecure [and] it casts those employing it into slippery and insecure successes" (11). More specifically, Gorgias suggests, arguments come and go on account of the artistic skills and the swiftness of thought of those who make them (13).

Gorgias concludes his speech by revealing his affinity for playfulness in rhetoric, "I wished to write a speech which would be a praise of Helen and a diversion to myself (ἐμὸν δὲ παίγνιον)" (21). In the light of the discussion of the stronger-weaker opposition, he seems to suggest that in and through his composition he has opposed the discourses blaming Helen, and at the same time diverted himself. But if this is so, the story of Helen has taken yet another turn, a fact that makes it far from over. Judging from the tone of the speech, Gorgias does not seem overly concerned whether his argument will ultimately unseat the arguments of his predecessors. He is content to have diverted himself by playing with language, playing, that is, with a malleable medium of dynastic powers and deceptive qualities (8). Put another way, he is content to have participated in the game of words, to have demonstrated to his audience that he is a splendid player, and to have tried to bring them into the game.

The third opposition that informs sophistical rhetoric is that between actuality and ideality with possibility serving as the third alternative.[25] Actuality refers to the way things are in the world. In rhetoric, actuality is what is believed to be known and understood about reality. Actual things are so by virtue of their presence and most people's conviction that they know what is the case about the world around them, how it works, and why. When speaking from the frame of actuality, the orator emphasizes the here, the now, and the is. More specifically, (s)he highlights those aspects of the world that exhibit a certain fixity by virtue of which they can be had or mastered cognitively. In so doing, (s)he not only draws the boundaries of the world as generally known but also confines his/her listeners within those boundaries. The ends of this rhetoric are within reach because they are construed as natural extensions or necessary implications of the way things are.

By contrast, ideality refers to the way things ought to be. In rhetoric, ideality is what is envisioned and known about a world that can never be made actual. Ideal things are so by virtue of their absence and a few visionaries' conception of things in their perfect form. When speaking from the frame of ideality, the orator emphasizes the nowhere, the never, and the should be. More specifically, (s)he highlights a world that, no matter how untenable, the audience should always strive to approach. In so doing, (s)he not only disparages the world as it is known but also prompts his/her audience to imagine an utopian world. The ends of this rhetoric are beyond reach but are construed as worthy of endless pursuit.

As a third alternative to the actuality-ideality opposition, possibility refers to things that are not but can be. Possible things are so by virtue of their absence and most people's proclivity to give primacy to what lies at a distance from their immediate grasp. When speaking from the awareness of possibility, the orator favors the there, the then, and the can be. As such, (s)he underscores the fluidity, the elusiveness, and the malleability of human experience. In so doing, the orator acknowledges the known boundaries of the world but urges his/her listeners to go beyond them. The ends of this rhetoric can be reached because people are endowed with the capacity to see themselves and the world not only as they are but also as they can become.

In its various forms, the possible confronts the actual-ideal opposition by negating the efficacy of either term, that is, by exposing the unactualizability of the ideal and the imperfections of the actual—it makes no sense to count on what can never become actual; and there is little or no incentive to stay where one is, perfectly content with the way things are. Recasting the ideal as a version of the impossible and the actual as a version of the unacceptable, the possible urges the kind of movement that oversteps the boundaries of the actual and undercuts the appeals of the ideal. Put differently, the possible refuses the actual-ideal antagonism and offers itself as a third option. In so doing, it declares that actuality can only furnish the ground for endorsements of the facticity of the world while ideality provides a wide open field of dreams. At the same time, it posits that the world need not be inhabited only by pedants and dreamers—there is always room for those between the extremities of immanence and transcendence. In effect, the possible cultivates the awareness that knowledge of and attachment to the actual hinders us from aspiring to transcend it while utopian ideals amount to unimpeded fantasy—the kind that refuses to come to terms with the materials of actuality. Finally, the possible advances the view that what is actual now has not always been so but has resulted from a sequence of possibles; by contrast, what is ideal now can always be expected to remain so.

In its proposed forms, the possible often meets with the resistance, objections, or rejection of audiences unable to see the world under a different light. This is so because the possible is a version of the novel, which is often dismissed on the grounds that it is really a variation of the old, that it demands too many changes, that it offers no guarantees of success, and that it has yet to be tested for its workability. But if the orator's display succeeds in firing the imagination of the listeners, and if their hopes triumph over their experience of the world as it is, the possibilities before them are well on their way to becoming actuality. When such a transformation does occur, the search for new possibilities starts over again.

To illustrate a way in which the possible emerges from the opposition between the actual and the ideal, let us turn to Thrasymachus' *The Constitution* (85B.1).[26] This fragmentary speech shows that rhetoric emerges as a response to a crisis. The rhetorical function of this speech is to depict the current state of affairs under a negative light, and to express dissatisfaction with the conditions of the present. Whether it suggests a specific course of action that would alleviate the prevailing ills, we cannot tell from what is preserved of the speech. What we can tell is that for Thrasymachus rhetoric constitutes the first step toward any kind of corrective action. This is so because rhetoric can display a more desirable future: a future free from the pain and suffering afflicting the present; a future often analogous to a nostalgically remembered past.

*The Constitution* points out that there is no need for rhetoric in times of order, calm, and contentment; during such times, silence will do: "I wish, Athenians, that I had belonged to that ancient time when silence sufficed for young people, since the state of affairs did not force them to make speeches and the older men were managing the city properly." But in times of disorder and discontent, "one really has to speak." In other words, when rhetoric is called into being during times of urgency and upheaval, it makes its objections heard and its alternative visions of possibility known. Throughout the speech, Thrasymachus takes for granted that his audience agrees with him that the current conditions are miserable: "instead of peace, we are at war; danger [has brought us] to such a pass that we cling to the day that is ending and dread that which is to come; instead of comradeship, we have fallen into mutual enmity and turbulence." One point of contention, however, is whether vocal protest is warranted. The speaker sees no reason why one ought to keep silent in the face of an intolerable situation: "Why should anyone put off speaking [what] is in his mind, if [it has fallen] to him to be injured by the present situation and he thinks that he is on to something that will put an end to such things?"

On the other side of the actuality of the present conditions (improper city management, war, danger, enmity) Thrasymachus imagines the ideals of proper city management, peace, safety, and comradeship. Yet, he surely knows these ideals are not perfectly attainable in the world of real politics—that is why politicians mention them so often in their speeches. Accordingly, Thrasymachus offers no prescription for their attainment. All he wants is to have people express their outrage and speak their dismay. Whether such speaking will remedy the present conditions is uncertain. Returning to the utopia of the good old days is not in the hands of his listeners; but speaking is something they can do. However, if this is so, the version of possibility Thrasymachus puts before the eyes of his audience is rhetoric itself.

*The Constitution* was read by Dionysius of Halicarnassus as an example of a hybrid rhetorical style—one that fuses the severe and the simple styles. In more recent times, Guthrie has read *The Constitution* as an argument "for efficiency and principle in government, and for reconciliation between the parties to that end."[27] For Havelock, the speaker portrays the actuality of rival politicians whose thoughtlessness has created a political crisis and expresses interest "in the possibility of agreement."[28] How agreement is to be reached, the speaker does not say. But even if he had, it must be noted that the question of how is addressed by the rhetoric of practicality. The rhetoric of possibility is mainly concerned with the creation of desire for a state of affairs that can be brought about.

As one of the chief exponents of the sophistic movement, Thrasymachus must have been sensitive to the notion of *dissoi logoi;* and as a sophistical orator, he must have been familiar with the notion of *kairos* and the *hetton-kreitton* opposition. If this is so, he cannot be said to speak about agreement as an abstraction that must be favored once and for all over another abstraction (conflict)—there is nothing inherently superior about agreement over conflict. What he delineates in *The Constitution* is not a speculative line of thought designed to arrange the world of ideas in a certain way; instead, he provides a specific rhetorical response to an alarming political crisis, a response aiming to evoke the indignation of his listeners and to firm their resolve to voice their own displeasure. Under different circumstances, the same Thrasymachus could have blasted the actuality of like-minded politicians in perfect cooperation with one another, and expressed interest in the possibility of dissent.

Thus far we have seen how three culturally grounded terminological oppositions play out in three sophistical discourses, and how each opposition is exploded by a third alternative term. Inasmuch as the oppositions and texts chosen are representative, and insofar as we can generalize from the above discussion, we are in a position to say that the rhetoric of the sophists is a rhetoric of third alternatives. Moving between commonly accepted versions of propriety and impropriety, sophistical rhetoric relies on clever uses of time to capitalize on and create opportunities for itself and its adherents. In this sense it is opportunistic. Operating within the polarities of discursive strength and weakness, this rhetoric exploits the paradoxical character of language to invent reversals and violate its rules. In this sense it is playful. Working in the midst of real actualities and unattainable ideals, it combines elements of both to point to actualizable possibilities. In this sense, it is prospective. With this preliminary characterization in mind, let us turn now to the receptions sophistical rhetoric occasioned in the fourth century B.C. First, let us turn to Plato's reception.

## Notes

1. Eric A. Havelock, *The Liberal Temper in Greek Politics* (London: Jonathan Cape, 1957), 157.
2. Ibid., 160.

3. Ibid., 157.

4. R. F. Holland, "On Making Sense of a Philosophical Fragment," *Classical Quarterly* 6 (1956): 215.

5. Ibid., 215–18.

6. Ibid., 219.

7. Richard M. Weaver, *The Ethics of Rhetoric* (Chicago: Henry Regnery Co., 1953), 211.

8. Ibid., 212.

9. See, for example, Raymond Williams, *Keywords: A Vocabulary of Culture and Society* (New York: Oxford University Press, 1976).

10. E. R. Dodds, "The Sophistic Movement and the Failure of Greek Liberalism" in E. R. Dodds, *The Ancient Concept of Progress and Other Essays on Greek Literature and Belief* (Oxford: Clarendon Press, 1973), 92.

11. These or any other term can be located almost instantaneously in the Greek texts thanks to recent computer technology and the TLG (Thesaurus Linguae Graecae) compact disk.

12. For a discussion of binary oppositions in Greek, see Richard Garner, *Law and Society in Classical Athens* (London: Croom Helm, 1987), 75–77.

Although τὸ ἰδανικόν is a later term, I am using it for lack of an equivalent.

13. Plato, *Laws* (716c).

14. One could also turn to the discourse referred to as *Dissoi Logoi* (90.1–9), but it does not serve as a good illustration because it mostly provides a discussion of the notion of contrary arguments and furnishes several examples.

15. Xenophon, *Memorabilia* (2.1.34). For various readings of *The Choice of Heracles* see Bromley Smith, "Prodicus of Ceos: The Sire of Synonymy," *Quarterly Journal of Speech Education* 6 1920: 51–68; Mario Untersteiner, *The Sophists*, trans. Kathleen Freeman (New York: Philosophical Library, 1954), 216–21; Eugene Dupréel, *Les Sophistes* (Neuchatel: Editions du Griffon, 1948), 119–21; W. K. C. Guthrie, *The Sophists* (Cambridge: Cambridge University Press, 1971), 277–78; Charles Picard, "Representations Antiques de l' Apologue dit de Prodicos," *Comptes Rendues de l' Academie des Inscriptions et Belles Lettres* 1951: 310–22; Charles Picard, "Nouvelles Remarques sur l' Apologue dit de Prodicos: Héraclès entre le Vice et la Vertu," *Revue Archeologique* 42 1953: 10–41.

16. Susan Biesecker, "Rhetorical Discourse and the Constitution of the Subject: Prodicus' *Choice of Heracles*," *Argumentation* 5 1991: 159–69.

17. For a discussion of *to prepon*, see Max Pohlenz, "Τὸ πρέπον: ein Beitrag zur Geschichte des griechischen Geistes," *Nachrichten von der königlichen Gesellschaft der Wissenschaft zu Göttingen, Philologische-historische Klasse* (1933): 53–92; Untersteiner, 195–99; W. Vollgraff, *L' Oraison Funèbre de Gorgias* (Leiden: E. J. Brill, 1952), 39–41; John Poulakos, "Toward a Sophistic Definition of Rhetoric," *Philosophy and Rhetoric* 16, no. 1 (1983): 41–42.

18. Accordingly, Isocrates (*Helen*, 14–15) faults the writer of an encomium of Helen (almost certainly Gorgias) on the grounds that he failed to observe the

difference between an encomium and a defense: "a plea in defence is appropriate only when the defendant is charged with a crime, whereas we praise those who excel in some good quality."

19. For discussions of the notion of *kairos*, see Untersteiner, 118–21 and 195–99; Kerferd, 82; Poulakos, 38–41; Vollgraff, 21–26; George Kennedy, *The Art of Persuasion in Greece* (Princeton: Princeton University Press, 1963), 67–68.

20. Eric C. White, *Kaironomia: On the Will-to-Invent* (Ithaca, N.Y.: Cornell University Press, 1987), 14.

21. Not generally regarded as a member of the first generation of sophists, Alcidamas' inclusion here is somewhat of an anomaly. Even so, his reported apprenticeship under Gorgias and his arguments in favor of orality justify such an inclusion.

Alcidamas' text can be found in Fridericus Blass, *Antiphontis Orationes et Fragmenta* (Lipsiae: Aedibus B. G. Teubneri, 1892), 193–205. For an English translation and commentary, see LaRue Van Hook, "Alcidamas Versus Isocrates: The Spoken Versus the Written Word," *The Classical Weekly* 12 (1919): 89–94. For other readings of *Peri ton Sophiston*, see Hazel L. Brown, *Extemporary Speech in Antiquity* (Menasha, Wis.: George Banta Publishing Co., 1914), 26–42; Marjorie J. Milne, *A Study in Alcidamas and His Relation to Contemporary Sophistic* (Philadelphia, Penn.: Westbrook Publishing Co., 1924); Tony M. Lentz, *Orality and Literacy in Hellenic Greece* (Carbondale, Ill.: Southern Illinois University Press, 1989), 136–44; Guthrie, 311–13.

22. White, 20.

23. For a relevant discussion of games, see James P. Carse, *Finite and Infinite Games: A Vision of Life as Play and Possibility* (New York: Ballantine Books, 1986).

24. For various readings of this speech, see Untersteiner, 102–24; Charles P. Segal, "Gorgias and the Psychology of the Logos," *Harvard Studies in Classical Philology* 66 1962: 99–155; John Poulakos, "Gorgias' *Encomium of Helen* and the Defense of Rhetoric," *Rhetorica* 1, no. 2 (Autumn 1983): 1–16.

25. This discussion of the actual-ideal opposition relies on but goes beyond the discussion in my "Rhetoric, the Sophists, and the Possible," *Communication Monographs* 51, no. 3 (September 1984): 215–26.

26. For various readings of this speech, see Havelock, 230–39; Untersteiner, 322–23; Guthrie, 295–98.

27. Guthrie, 296.

28. Havelock, 238.

# Chapter 3

# Plato's Reception
# of the Sophists

If there is only one preoccupation in the Platonic corpus, it is the sophists and their rhetoric. Plato is intrigued by the sophists, who they are, what they say and do, how they think. At the same time, he is intensely troubled by them. In many of his dialogues, he seldom misses a chance to attack their rhetorical practices, to ridicule their promises to prospective students, to condemn their teaching methods, and to dissect their claims beyond recognition. Throughout this all consuming literary campaign of dismissal and vilification, Plato portrays the sophists as formidable adversaries whom he opposes with all the might that his own ideational project affords. In doing so, he draws the outline of an epical struggle between two irreconcilable ways of being in the world—the rhetorical and the philosophical.[1]

Thus understood, Plato's relationship to the sophists is simultaneously one of dependence and antagonism. He wishes to preserve and eliminate them at the same time. Their preservation provides a background against which he can argue for the superiority of his polished philosophical system over their indefensible rhetorical enterprise. On the other hand, their elimination promises to clear the path leading to the utopia of the perfect polis. Without the sophists, Plato would have had little or nothing to challenge—his only option would have been to add his insights to the collected wisdom of the past. But one's insights rarely stand out when simply added to those of others; it is when they question past traditions or current practices that they are more likely to receive notice. This, however, is not to suggest that Plato's calculations for effectiveness were motivated by this line of thought; rather, it is to point out that his enormous impact on posterity is, in large measure, due to his masterful orchestration of a set of well-staged discursive battles in which his protagonist, Socrates, fights valiantly against the forces of corruption and evil embodied by sophistry. Absent these forces, it is hard to imagine the Plato we have come to know.

Although much of what Plato has to say about the sophists and their rhetoric is still interesting, it is no longer persuasive. Nobody, for example, today believes that taking fees for instruction or speech writing is a reprehensible practice. Likewise, nobody holds that a given argument is always and for all either weak or strong. And only very few people still regard rhetoric as an inherently decadent enterprise. Judging from the sophistical scholarship of the last one hundred and fifty years, the sophists are generally thought to have made a much greater mark on Western thought than Plato or his disciples would have liked. Of course, this was not always so. Not too long ago, a whole generation of scholars was taught to believe that "in his quarrel with the Sophists Plato was right. He was what he claimed to be, the real philosopher or lover of wisdom, and the Sophists were superficial, destructive, and at worst deliberate deceivers, purveyors of sophistry in the modern sense of that term." Our modernity, however, seems to have turned its head away from the legacy of Plato. Why this may be so is far from obvious. What is more obvious is that, at least among students of rhetoric, the sophists' views are being given unprecedented attention, while Plato is being portrayed as "a bigoted reactionary" who dedicated himself to the task of trivializing or dismissing whoever or whatever opposed his thinking.[2] But if Plato's depiction of the sophists and their rhetoric has lost its appeal, and if Plato has fallen out of favor, why consider what he has to say about them?

First, even the most zealous defenders of the sophists would grant that Plato's attempts to define and revile the teachers of rhetoric have been effective for many centuries. But if this is so, how can we explain the recent interest in sophistical rhetoric? Is it a random phenomenon? Is it a sign of intellectual regress? Could it be the outcome of a deep-seated dissatisfaction with Platonic doctrines and a search for more satisfactory theories explaining our present predicament? Could it be the result of a protracted and persistent scholarly struggle against the grand authority of the priestly tradition of Platonism? While there is room for speculation on these questions, it seems that without Plato's hostile reception of the sophists, the historical significance of their return could hardly be appreciated. His views on them, then, need to be taken into account if only to remind us of the enormous opposition that had to be overcome before the sophists could begin, once again, to be considered worthy of study—even among students of rhetoric.

Second, for most rhetoricians Plato has always played the same role he assigned to the sophists—the enemy. In that capacity, he has been attacked frequently by admirers of the sophists as a bitter misanthrope whose illiberal temper has earned him a prominent place among the opponents of the open society.[3] In and through these attacks, many commentators have attempted to answer Plato on the sophists' behalf. Specifically, they have sought to establish that had the sophists been free from Plato's dialectical strangleholds the sophists could have easily answered his charges; that a dialectically certified rhetoric makes as much sense as a rhetorically certified dialectic; and that Plato's prescriptions for a reformed rhetoric point not to the way but to one alternative among several. The pleasure rhetoricians seem to derive from making these points on their way to self-affirmation is so great that, had Plato not existed, they would have found it necessary to invent him.

A third reason for considering what Plato has to say about the sophists revolves around the attempt to entertain his arguments on the shortcomings of sophistical rhetoric. No matter how caustic or unfair his comments may be, it still behooves students of rhetoric to understand the art of discourse as an issue and, in the spirit of Protagoras' notion of *dissoi logoi*, attend to the other (in this case, the Platonic) side. Lastly, Plato's vitriolic comments about the sophists and their discourses constitute excellent examples of rhetorical strategizing meant to outdo the tactics of the sophists. As such, Plato's comments merit attention by those interested in rhetoric's doubleness, in its capacity, that is, to praise and blame itself.

One way to discern Plato's reception of the sophists and their rhetoric is to read his various accounts of the sophists' personalities, their activities, and their professed *technai*. But because these accounts are interspersed throughout his dialogues, the search for his perception of sophistical rhetoric inevitably leads to a discourse that Plato himself did not write but whose parts are from Plato's own works as we have them today. Naturally, this task does not concern itself with the chronology, the form, the purpose, or the meaning of each dialogue. Rather, it concerns itself with constructing a narrative out of Platonic passages, and arguing that this narrative reflects Plato's complex attitude toward the instructors of rhetoric and disputation. Such a narrative would include not only his references to specific characters in his dialogues (i.e., Gorgias, Protagoras, Hippias, Prodicus, Thrasymachus), it would also take into consideration his comments about the sophists as a class, the sophist as a type of operator, and rhetoric as a cultural practice. Although Plato devotes an entire dialogue (*Sophist*) to the portrayal of the sophist, many of his other works anticipate, supplement, extend, and qualify what he says there. Drawing from all of his works, then, allows us to develop a more complete sense of a major Platonic preoccupation. More importantly, the kind of crosstextual reading I am advocating here permits us to show that, even though the topics of each Platonic dialogue may differ, the referent sophist stays relatively stable.

If, as Aristotle argued, the intelligibility of what is said is affected by the way in which it is said (*Rhetoric*, 1404a.10), we need to attend to the manner in which Plato depicts the sophists before discussing what he says about them.[4] For the most part, he casts them as participants in a round of dialectic, a language game in which he is proficient and they are not especially interested or particularly well versed (*Gorgias*, 448e, 471d; *Phaedrus*, 266c). Time and again, Plato has Socrates invite the sophists to discuss intellectual issues of his choice (i.e., Can virtue be taught? Is it better to commit or suffer wrong? How can one tell the difference between the genuine and the counterfeit?). Without exception, the sophists are made to agree, although at times reluctantly, to play along (*Protagoras*, 338e). But as the interchange between Socrates and the sophists unfolds, it soon becomes apparent that part of the game includes accepting his procedural rules, answering his questions, observing the laconic norm of brevity (*Protagoras*, 334d, 343b; *Gorgias*, 449b–c), and being led to his conclusions.[5]

During the course of their dialectical misadventures, the sophists find themselves inside labyrinthine discourses, wandering in the mazes of Socrates' countless divisions and subdivisions, avoiding one logical trap only to fall into another, and ultimately walking right into the jaws of the philosopher/minotaur. By the end of their discussions, the sophists are either found wanting in dialectical skill or caught committing the cardinal sin against philosophy—contradiction.[6] Once in a while, they register feeble or seemingly unreasonable objections against the way Socrates conducts the discussion but they are always given the same standard response: "Stay with me. Do not walk away. I have nothing personal against you. It is our argument that demands this kind of interrogation. Besides. The search for the truth must go on. And by the way: if I am making bad arguments, do refute me."[7]

The way Plato has scripted the debates between Socrates and the sophists has been discussed extensively by several commentators. While most agree that Plato is not especially kind to Socrates' antagonists, they differ on whether he was fair to the historical sophists. According to Havelock, for example, "Platonists have a great deal of difficulty accepting the fact that he could be unfair to anybody. How could the prophet of personal sincerity and scientific clarity be himself a propagandist muddying the waters of history?"[8] Havelock answers the Platonists categorically, "No philosopher in his senses will take the trouble to report with historical fidelity views which intellectually he cannot accept. What he [Plato] is committed to is a critical examination of them [the sophists], which passes judgment by the light of his own system, and the judgment becomes part of the report."[9] Some commentators defend the plausibility of Plato's portrayals of the historical sophists on the grounds of his presumed sensitivity to his audience. Plato could not have risked, so the thinking goes, producing the kinds of portrayals that his readers could dismiss as pure fabrication. Although sensible, this line of thought overestimates readers in general and underestimates the capacity of a good writer to invent or manipulate reality. Given the inevitability of personal perspective and bias, the issue here is not how accurate Plato's representations of the sophists may be; rather, it is why these representations were undertaken in the first place, and what we make out of them today. An answer to the first question is provided in the last section of this chapter; the second question is entertained in the last chapter of this book.

In several of his dialogues, Plato as a rule does two things to the sophists. First, he replaces their large audiences with Socrates and a small coterie of intellectuals. Second, he takes away from them the oration, the principal form of discourse they were known for, and puts in their mouths plausible, short responses to Socrates' exact questions. In so doing, he dresses them up as incompetent dialecticians and assigns them the supporting role of fellow interlocutors. This transformation in effect denies them their own intellectual identity and power. In their Platonic costumes, the sophists are unrecognizable and impotent because they are out of their element. As Havelock notes, if the sophists are "put in the witness box and allowed only a yes or no to the questions selected by the prosecuting counsel, [they are] likely to stutter and stumble. [They are] not being allowed the privilege of speaking [their] own language."[10] Accordingly, the Gorgias of the *Helen* or the *Palamedes* and the Gorgias of Plato's *Gorgias* are two different personages; and the difference is as great as that between Plato's Socrates and a would-be Socrates portrayed as an inept orator competing against other, more accomplished orators before large crowds in the agora or any other public gathering![11] To accept Plato's representations of the sophists unquestionably, then, would be to disregard the motives and the artistry of their author.

Plato's theatrical ingenuity, however, is not limited to the teachers of rhetoric and disputation. When Socrates is not facing an accomplished sophist, he is conversing either with an immature youth, intoxicated with rhetoric (i.e., Hippocrates in the *Protagoras*, Phaedrus in the *Phaedrus*, Polus in the *Gorgias*), or a father wondering how best to educate his son (i.e, *Theages*, 121d–22a; *Euthydemus*, 306d–7c; *Laches*, 186a). The intoxication of the youths is usually explained away in terms of their impressionable age and the enchanting power of the words of the sophists. As for the parents' concern for their sons' education, it needs no explanation—every father wants a good education for his offspring. In both cases, however, Socrates attempts to convince his interlocutor that the promise of the sophists—eloquence and the power that comes with it—is not worth considering because it can only deliver worldly goods acquired by conceptually questionable and ethically reprehensible means. The sophists' students, in other words, can only hope to learn from their teachers how to become powerful political figures in a corrupt polis, quasi-ignorant leaders of the ignorant masses, and famous people in an ephemeral world. By contrast, a philosophical (Socratic) education promises power over one's own appetites, certainty of knowledge, perhaps a glimpse of the truth, and a secure place in the eternal world of the afterlife.

What is especially noteworthy in Plato's portrayal of impressionable youths and ambivalent parents conversing with Socrates is a certain double standard that often escapes notice; if they are leaning toward rhetoric, we are led to believe that it is because they do not know any better or because they have let themselves be bewitched by the magical spell of the sophists' speeches (i.e., *Cratylus*, 403e; *Sophist*, 233b, 234c; *Protagoras*, 315a). If, on the other hand, they are willing to entertain the questions of the master dialectician, it is because they somehow suspect philosophy to be superior to rhetoric, and all that is left for Socrates to do is help them confirm their suspicions. Plato, however, cannot have it both ways. If youths are immature and impressionable, they are so both when listening to sophists and when talking with Socrates. Likewise, if the parents' outlook is informed by the parental care for the intellectual development of their sons, that outlook is the same regardless if they are entertaining a rhetorical or a philosophical education for their children. Because Socrates tries to convert to philosophy those already attracted to or persuaded by the sophists, his successes cannot be attributed to the superiority of his philosophy and his failures blamed on the intellectual inferiority or the rhetorical preconceptions of his interlocutors.

### Plato's Representations of the Sophists

For Plato, the sophists are the unacceptable other whose thinking and practices he has internalized all too well. Generally, what makes the sophists unacceptable is their discourse, which he finds groundless but also immensely influential. Because it is driven by the ignorant masses it caters to, sophistical rhetoric is conceptually deficient; because it emerges in response to the flitting events of the day, it is inconsistent, unreliable, of no permanent value; and because it is fueled by the ignoble ambitions of its makers, sophistical rhetoric is suspect. Quite simply, what the sophists have to say is (philosophically) senseless. On the other hand, Plato does acknowledge that sophistical rhetoric is a potent force behind all symbolic operations. Yet, because it is disorderly and self-contradictory, it can only prompt its listeners to act in sociopolitically incoherent ways. True, its appeal is widest among the many but, as a rule, mobs have no feeling or regard for the truth. Thus, Plato seems to reason, sophistical rhetoric can only have disastrous consequences. Produced by the ignorant few (the orators), the discourse of the sophists is directed to the ignorant many (the public), whose practices affect the character of and life in the polis; then the discourse returns to the orators via their readings of the public. As participants in and slaves to this vicious cycle, the Platonic sophists are powerful voices in the cultural horizon of the Hellenic world but can only lead those persuaded by them to their own demise. Accordingly, Plato has Anytus exclaim in the *Meno* (91c): "May no kinsman or friend of mine . . . be seized with such madness as to let himself be infected with the company of those men [the sophists]; for they are a manifest plague and corruption (λώβη τε καὶ διαφθορὰ) to those who frequent them." The point Anytus drives home is this: the corruption of the sophists is so powerful that it spreads insidiously and infects great parts of the upstanding segment of the population. To be in their company is pure folly because their ways can destroy everything that is decent and honorable in a society.

Insofar as the sophists enjoyed considerable popularity during their time,[12] Plato's wish to expel them from the mind of the public must have entailed the difficulty of reversing popular discursive tastes and sensibilities, a difficulty accentuated by the fact that disgracing the sophists also meant offending liberal democratic attitudes and condemning a fairly strong educational trend among the aristocratic gentry. Even among the narrower circle of his disciples, such a reversal must have been no small task. The problem Plato's critical project must have been facing is the perennial problem of all philosophy: suspending the assumed clarity of the commonsensical and throwing it into the haze of systematic doubt. Hence Callicles' response to Socrates' convoluted argument that rhetoric is of no use to those who have no intention of doing wrong, or that it is useful only to accuse oneself or one's relations, and to deprive a criminal his due punishment so as to keep him in a state of eternal suffering (*Gorgias*, 480a–81b): "Tell me, Socrates, are we to take you as serious just now, or joking? For if you are serious and what you say is really true, must not the life of us human beings have been turned upside down, and must we not be doing quite the opposite, it seems, of what we ought to do?" (*Gorgias*, 481c). To see how Plato attempted to address the perennial problem of philosophy, let us turn to his representations of the sophists.

Before doing so, a brief note is in order. Because I am not concerned with the sophists' place within Plato's vast philosophical project, I am only looking at what and how Plato writes about them; how he wanted to be understood by his contemporaries or posterity is beyond me. In other words, I do not wish to discover whether Plato's representations of the sophists are consistent with his metaphysical, epistemological, or ontological notions in their intricacies and interconnections. In this regard, all I assume is that Plato found the sophists provocative enough to write extensively about the assumptions and implications of their rhetorical practices. Despite his well-known view of the philosopher as a reflective thinker exclusively concerned with matters of inwardness (*Theaetetus*, 173c–e, ff), Plato the philosopher does recognize the sophists' impact on the culture of his time and treats their influence as a social phenomenon with concrete, if only undesirable, results. That he also treats the sophists according to the postulations of his philosophy does not deny their public status and cannot reduce them to a mere idea. Plato himself directs our attention to the fact that the sophists exist and operate very near, but still outside, the borders of philosophy (*Euthydemus*, 305c–d); and in his mind, this is precisely what makes them dangerous. To portray them, then, as he does, is to bring them within philosophy's borders, define them unambiguously, expose them from top to bottom, and declare them wolves in sheeps' clothing.

Even though Plato finds it easy to denounce the sophists as a class, he also observes that the sophist, as a type of operator, is not the easiest thing in the world to catch and describe; the whole family (τὸ γένος) of sophists is troublesome and hard to hunt down (χαλεπὸν καὶ δυσθήρευτον) (*Sophist*, 218c–d; 261a). The sophist is a many-sided beast (ποικίλον εἶναι τοῦτο τὸ θηρίον) that cannot be caught with one hand (*Sophist*, 226a).[13] He appears in many forms (πολλὰ πεφάνθαι) and it is nearly impossible to hold him down to only one and define him exactly (*Sophist*, 231c). Because the sophist is multiheaded (πολυκέφαλος), he can raise repeatedly multiple objections and difficulties (ἀντιλήψεις καὶ ἀπορίας) for his hunter (*Sophist*, 241b). In other words, the sophist does not lend himself easily to definition. In the same regard, he can be said to have numerous lines of defense (προβλημάτων γέμειν); when he throws one of them up, his opponent has to fight first through it before he can reach the man himself (*Sophist*, 261a). In these two senses, he is like Hydra, the mythical beast that sent out two heads for every one Heracles cut off (*Euthydemus*, 297c).[14] He is really a fascinating man and very hard to keep in sight (ὄντως θαυμαστὸς ἀνὴρ καὶ κατιδεῖν παγχάλεπος) for very long (*Sophist*, 236d). These latter two traits make him resemble the philosopher (*Sophist*, 253e). But whereas the philosopher is hard to see by virtue of the blinding light of being,[15] the sophist escapes into the obscurity of nonbeing, feeling his way in it by practice, and is hard to see on account of the darkness of the place of nonbeing (*Sophist*, 254a). The sophist is also hard to see because he hides behind the claim that there can be no falsehood or contradiction. In particular, he claims that nonbeing can be neither conceived nor uttered, since nonbeing does not in any way participate in being (*Sophist*, 260c–d). To catch the sophist, then, one has to bring him out in the light by proving that falsehood does exist in relation to opinion and speech (*Sophist*, 261a), that is, by establishing that nonbeing is part of being.

The difficulty of defining the sophist, however, extends beyond his polymorphic, ambiguous, and everchanging nature. Besides his Protean character, he is also a masterful imitator of the orator, the philosopher, and the statesman. So good are his imitations of these three types of people that one cannot easily tell him apart from them. As Socrates explains to Polus in the *Gorgias*, even though rhetoric and sophistic do differ, they are also so similar that "sophists and orators are jumbled up as having the same field and dealing with the same subjects, and neither can they tell what to make of each other, nor the world at large what to make of them" (465c). Socrates repeats the same point while addressing Callicles: "Sophist and orator, my estimable friend, are the same thing, or very much of a piece" (520a). Yet another juxtaposition between orator and sophist occurs in the *Cratylus*, where Socrates shows that from the standpoint of the etymology of the verb *legein* (to speak) the race of heroes (ἥρωας) can be understood as a class of orators and sophists (ῥητόρων καὶ σοφιστῶν) (398d–e). In the *Sophist*, Socrates alludes to the apparent similarity between philosopher and sophist/orator by telling Theodorus that philosophers appear sometimes disguised as sophists (216c–d). Later on in the same dialogue, the Eleatic Stranger tells Theaetetus that, given the near identity of philosopher and sophist, it is possible that their search for the sophist has led them to the philosopher (253c).[16] The same kind of confusion can also take place because the sophist often imitates the dialectician/philosopher by engaging students in cross-questioning (*elenchus*) (*Sophist*, 230e–31a). Relying once again on the etymological argument, Plato has the Younger Socrates suggest that because the term sophist can be applied virtually to all leaders of the various forms of government, it is not very far from the term statesman (*Statesman*, 303c). Part of the confusion surrounding the precise identity of the sophists arises from the fact that they, like the orators, compose clever speeches (δεινοὺς λόγους συντιθέναι). Moreover, they are moderately versed in both philosophy and politics (μετρίως μὲν γὰρ φιλοσοφίας ἔχειν, μετρίως δὲ πολιτικῶν)—in fact, Plato observes, that is why Prodicus has placed the sophist on the borderline between the philosopher and the politician (*Euthydemus*, 305c–d). Asserting the sophist's capacity to imitate, the Eleatic Stranger warns that one must be on guard for resemblances because they are slippery; so slippery, in fact, that one can easily mistake the dog, the tamest of animals, for the wolf, the wildest of animals (*Sophist*, 231a). The lesson of all these formulations comes in the form of a clear warning—one should be careful not to fall in the hands of the sophist while looking for the company of the philosopher.[17] Although Plato nowhere clarifies exactly the difference between sophist and orator, he never tires of addressing the distinction between the philosopher on the one hand and sophists and orators on the other.

Aware of the difficulties of defining the sophist precisely and unambiguously, Plato attempts to dispel the popular belief that a sophist is what the name σοφιστής implies, a knower of wise matters (τῶν σοφῶν ἐπιστήμονα) (*Protagoras*, 312c). In the *Sophist*, Theaetetus agrees with the Stranger that the sophist is "very far from being wise, although his name implies wisdom" (221d). According to the Stranger, a name by itself cannot be relied upon to yield a proper conception of the nature of the object under investigation: "For as yet you and I have nothing in common except the name [σοφιστής]; but as to the thing to which we give the name, we may perhaps each have a conception of it in our minds; however, we ought always in every instance to come to agreement about the thing itself by argument rather than the mere name without argument" (*Sophist*, 218b–c).[18] Plato's massive hunt in the *Sophist* and elsewhere is designed to catch, by means of rational argument, the cunning beast that is the sophist.

Armed with the nets of logical devices (*Sophist*, 235b) and the traps afforded by the dialectical method of division (διαίρεσις) (*Sophist*, 235c, 264e–65a), the Eleatic Stranger and Theaetetus set out to track their prey down, that is, to define it. Before doing so, they practice their hunting skills on the angler because "everyone has agreed long ago that if investigations of great matters are to be properly worked out [one] ought to practice them on small and easier matters [the angler] before attacking the very greatest [the sophist]" (*Sophist*, 218c–d). Having caught, that is, having defined, the angler (*Sophist*, 221a–b), they then apply the same method to the sophist (*Sophist*, 221c). Their pursuit is lengthy and tiresome but they are determined not to relax their efforts until they get a good view of the sophist (*Sophist*, 254b); and once they do, they are careful not to let the beast escape (*Sophist*, 235b). Dividing and subdividing, they anticipate its many reactions (countermoves) and eliminate its many hiding places (counterarguments) until, finally, they have it cornered, where it can no longer elude their indivisible argument (*Sophist*, 231c, 235c).[19]

In the earlier part of the *Sophist*, Plato represents the sophist as a hunter after youths and the rich, (νέων καὶ πλουσίων θηρευτής) (231d, 222a); but in a curious reversal, he later turns the sophist into the hunted, thereby making himself a hunter of sophists. For Plato the sophist succeeds as a hunter only in part because his hunting methods are unscientific and irrational. Although most of the sophist's successes are accidental, some are due to his deceptive practices (*Sophist*, 240d) and the low intelligence of his prey; more importantly, the sophist's hunt of youths and money is illegitimate because it is carried out in the service of unreason and nonbeing. By contrast, the philosopher's hunting method is always and in all cases successful because it is scientific and systematic; moreover, his mission is perfectly justified because he is executing the orders of reason and because he is serving the cause of truth. At one point during the hunt, when the sophist has been found to belong to the class of conjurers (θαυματοποιῶν) (*Sophist*, 235b), the Stranger explains confidently the procedure he and Theaetetus are about to follow:

> It is decided, then, that we will as quickly as possible divide the image-making art and go down into it, and if the sophist stands his ground against us at first, we will seize him by the orders of reason, our king, then deliver him up to the king and display his capture. But if he tries to take cover in any of the various sections of the imitative art, we must follow him, always dividing the section into which he has retreated, until he is caught. For assuredly, neither he nor any other creature will ever boast of having escaped from pursuers who are able to follow up the pursuit in detail and everywhere in this methodical way. (*Sophist*, 235b–c)

Following this procedure, Theaetetus and his mentor discover that the sophist possesses seven forms: (1) a paid hunter after the young and wealthy, (2) a kind of merchant in articles of knowledge for the soul, (3) a retailer of these same kinds of knowledge, (4) a seller of his own productions of knowledge, (5) an athlete in contests of words concerned with the art of disputation, (6) a purger of souls, who removes opinions that obstructs souls (*Sophist*, 231d–e), (7) a practitioner of "the imitative kind of the dissembling part of the art of opinion (δοξαστικῆς) which is part of the art of contradiction (ἐναντιοποιολογικῆς) and belongs to the fantastic class (φανταστικοῦ γένους) of the image-making art (εἰδωλοποιικῆς), and is not divine, but human, and has been defined in arguments as the juggling part of productive activity (θαυματοποιικὸν μόριον)" (*Sophist*, 268c–d).[20] Although more or less apt, these forms or definitions can keep one from seeing the common principle that informs all seven (*Sophist*, 232a). The Stranger suggests that one statement, the sophist is a disputer (ἀντιλογικός), characterizes him more plainly than does any other (*Sophist*, 232b).

Even so, Plato repeats, supplements, extends, explains, or reinforces most of these definitions in other dialogues as he discusses the sophists' practices and activities, their claims, and their impact on the wider culture of his time. The sophists are represented in his texts as practicing and teaching the arts of language (τέχναι λόγων), which include rhetoric and disputation. As teachers, they travel from city to city (*Protagoras*, 315a; *Apology*, 19e; *Timaeus*, 19e) giving exhibitions (ἐπιδείξεις) of their arts (*Euthydemus*, 274a–b, 275a; *Gorgias*, 447c; *Hippias Major*, 282b), and teaching anyone who agrees to pay the fees they charge for instruction (*Apology*, 19e–20a; *Laches*, 186c).[21]

As disputers, the sophists are known for their affinity for verbal contests, battering each other's arguments with counterarguments (*Theaetetus*, 154e). In addition to being clever disputers (ἀντιλογικοί) themselves, they are also known as teachers who can make disputers out of others (ποιεῖν ἀντιλογικούς), and as authors of handbooks on the art of disputation (ἀντιλογικῆς τέχνης) (*Sophist*, 232b, e). For the sophists, disputation is an art of answering one's opponents (ἅ δεῖ πρὸς ἕκαστον . . . ἀντειπεῖν) (*Sophist*, 232d), of holding one's views beyond refutation (*Hippias Major*, 286e–87b), and of producing, highlighting, and shading resemblances between things (*Phaedrus*, 261d–e). Alternatively, disputation is the capacity for arguing about everything (περὶ πάντων πρὸς ἀμφισβήτησιν ἱκανή τις δύναμις) (*Sophist*, 232e).[22] The topics or subjects of sophistical disputation include divine things that are invisible, visible things of earth and heaven, generation and being, laws and public affairs, in a word—everything (*Sophist*, 232c–e).

As rhetoricians, the sophists are represented as asserting that rhetoric is the finest of all arts (καλλίστη τῶν τεχνῶν) (*Gorgias*, 448c) and dissembling in lengthy speeches before a multitude of people (*Sophist*, 268b). They are known for their prose eulogies to mythical figures such as Heracles, or to such mundane commodities as salt (*Symposium*, 177a–c), for their declamations at public funerals (*Menexenus*, 234b–35d), and for their technical discoveries in rhetoric (*Phaedrus*, 266c–67d). Among the better known sophists, Prodicus is repeatedly mentioned for being the best at analyzing the meaning of words (*Laches*, 197d; *Protagoras*, 337a; *Meno*, 75e), for arguing that speeches should be neither long nor short but of reasonable length (*Phaedrus*, 267b), and for insisting on the primacy of knowing the correctness of names (ὀρθότης ὀνομάτων) (*Euthydemus*, 277e). Protagoras is depicted as a universally praised man whose reputation is based on his mastery of speech (*Protagoras*, 310e), which includes his notion of ὀρθοέπεια (correctness of diction) and many other fine things (*Phaedrus*, 267c). Gorgias is also portrayed as an accomplished rhetorician (*Gorgias*, 449a), known for his interest in probabilities over truth, his ability to make small things seem great and great things small, as well as his ability to make new things seem old and old things new all through the power of words (*Phaedrus*, 267a–b). Both he and Protagoras are presented as masters at making their students clever speakers (*Protagoras*, 312d; *Gorgias*, 449a–b, 455c, 458a; *Meno*, 95c). Finally, Thrasymachus is portrayed as the best at composing "tearful speeches to arouse pity for old age and poverty . . . and . . . a genius at rousing large companies to wrath, and soothing them again by his charms when they are angry, and most powerful in devising and abolishing calumnies on any grounds whatsoever" (*Phaedrus*, 267c–d).

There are several commonalities among all sophists that permit Plato to treat them as a class. First, they are all in the business of teaching (παιδεύειν ἀνθρώπους) (*Apology*, 19e; *Protagoras*, 317b) and making money by doing so.[23] Second, insofar as their art is about words (περὶ λόγους) (*Sophist*, 234c; *Gorgias* 449d), they are all interested in the workings and uses of language. Third, they all tend to believe that philosophy is worthless;[24] in fact, some go as far as to think that "none but the followers of philosophy stand in the way of their universal renown. Hence they believe that, if they can reduce the latter to a status of no esteem, the prize of victory will by common consent be awarded to them" (*Euthydemus*, 305b–d). A fourth commonality among the sophists is their claim to know many things, if not everything. Gorgias, for example, is made to boast that he could answer any question anyone posed to him (*Gorgias*, 447c–48a, 458e; *Meno*, 70b–c). Likewise, Hippias is made to brag that he could speak on anything related to his prepared linguistic displays, and that he could answer any questions that any one asked him (*Hippias Minor*, 363c–d). Fifth, the sophists are long-winded (*Gorgias*, 449b, c, 461d; *Statesman*, 286b–c). When asked a question, they extend their speech over a full length course. In that sense, they are like brazen vessels which ring a long time after they have been struck and prolong the note unless you put your hand on them (*Protagoras*, 329a–b).[25]

Many sophists claim to be clever and wise (δεινοὶ καὶ σοφοὶ) (*Theaetetus* 154d), and to teach others how to become virtuous (*Laches*, 186c; *Euthydemus*, 273d; *Meno*, 91a–b, 95b–c). Their idea of virtue (ἀρετή, καλοκαγαθία) is material rather than formal. Accordingly, they hold that virtue is a relative matter, not the same for all people or all things. At least for Gorgias, we are told, a man's virtue consists of being "competent to manage the affairs of his city, and to manage them so as to benefit his friends and harm his enemies, and to take care to avoid suffering himself." A woman's virtue, on the other hand, is "the duty of ordering the house well, looking after the property indoors, and obeying her husband" (*Meno*, 71e). Under pressure from Socrates to define virtue formally, Meno identifies it with the power of governing humankind (ἄρχειν τῶν ἀνθρώπων) (*Meno*, 73c–d) or the desire for what is honorable and the ability to procure it (ἐπιθυμοῦντα τῶν καλῶν δυνατὸν εἶναι πορίζεσθαι) (*Meno*, 77b).

Meno's definition notwithstanding, there is no indication from Plato that all the sophists subscribed to the same notion of virtue. Protagoras, for example, is shown to be an educator of culture and virtue (παιδεύσεως καὶ ἀρετῆς διδάσκαλον) (*Protagoras*, 349a) teaching a student "good judgment (εὐβουλία) in his own affairs, showing how best to order his own home; and in the affairs of his city, showing how he may have most influence on public affairs both in speech and in action" (*Protagoras*, 318e–19a). Socrates takes this to mean that Protagoras taught the political art (πολιτικὴν τέχνην) so as to make people good citizens (ἀγαθοὺς πολίτας) (*Protagoras*, 319a). Hippias' view of what is virtuous is given an exclusively rhetorical bent: "the ability to produce a discourse well and beautifully in a court of law or a council-house or before any other public body before which the discourse may be delivered, to convince the audience and to carry off, not the smallest, but the greatest of prizes, the salvation of oneself, one's property, and one's friends" (*Hippias Major*, 304a–b). Finally, Gorgias is said to have laughed at other sophists for claiming to teach virtue, and to have focused his teaching on making clever speakers (*Meno*, 95c). For all their differences, nearly all the sophists are portrayed as purveyors of some form of wisdom, virtue, or excellence.[26]

Partly because of the their exaggerated promises to prospective students (*Sophist*, 233e–34a; *Euthydemus*, 274a) and partly because of their own reputation as accomplished public people,[27] the sophists are portrayed as attracting youths who wish to gain consideration in their cities (ἐλλόγιμοι γενέσθαι ἐν τῇ πόλει) (*Protagoras*, 316c). As already pointed out, this attraction is explained in terms of the youths' impressionable age and the sophists' bewitching words (*Sophist*, 234c; *Cratylus*, 403d–e).[28] When the teachers of rhetoric go to a city, they "persuade the young men, who can associate with whomsoever they wish among their fellow citizens, to give up the association with those men and to associate with them and pay them money and be grateful besides" (*Apology*, 19e–20a). Insofar as many youths are persuaded to join the circle of a particular sophist, they are, in effect, uprooted from their local communities. But, as we have noted, because this phenomenon was apt to cause resentment among the people of the cities and give rise to considerable jealousies and numerous enmities, the sophists are said to have exercised great caution (*Protagoras*, 316c–d). Indeed, Protagoras jokes that in earlier times experts in poetry, mystic rites, soothsaying, athletics, or music felt obliged to shun the title sophist for fear of the odium it evoked (*Protagoras*, 316d–e). Protagoras, however, opposes the practice of disguising his profession and art. Hence he declares openly: "I admit that I am a sophist and that I educate men" (ὁμολογῶ τε σοφιστὴς εἶναι καὶ παιδεύειν ἀνθρώπους) (*Protagoras*, 317b).

## Plato's Critique of Sophistry

Plato's representations of the sophists and their rhetoric are intertwined with an explicit critique of their activities as itinerant teachers, their claims as intellectuals, and their impact on those they instruct. Because this critique has been the subject of many a commentary, and because our main task in this chapter is to explain Plato's reception, we need concern ourselves with his critique only in passing. As critiques go, Plato's is as comprehensive as they come. Take, for example, the sophists' claim to teach virtue. Socrates not only challenges the possibility of teaching virtue (*Protagoras; Laches*, 186b–c), he also doubts seriously whether one can teach anything at all (*Apology*, 20c). When it comes to the sophists, he suggests that their claims are so inflated that one cannot take them seriously. Accordingly, the Stranger asks in the *Sophist:* "when a man says that he knows all things and can teach them to another for a small price in a little time, must we not consider that a joke?" (234a).[29] Likewise, Socrates responds to Euthydemus and Dionysodorus' claim to teach virtue expeditiously by saying: "the vastness of your promise gives me some excuse for disbelieving" (*Euthydemus*, 274a). That the sophists cannot teach virtue, an example of which is fairness, is evident to Socrates from their students' occasional refusal to pay them for their services (*Gorgias*, 519c). In Socrates' estimation, nonpayment from their students serves them best: "I always regarded public speakers and sophists as the only people who have no call to complain of the thing that they themselves educate, for its wickedness towards them" (*Gorgias*, 520b).

Socrates also condemns with no hesitation the sophistical practice of charging money for instruction. As he tells Callicles, when it comes to the "business of finding the way to be as good as possible, and of managing one's own household or city for the best, it is recognized to be a disgrace for one to decline to give advice except for a payment in cash" (*Gorgias*, 520e). Money in this regard is an issue for Plato because it trivializes education by turning what is a serious intellectual exchange of the first order into merchandise for the soul (*Protagoras*, 313c), a commodity that can be bought and sold. If money determines who does and who does not get educated, the distinction between the serious and the nonserious or the intelligent and the nonintelligent is eliminated. Consequently, a teacher agrees to instruct any and all so long as they promise to pay at the end. If we can rely on Xenophon's account of a conversation between Socrates and Antiphon (87A.8.13), the Platonic view is that selling wisdom for money is no different from selling one's body for money; both practices amount to prostitution. Beyond the issue of money, Plato also questions the quality of the sophists' intellectual wares. Since they teach for monetary profit, there is nothing to prevent them from selling goods unfit for mental consumption; what is more, most people do not know how to differentiate between good and bad products be they material or immaterial (*Protagoras*, 313d–e).[30] Therefore, youths should seek the advice of their elders, friends, and relatives before rushing to buy wisdom from the sophists (*Protagoras*, 313a–b, 314b).

As can be expected from a polymorphic and polytropic teacher, the art of the sophist is multifarious (εὖ μάλα ποικίλης) (*Sophist*, 223c), claiming to encompass a great variety of purposes and subjects. Moreover, it is a deceptive art (ἀπατητικὴ) (*Sophist*, 240d); through it, the sophist deceives his students by "exhibiting to them spoken images (εἴδωλα λεγόμενα) of all things, so as to make it seem that they are true and that the speaker is the wisest of all men in all things"

(*Sophist*, 234c). If the sophistical art has any ground, that ground is opinion, not true knowledge (*Sophist*, 233c). The sophist is among those who imitate various realities, not among those who know them (*Sophist*, 267e). As such he must be understood as a juggler whose real business is entertainment (*Sophist*, 235a). For all these reasons, the sophist's claim to teach virtue is empty, because virtue is a form of knowledge. Likewise, the sophists' promise to teach politics and law cannot be kept because they have no knowledge about these matters (*Statesman*, 291b–c). Yet they promise to deliver what, in reality, they cannot; otherwise nobody would attend their classes (*Sophist*, 232d). As if deceiving their students were not enough, the sophists also put them, once in a while, through initiation rites (*Euthydemus*, 277d–e) and make sport of them (*Euthydemus*, 278c). Finally, when their words fail to persuade their students, they chastise them with loss of civic rights and fines and death (*Republic*, 492d–e). For all these practices, the sophists ought to be ashamed.[31]

Sophists who engage in and teach disputation are known for their adeptness in fighting and winning legal battles and for their faculty of "wielding words as their weapons and confuting any argument as readily if it be true as if it be false" (*Euthydemus*, 271d–72a). But when one sees beyond their tricks, one can see that disputers generally make an absurd ado about matters of no consequence (*Euthydemus*, 304e). As for those sophists who teach rhetoric, they are basically inviting their more accomplished students to commit the injustice of helping the unjust escape due punishment. Furthermore, they are instructing people, if only indirectly, to prefer the ease of beliefs and probabilities over the rigor of knowledge and certainty, to indulge in sensual over mental pleasures and bodily over spiritual appetites, to favor power over goodness—in short, to attend exclusively to mundane tasks rather than focusing on the principal task befitting all free persons, the improvement of their soul.[32] As we noted earlier, the sophists are portrayed as "a manifest plague and corruption to those who frequent them" (*Meno*, 91c). But the blame is not entirely theirs; one should also consider blaming "the young men who pay them money, and still more the relations who entrust young men to their charge; and most of all the cities that allow them to enter, and do not expel them" (*Meno*, 92a–b). In truth, a student stands to gain more and better insights from any Athenian citizen he may encounter than from the sophists (*Meno*, 92e).

As we noted earlier, one of the effects of the sophists' recruiting practices is the gradual erosion of the communal bonds in the cities they visit (*Apology*, 19e–20a; *Protagoras*, 316c–d). Youths either leave their homeland in search of sophistical wisdom and deprive their local communities of their services as workers and citizens, or they remain but forsake their family and friends. However, the greatest impact on the young is made, not by any individual sophist, but by the multitude, the greatest sophist of them all. When it assembles, the level of its noise is so powerfully loud that it can sweep a person away from any privately acquired insight, and force him/her to conform to its views (*Republic*, 492a–d).

What the sophists say originates from the commonly held opinions of the lay public (οἱ πολλοί, δῆμος, πλῆθος). Because the sophists are in the business of flattering crowds (*Gorgias*, 463a), they only speak according to what their audiences want to hear. Unlike the philosopher, who is indifferent to the crowd's appetite for flattery, and who always says the same things about the same subjects, the sophists never say the same thing (*Gorgias*, 481d–82a, 490e–91c). This makes them as inconsistent and unreliable as the fickle crowds they address—in fact, it makes them slaves to their ignorant listeners. Even so, the sophists claim that what they have to say is wisdom, when it is really nothing more than a version of the public's beliefs. Plato explains the sophist's relationship to the crowd at length (*Republic*, 493a–c):

> It is as if a man were acquiring the knowledge of the humours and desires of a great strong beast which he had in his keeping, how it is to be approached and touched, and when and by what things it is made most savage or gentle, yes, and the several sounds it is wont to utter on the occasion of each, and again what sounds uttered by another make it tame or fierce, and after mastering this knowledge by living with the creature and by lapse of time should call it wisdom, and should construct thereof a system and art and turn to the teaching of it, knowing nothing in reality about which of these opinions and desires is honourable or base, good or evil, just or unjust, but should apply all these terms to the judgements of the great beast, calling the things that pleased it good, and the things that vexed it bad, having no other account to render of them, but should call what is necessary just and honourable, never having observed how great is the real difference between the

necessary and the good, and being incapable of explaining it to another.

In this double dismissal of sophists and their audiences, Plato, once again, makes his point analogically: just as the animal trainer becomes acquainted with the behaviors of the wild beast he attempts to tame, so too the sophist learns the ways in which crowds tend to act by virtue of his frequent contact with them. But the sophist is worse than animal trainers because he accepts the masses' notions of honor, goodness, and justice—notions whose nature the masses are too ignorant to determine for themselves. Once again, the greatest liabilities of the sophist are that he does not know the difference between the pleasant and the good; that he cannot explain what he does to another; that he teaches a false wisdom; and that he caters to the crowds. In short, the sophist's greatest shortcoming is that he is not a philosopher.

Thus far we have seen that Plato's reception of the sophists follows the outline of a sharp antagonism between the rhetorical and the philosophical ways of being-in-the-world. Using the sophists now as a pretext for articulating his own philosophical program, now as an obnoxious societal malady, Plato offers his dialectic as a radical alternative to their rhetorical and disputatious discourses, an alternative designed to cure the ills of sophistry. In and through a series of dramatic plays (the dialogues), Plato portrays the sophists as intellectually inferior, ethically corrupt, and technically inept. According to Plato, what drives the sophists is ambition for success in a corrupt world, greed for material gains, and the desire for sensual pleasure. Their language, largely imagistic and undisciplined, impresses the many, who have no critical capacity to see through the fraudulent and deceptive properties of such language. Because the sophist is not easily distinguishable from the philosopher, Plato attempts to define him unambiguously, to hunt him down, to arrest him, and to bring him out of the blurred terrain of ambiguity with the help of the method of definition that relies on the procedure of division. This is another way of saying that Plato tries to integrate the sophists into his despotic system of thought. Their role in that system is that of imitators of philosophers, statesmen, and orators. Finally, Plato concludes that the sophists' discursive practices, by virtue of their ambiguous, deceptive, or imitative character, have detrimental consequences for the society around them. Therefore, if the sophists are to be integrated into his ideational framework, they must be disabused of their dangerous notions and harmful practices.

Why did Plato portray the sophists in such an unflattering manner and under such a negative light? Why did he attack them so fiercely? The next section of this chapter attempts to answer these questions.

### Plato's Rejection of the Sophists

Plato's hostility toward the sophists and their rhetoric has attracted a great deal of attention from many commentators of Greek antiquity.[33] Even so, most explanations of the intense antagonism between the dialectical philosopher of the fourth century B.C. and the itinerant instructors of the fifth are limited to a discussion of personal, intellectual, class, and citizenship differences. Plato disliked the sophists, so the thinking goes, because they were different from him. They were popular; he was not. They were liberal; he was conservative. They were members of the middle class; he was a member of the aristocracy. They were resident aliens; he was an Athenian citizen.

In 1857 George Henry Lewes posed the same question many historians of rhetoric are asking today, "Why . . . did Plato speak of the Sophists with so much asperity? Why did he consider their teaching so dangerous?"[34] Lewes answered categorically: "Because he differed from them *in toto*."[35] Calling the difference between Plato and the sophists a "difference in creed," Lewes went on to qualify his answer in terms of his view of human nature, a view according to which people are envious of the success of others, and indignant when feeling ignored.[36]

> The Sophists were wealthy; the Sophists were powerful; the Sophists were dazzling, rhetorical, and not profound. Interrogate human nature—above all the nature of philosophers—and ask what will be the sentiment entertained respecting these Sophists by their rivals. Ask the solitary thinker what is his opinion of the showy, powerful, but shallow rhetorician who usurps the attention of the world. The human of conviction has at all times a superb contempt for the human of mere oratorical or dialectical display. The thinker knows that the world is ruled by Thought; yet he sees Expression gaining the world's attention. He knows, perhaps, that he has within him thoughts pregnant with human welfare; yet he sees the giddy multitude intoxicated with the enthusiasm excited by some

plausible fallacy, clothed in enchanting language. He sees through the fallacy, but cannot make others as clear-sighted. His warning is unheeded; his wisdom is spurned; his ambition is frustrated: the popular Idol is carried onward in triumph. *The neglected thinker would not be human if he bore this with equanimity.* He does not. He is loud and angry in lamenting the fate of a world that can be so led; loud and angry in his contempt of one who could so lead it. (emphasis added)[37]

Following the same line of thinking, George Grote argued in his *A History of Greece* that Plato's quarrel with the sophists must be understood in terms of the distinction between the contemplative and the active life:

The hostility of Plato against these teachers [the sophists] . . . may be explained without at all supposing in them that corruption which modern writers have been so ready not only to admit but to magnify. *It arose from the radical difference between his point of view and theirs.* He was a great reformer and theorist: they undertook to qualify young men for doing themselves credit, and rendering service to others, in active Athenian life. (emphasis added)[38]

Explicating further Plato's reform-mindedness, Grote noted that the sophists were only a small part of Plato's radical and comprehensive program for change: "His [Plato's] criticisms are dictated by his own point of view, according to which the entire society was corrupt, and all the instruments who carried on its functions were of essentially base metal."[39]

In more recent times, Havelock has pointed out that Plato's contempt for the sophists was due, at least in part, to "the pressure of professional competition" and to his fear of their ideas, which were abundantly present in many expressions of public life long after their proponents were gone.[40] Similarly, Vickers has suggested that Plato's adverse disposition toward sophistical rhetoricians can be explained by his jealousy of their success, and the prominent role their rhetoric had played in shaping the culture of his time.[41] Finally, Guthrie has proposed that the antagonism of Plato and the sophists can be explained in terms of two mutually exclusive philosophical views:

The first view is typified by the sayings of Protagoras . . . that man is the measure of all things and the existence of gods an undemonstrable assumption. The second . . . culminates later in Plato's ideal theory, according to which such concepts as justice and beauty . . . have an existence apart from the human mind.[42]

However meritorious, these explanations overlook two important facts. First, Plato grew up during the age of the sophists, which means that he must have been acquainted with their practices and notoriety; and second, he lived his adult life under the weight of their continuing influence. If the *Seventh Letter* can be relied on, the latest part of the fifth century B.C. and the earliest part of the fourth was a time in which people were living out the implications of the adopted lessons and practices of the older sophists—at least this is what Plato thought. But if this is so, his hostility against them was not so much a function of his differences from them as it was a symptom of his disgust with the political chaos in the Hellas of his adult life. In his mind, the chaos he was experiencing was a direct consequence of sophistical thought and practice. Whether his conclusion was warranted is beside the point. The fact is that Plato rejected the sophists; and he did so because he believed them responsible for the sociopolitical deterioration he was witnessing all around him. Therefore, the logic of his rejection is not the logic of difference but the logic of cause and effect (to reject the effects of something often requires the rejection of its causes). To see how this logic plays out in Plato, we need to attend to his circumstances the way we attended to the circumstances of the sophists. To do this we must go against tradition, which portrays Plato as an eccentric thinker, an elitist mind, or an unrepresentative intellect of the Hellenic world.[43] To follow the tradition would be to admit that he, or any thinker for that matter, can be considered apart from the historical moment in which they lived and thought.

## Plato's Discursive Circumstances

In chapter 1, we discussed the sophists and their practices and doctrines in the light of the adventuresome age of Pericles, an age whose character they helped crystallize. Considering the logic of their circumstances, the prevailing ethic of competition, and the dominant aesthetic of spectacles, we treated them as agents of the perpetuation of certain cultural practices and as catalysts of the emergence of new practices. By the time of Plato's adulthood, the rhetorical innovations of the older sophists had already demonstrated their versatility and influence as they had found impressive expressions in the drama of Euripides, the history of Thucydides, and the medical science of Hippocrates. But now the sophists were becoming commonplace. At the same time, they were losing their earlier appeal largely because they, like the age they represented, had failed to live up to the expectation of fulfilling their promise to make men good citizens (ποιεῖν ἄνδρας ἀγαθοὺς πολίτας).[44] Thus it was not unreasonable for thoughtful people in Plato's time to ask: Were the sophists the worthy teachers of the Hellenes of the fifth century? Could their lessons sustain the social, political, and intellectual life of the Hellenic world during the fourth? Was a sophistical State possible? In the post-Peloponnesian War era, one had many reasons to be skeptical.

If we can rely on Isocrates, Plato's contemporary rival, rhetorical education, initially sought as a means to a political career or effective citizenship, had turned into a skill desired for achieving individual purposes with no regard to the common good. Verbal competition, at first a mechanism for testing one's intellectual agility against that of others, had turned into a matter of technique indifferent to fair play—a channel for pursuing legal and other kinds of victories at any cost. And display oratory, originally designed to entertain a public and critique its institutions at the same time, had lost its sense of purpose, becoming in the process an activity for its own sake.[45]

Assuming a strong connection between discourse and actions, and viewing specific political conditions as consequences of historical causes, Plato must have concluded that the sophists were unworthy teachers because they had taught the public that any and all actions could be justified as long as one had polished rhetorical skills. For Plato, such a lesson was doomed to failure because it had left out of the equation for a good State the respect for order, proportion, and authority. The prevailing conditions at the time seem to confirm Plato's belated prophesy of doom. A person did not have to go very far to see the influence of the sophists in action. In Plato's mind, opinion leaders and common citizens alike were thinking and acting rhetorically. The results of such an orientation within the polis included irresponsible management of the State, competition for personal victory or conquest, theatricalized political and legal proceedings, discursive exhibitions for their own sake, and the kind of general uneasiness that goes hand-in-hand with civic disorder. In politics, the eloquent politician could sway crowds at will, without considering the soundness of his plans or the long-term effects of his policies on the State and its people. For their part, the crowds, always unruly and fickle, were all too eager to be persuaded by anything that sounded good, and too ready to disregard the consequences. In the courts, mob rule was the order of the day as the causes of justice suffered indignities in the hands of large ignorant juries and shrewd orators reciting the rhetoric of unscrupulous logographers. In state festivals, orations had turned into idle shows of linguistic dexterity without regard for the moral refinement of their audiences.

Beyond these observations, Plato reasoned that a sophistical State, if at all possible, would be "one great mass of turmoil and lawlessness" because it would have too many standards, too many individual purposes, too many competing opinions, too much disregard for what is best for itself, and too much blindness to see the truth.[46] In a well-known passage in the *Seventh Letter* (324b–326b), Plato gives the impression that during his early twenties this is precisely the kind of State he lived in. In what has been regarded as his explanation for not going into politics, Plato recounts a terrible state of political affairs: one revolution after another, empty promises of reform and proper city management, countless instances of wickedness, abuses of the worst kind, injustice after injustice, and a general atmosphere of mistrust and corruption.

Even though these conditions dashed his hopes of entering politics, they offered Plato the opportunity to argue against the sophists' opportunistic management of circumstances, to posit that improvised rhetorical responses to critical situations are often premature, uninformed, and potentially regrettable both to the orator and those persuaded by him.[47] What was needed, Plato thought, was a more enlightened approach, an approach that could treat circumstances not circumstantially, but from a more solid standpoint, the standpoint of definition and principle.[48] The man who does the former, Plato must have thought, is generally unprepared to act thoughtfully and as a result, circumstances tend to overwhelm him. But the man who does the latter, enters circumstances ready to address them from a certain distance with confidence and conviction, and the result is that he usually makes the best out of them. In the first instance, the circumstances control the man; in the second, he controls the circumstances. Clearly, both the sophists and Plato expressed their radically disparate views from within a set of particular circumstances. But while the sophists had adapted to theirs by fashioning circumstantial re-

sponses, Plato resisted his by means of supposedly extra-circumstan-
tial (that is, philosophical) principles and definitions.

Plato's philosophical resistance to the force of his circumstances is
reflected in his view of sophistical rhetoric. It has often been said that
Plato disliked, not rhetoric, but only the kind of rhetoric the sophists
and their disciples were practicing. While this issue remains open, it
is noteworthy that the sophists in his dialogues claim to be able to address every subject intelligently, speak on any issue persuasively, and
charm a crowd with their speeches at will. But ask the sophists to define their art and you will find that they cannot (*Gorgias*, 449c–60e). Of
course, this does not mean that they were ineffective. Plato knew otherwise. Not blind to the immense power of rhetorical discourse in
guiding human thought and action, Plato also knew that, if one were
to judge from the social and political conditions at the aftermath of the
Peloponnesian Wars, one would see that the sophists' rhetoric had
not served the Hellenic states well. In his mind, their kairotically fash-
ioned responses to ephemeral situations had led to short-sighted and
ill-conceived courses of action; their competitive spirit had promoted
self-serving behavior and a lack of cooperation; and their spectacular
rhetorical displays had lulled the citizenry to intellectual sleep.

What was needed, for Plato, was a rhetoric that could go beyond
the love of paradox (Lysias' speech in the *Phaedrus*) or the urgency of
circumstances (Gorgias' *Palamedes*). More specifically, what was
needed was a self-conscious rhetoric, a rhetoric that stood on clearly
defined grounds, followed a set of wise rules, explained the logic of
its procedure, and persuaded "men to justice thereby helping to steer
the ship of the state" (*Statesman*, 303e–4a). Plato offers us examples of
this kind of rhetoric in Socrates' second speech in the *Phaedrus* and in
the *Apology*.[49] Moreover, he also lays down in the *Phaedrus* a blueprint
for a general theory of rhetoric. In a well-known passage summariz-
ing his discussion with Phaedrus on the requirements for a proper
rhetoric, Socrates says:

> A man must know the truth about all the particular things of which
> he speaks or writes, and must be able to define everything sepa-
> rately; then when he has defined them, he must know how to di-
> vide them by classes until further division is impossible; and in the
> same way he must understand the nature of the soul, must find
> out the class of speech adapted to each nature, and must arrange
> and adorn his discourse accordingly, offering to the complex soul

elaborate and harmonious discourses, and simple talks to the simple soul. Until he has attained to all this, he will not be able to speak by the method of art, so far as speech can be controlled by method, either for purposes of instruction or of persuasion. (277b–c)

Plato's direct call for this kind of rhetoric amounted to an indirect call for dialectic. For him, dialectic constituted a new discursive orientation, an orientation that could alter for the better the rhetorical practices of his contemporaries. More specifically, it could put orators, political leaders, and intellectuals alike on the road to the dual discovery of disciplined reflection on the issues of the day and thoughtful governance of the State. Relying on the traditions of disputation and eristic, Plato developed dialectic as a mode of discourse that could resist the force of circumstances and critique popular conceptions and practices dominating the cultural horizon of his times.[50] As a first order of business for the philosopher, dialectic sought to rearticulate the meaning, the form, and the direction of discourse. To that end, it was made to work outside the discursive parameters already drawn by the sophists. Had Plato been a reformer rather than a detractor of sophistry, he would have argued for a rhetoric revolving around the notions of goodness rather than opportunity, truth rather than playfulness, and ideals rather than possibilities. But as it turns out, he settled new discursive frontiers instituting the regime of dialectic.

In and through this regime, Plato attempted to transcend the realms of appearance (φαίνεσθαι) and opinion (δόξα), and argue for the existence of reality (εἶναι) and the necessity of knowledge (ἐπιστήμη). In the case of his resistance to his circumstances, the point for him was not which one out of a multitude of discursive appearances was the most appealing, but what discursive formulation could stand against all appearances. Likewise, the question was not which opinion in a sea of opinions may be the most persuasive, but what discursive construction could oppose all opinions. Accordingly, he created an elaborate set of new oppositions, placing the sophists with their rhetoric on the one side and the philosopher with his dialectic on the other. In so doing, he made his own preferences known: one idea rather than myriads of linguistic representations already in circulation; one knowledgeable specialist rather than all the opinionated generalists in the society; and one truth above all the deceptions in the world. This was Plato's philosophical stance, a stance suggesting a compensatory project designed to return to order a disorderly world. The general structure, as well as the particularities of this project, found their most eloquent expression in his *Republic*. Thus understood, Platonic philosophy emerged out of one set of cultural tensions and introduced another.[51]

The new problem for Plato, as for any radical reformer, was how to make his views authoritative. Insofar as reformers can establish their authority by discrediting the work of their predecessors, Plato must have been quite aware that his own intellectual project could not be launched before exposing the weaknesses and untenability of the sophistical enterprise. But he must have also known that the sophistical mentality could not be discredited easily. As we have seen, all its manifestations (interventional, competitive, and exhibitionary) had deep cultural roots. Accordingly, his answer was the form of dialogue, a form that could lend itself to and simultaneously call into question the logic of circumstances, the ethic of competition, and the aesthetic of spectacles.[52]

Intended as an invitation to philosophy,[53] Plato's push for dialogical discourse did several things. For one, it introduced a challenge to the rhetorical establishment by arguing that behind the apparent duality of discourse (*dissoi logoi*) there exists a singular truth, a truth one could arrive at in conversation with an accomplished dialectician (usually Socrates). For another, it announced that, far from an agonistic enterprise, discourse was a cooperative endeavor, an endeavor depending on the give-and-take of disciplined discussion. For yet another, it declared that the main aim of discourse is inward reflection, not outward exhibition—its purpose should be to problematize its listeners and cleanse them of their ignorance, not to dazzle its spectators and feed their appetite for show. Finally, it reduced the size of the audience and rearranged the flow of discourse; instead of a passive crowd listening to the orator's uninterrupted and self-enclosed discourse, dialogue required a small company of actively engaged interlocutors expressing their views, asking and answering questions, registering objections, and seeking clarification from each other without necessarily arriving at a definite conclusion. In all these ways, dialogical discourse opposed its rhetorical counterpart, and gave birth to the philosopher as the new intellectual leader of the culture. For Plato, the main task of the new leader was to challenge the domination of rhetoric.

Unlike an oration, a form of discourse making up one part of a larger setting, many Platonic dialogues include a setting making up one part of a larger discourse. The setting itself (e.g., Socrates' jail cell in the *Crito*), the affairs of the characters (e.g., Hippias' travels and exhibitions in the *Hippias Major*), their circumstances (e.g., Theages' dilemma over his son's education in the *Theages*), their reputation (e.g., Protagoras' notoriety in the *Protagoras*), as well as their conduct during the course of the dialogue (e.g., Callicles' uncooperative behavior in the *Gorgias*) are all targets for commentary. But as the dialogue proceeds, all these circumstantial elements fade into the background and the main idea begins to emerge and take center stage. By the end of the dialogue, say the *Gorgias*, the focus is not on Gorgias' fame as a brilliant declaimer, Polus' youthful immaturity, or Callicles' impolite behavior; rather, it is on a set of significant questions: What is rhetoric? Is it better to commit or to suffer wrong? What does it mean to be powerful? Which life is superior, the active or the contemplative? In this way, the circumstantial elements represented in and occasioning or facilitating the internal workings of the dialogue are ultimately subordinated to the ideas the dialogue expounds. But if this is so, the reader must acknowledge (along with Gorgias, Polus, and Callicles) that in the final analysis, rhetoric needs to concern itself with justice; that to be powerful means to be in control of one's appetites; and that the contemplative life is superior to a life of action.

In addition to the oppositional tension between circumstances and ideas, some Platonic dialogues portray the full force of one idea in competition with another. Time and again, Socrates, feigning innocence and ignorance, entertains a competitive sophist willing to engage in symbolic combat over an issue of common interest. During the course of the discussion, it becomes apparent that even though the sophists' ideas are widely believed, they finally bend under the weight of the dialectical scrutiny (ἔλεγχος).[54] Without exception, Socrates gets the better of his opponents not because he is a better contestant (ἀγωνιστής) but because he is a lover of wisdom (φιλόσοφος) (*Theaetetus*, 164c). This means that he is less interested in winning and more in following the argument wherever it may lead. By the end of the dialogue, the very competition taking place between Socrates and the sophists has been undermined by their cooperation, which has led either to a truth or to a state of ἀπορία, perplexity. In the former case, competition is shown to be unnecessary because the truth is incontestable; in the latter, characters and readers alike must put their agonistic predispositions aside, and press on together to discover what eludes them. In and through his dialogues, then, Plato competes with the sophists so as to undermine and endorse competition at the same time: if his dialogical project is to succeed, Plato must ultimately subordinate the sophists' rhetorical competitiveness to dialogical cooperation in search of the truth. Put another way, Plato must enter several contests with the sophists in order to demonstrate the shortcomings of their agonistic orientation and discuss the advantages of his version of cooperation.

Beyond their competitive characteristics, another feature of the Platonic dialogues is their resemblance to theatrical dramas. Like the plays of the tragedians of the fifth century B.C., Plato's dialogues portray characters acting out their pride, false certitude, and invincibility only to see their views ridiculed and exposed as faulty, inadequate, and unreliable. Like the actors on the stage, who are torn between the human and the divine worlds, the characters in Plato's pages find themselves compelled to choose between the mundane world of sophistical rhetoric and the semi-divine world of philosophy. But as in the case of drama, where the typical protagonist faces divine sanctions for acting according to human laws, or human sanctions for acting according to divine ones,[55] the choices that are philosophy or rhetoric have a price, too. To choose philosophy means to be prepared to live neglected, dismissed, and ridiculed by the many, who do not know.[56] By contrast, the price of choosing rhetoric is a life of shameful compromises, personal disharmony, hypocrisy, dishonesty, and lies. In all these senses, the Platonic dialogues can be viewed as spectacles for a new generation of spectators, readers. But while the spectators of theatrical or rhetorical shows had been accustomed to looking outward for the sensual pleasures afforded by "tones and colors and shapes and everything that art fashions out of these," Plato's readers were urged to turn inward, apprehend, and take intellectual delight in the idea of beauty itself (*Republic*, 476b). Once again, Plato produced a new kind of spectacle in order to undermine the popularity and appeal of rhetorical spectacles.

As it relates to the sophists, then, the discourse of the dialogue embodied, at least in its form, circumstantial, competitive, and exhibitionary elements. But at the same time, it brought its own form into sharp opposition with its content. The result was the subordination of circumstances to ideas, of competition to cooperation, and of exhibition to reflection. Whether addressing political, social, educational, or

intellectual topics, Plato's dialogues as a whole constituted an opportune response to an undesirable situation. In this sense, they differed
little from the rhetorical discourses of the sophists.[57] But in contrast to
sophistical rhetoric, which had found its inspiration and arguments in
the manifestations of public life, the dialogues turned inward, into
the reservoir of human intelligence, in order to recollect what was already there. In so doing, the dialogues not only rejected the rhetoric
of the sophists; they also articulated a new politics, the politics of
ideas. Moving from consequences to causes, Plato was attempting to
show that the sophistic movement had not led to a better world;
worse, it had reduced the world it had inherited to virtual ruins.
Therefore, it was time to start the process of reparation. Plato's dialogues also constituted an agonistic undertaking, an undertaking aiming to overthrow the sophistical culture of rhetorical and disputatious
practices. But if this is so, the difference between sophistical disputation, as portrayed in the *Euthydemus* for example, and a Platonic dialogue of the refutative (ἀνατρεπτικὸς) kind (i.e., the *Gorgias*) is not
great. Yet, unlike sophistical agonistics, which was thought to violate
normative rules of competition and to be seeking only victory, Platonic agonistics was to observe faithfully a set of rules and to aim at
the discovery of the truth, not the replacement of the stronger argument by the weaker. In this regard, Plato's dialogues were concerned
not so much with who won a particular discursive contest but with
whether the participants competed fairly (rationally). Finally, the Platonic dialogues constituted theatrically inspired productions seeking
to dislodge the sophistical culture of display rhetoric. But if this is so,
Plato's dialogical discourses did not vary substantively from their sophistical counterparts—they, too, were seeking to stage playful discursive encounters, the kind that would guide their readers through a
specific path and point them to a specific goal. But unlike sophistical
rhetoric, which had relied on the susceptibility of large crowds to enchanting language performed in a public place, Plato's dialogues
aimed at the singular reader who could follow an intelligent conversation and adopt its lessons for life.

In this chapter we have taken a look at Plato's reception of the
sophists. What we have seen is a large cluster of unflattering portrayals, which I have explained by reference to Plato's own view of the
sociopolitical conditions in the Hellenic world of his adult life. Convinced that the sophists were to blame for these conditions, Plato attacked their rhetorical activities wherever he saw them spring up. In

his mind, the sophists had to go. Because they practiced linguistic athletics, using words as weapons and aiming at victory at any cost, they were not beyond unethical conduct. Because they performed like actors, using words as masks and seeking to please large crowds of spectators, they were not beyond exaggerated promises and deceptive talk. Because they taught for pay, using words as commodities and promising power, they were not beyond dishonest deals. And because they imitated philosophers, using words as self-referential entities and pretending to instruct their pupils, they were not beyond the dissemination of untruths. For Plato, the State did not need verbal gymnasts, virtuosos of rhetorical performances, greedy merchants, or ignorant teachers. Rather, it needed philosophically minded political rulers or politically minded philosophers—in short, the State needed the kinds of people the sophists were incapable of producing.[58] Only through philosopher-kings or king-philosophers could the State recover its compass to the happy life.

What we have also seen in this chapter is Plato's many attempts to define the sophists, to draw clear lines separating what they are from what they are not. Aware that they roamed from city to city without a fixed political or intellectual identity, Plato toiled to codify their practices and doctrines in his new vocabulary of ideas. For him, the sophists had to be identified. Because they argued now for one side of an issue, and for the opposite side later, one could not tell what a sophist's own position was. Because they occupied many discursive locations, one could not at a given moment in time find them in any one place. And because they were accomplished imitators, one could not distinguish them from statesmen, philosophers, or orators. For Plato, the world of thought required correct names as well as clear and distinct ideas, not discourses with blurred lines on matters of knowledge and ethical conduct. By way of strict definitional procedures and imaginative portrayals, Plato identified the sophists, in effect naming them opportunists, verbal athletes, deceiving entertainers, pretenders of knowledge, multiheaded beasts, and the like. With these definitions in mind, his contemporaries and successors could decide more intelligently what to do with their sophists.

With the advent of Plato, there began a new epoch in the history of Hellas. It was an epoch marked by the will to heal the wounds of the Peloponnesian Wars, to rethink the relationship between the individual and the State, to institute legal reforms, to articulate new desires for the culture, and to provide new discursive means of satisfying them. From Plato's perspective, the creation of new cultural desires went hand-in-hand with the rejection of the desires the sophists had instilled in the Hellenes—most notably the desire for rhetoric. As practiced by the rhetoricians of his time, rhetoric amounted to unruly discourse, which promoted unruly social and political behavior, which led to an unruly State.

Plato's response to sophistical rhetoric was not the only one from the intelligentsia of the new epoch. His contemporary rival, Isocrates, had a different response. To see what this response entailed, let us turn to the next chapter.

## Notes

1. See, for example, *Gorgias* 500c–ff.
2. W. K. C. Guthrie, *The Sophists* (Cambridge: Cambridge University Press, 1971), 10.
3. See Friedrich Nietzsche, *The Will to Power*, trans. Walter Kaufmann and R. J. Hollingdale (New York: Vintage Books, 1968), 141–43, 429, 434–38; Eric A. Havelock, *The Liberal Temper in Greek Politics* (London: Jonathan Cape, 1957); Sir Karl R. Popper, *The Open Society and Its Enemies*, vol. 1 (Princeton: Princeton University Press, 1971).
4. As Havelock points out (159), Plato defined the sophists "by creating dramatis personae for his dialogues and naming them after the five. This is the safe way to put it, rather than saying that he took historical characters and put them into dialogues. Identity between original and portrait cannot be taken for granted. . . . . Plato was a philosopher, not an historian, and the standards governing the literary composition of his day gave wide latitude to the dramatic manipulation of historical figures."
5. Regarding the language game of dialectic, Havelock (167–68) observes that the contemporary reader of Plato's dialogues needs to be aware that "the way in which the problems set by Plato in his dialogues for the Sophists to solve, or to fail at solving, are Platonic questions to which sophistic was not equipped to give an answer; and quite properly so, because it did not ask them."

Following Havelock, we may add that Plato's typical procedure is to have Socrates ask the questions and a sophist answer them. However, see *Protagoras* (328c–d, ff), where this procedure is reversed, with Protagoras doing the asking and Socrates the answering. But even in this case, it is safe to assume that the questions are more Platonic and less Protagorean.
6. In the *Gorgias*, for example, Polus points out that Socrates loves to see his

interlocutor contradict himself (461c). Later on, Callicles makes the same point (482d).

7. See *Theaetetus*, 166–68; *Gorgias*, 461c–d, 467b–c, 482d–83a, 489b, 496b, 501c, 505c–6a, and 510a; *Protagoras*, 334c–38e.

8. See Havelock, 160. One of these Platonists is W. K. C. Guthrie, who writes: "I do not understand how anyone can read the brilliant and sympathetic speech of Protagoras in the *Protagoras* from 323c to 328c and still hold that Plato in his representations of the best of the Sophists was setting out to blacken their memory" (39, n. 2).

9. Havelock, 165. Elsewhere, (87–88), Havelock explains his position at greater length: "Scholars eager to grasp any available testimony to the teaching of the Sophists have sometimes assumed that Protagoras' speech reproduces Protagoras' teaching. Plato's methods elsewhere in his writings are not those of a reporter. Why should he report when he himself has so much to say? Why in particular should such a genius take the trouble to advertise in his own writings a system already in circulation and put out by a representative of a school of thought which he distrusted? . . . . Taking such trouble, he could have had only one purpose—to replace the original by his own version and to destroy so far as possible the effect of the original by dramatizing his own as though it were the original. This, indeed, is a general law of composition applicable to others of Plato's dialogues, and it is to be noted that it proved effective. Later antiquity, as it treasured the dialogues which pretended to memorialize the leading Sophists, ceased to take the trouble to read or to preserve the originals of these Sophists' works."

10. Ibid., 168.

11. Interestingly, Plato seems quite aware of the awkwardness of public men engaging in philosophy and philosophers engaging in public matters. In the *Gorgias* he has Callicles tell Socrates that "when they [philosophers] enter upon any private or public business they make themselves ridiculous, just as on the other hand, I suppose, when public men engage in your studies and discussions, they are quite ridiculous" (484d–e); see also *Theaetetus* (172c).

12. See, for example, *Meno*, 92a.

13. Plato attaches the term beast (θηρίον) not only to the sophist as a type but also to Thrasymachus, a particular sophist: "But when we came to a pause [in the discussion] after I had said this, he [Thrasymachus] couldn't any longer hold his peace. But gathering himself up like a wild beast he hurled himself upon us as if he would tear us to pieces" (*Republic*, 336b).

14. For a discussion of the many-headed beast in relation to justice and injustice, see *Republic*, 588c–ff.

15. The full citation regarding the philosopher and his similarity to and difference from the sophist reads as follows: "the philosopher, always devoting himself through reason to the idea of being, is also very difficult to see on account of the brilliant light of the place; for the eyes of the soul of the mul-

titude are not strong enough to endure the sight of the divine" (*Sophist*, 254a–b).

16. The Stranger, however, ultimately distinguishes between "the one who can dissemble in long speeches in public before a multitude, and the other who does it in private in short speeches and forces the person who converses with him to contradict himself" (*Sophist*, 268b). Clearly, the former refers to the orator and the latter to the sophist; or the former refers to the sophist who specializes in rhetoric and the latter to the sophist specializing in disputation.

17. This is precisely the idea behind Socrates' advice to the young Hippocrates on their way to meet Protagoras (*Protagoras*, 312b–14c).

18. For a similar point on the significance of defining the object of a given discussion, see *Phaedrus*, 237b–d.

19. Explaining division as a procedure of getting to the essence of something, the Stranger says: "Let us divide in two the class we have taken up for discussion, and proceed always by way of the right-hand part of the thing divided, clinging close to the company to which the sophist belongs, until, having stripped him of all common properties and left him only his own peculiar nature, we shall show him plainly first to ourselves and secondly to those who are most closely akin to the dialectical method" (*Sophist*, 264e–65a).

20. For an interesting discussion that matches each of these definitions with a particular sophist, see Frederick S. Oscanyan, "On Six Definitions of the Sophist: *Sophist*, 221c–31e," *Philosophical Forum* 4 (1973): 241–59.

21. For other references to the fees the sophists charged for their instruction, see *Protagoras*, 310d, 311b and d–e, 313b; *Hippias Major*, 282b and d–e; *Sophist*, 225e; *Theaetetus*, 167c; *Theages*, 121d.

22. See also *Meno*, 75c–d and *Protagoras*, 337b–c.

23. Hippias is made to claim that Gorgias, Prodicus, and Protagoras made much money from their teaching as well as their private exhibitions and public speaking. He is also made to boast that he himself has made more money than any two sophists put together (*Hippias Major*, 282b–e).

24. See Callicles' contempt for philosophy as a useless enterprise (*Gorgias*, 484c–86c). See also Hippias' comment on Socrates' dialectical procedure: "But you see, Socrates, you do not consider the entirety of things . . . but you all test the beautiful and each individual entity by taking them separately and cutting them to pieces" (*Hippias Major*, 301b). Further down, (304a), Hippias calls Socrates' talk "mere scrapings and shavings of discourse . . . divided into bits" (κνήσματά τοί ἐστι καὶ περιτμήματα . . . κατὰ βραχὺ διῃρημένα). Finally, see Crito's report to Socrates that the sophists regard philosophy as worthless and ridiculous (*Euthydemus*, 305a).

25. For a discussion of the relative merits of lengthy (rhetorical) and brief (dialectical) discourses, see *Protagoras*, 334d–38e. For a discussion of the issue of lengthy discourses in Plato, see Harold Barrett, *The Sophists: Rhetoric, Democ-*

*racy, and Plato's Idea of Sophistry* (Novato, Calif.: Chandler & Sharp Publishers, 1987), 55–62.

26. In the *Meno*, 91b, for example, the sophists are treated collectively as "these men who profess to be teachers of virtue and advertize themselves as the common teachers of the Greeks, and are ready to instruct anyone who chooses in return for fees charged on a fixed scale."

27. Protagoras, for example, was a political advisor to Pericles in the formulation of the constitution of Thurioi. Gorgias was an ambassador of Syracuse, and Hippias an ambassador of Elis. Antiphon and Critias were influential politicians with oligarchic leanings.

28. Consider the Stranger's reference to an art "which has to do with words, by virtue of which it is possible to bewitch the young through their ears with words while they are still standing at a distance from the realities of truth, by exhibiting to them spoken images of all things, so as to make it seem that they are true and that the speaker is the wisest of all men in all things" (*Sophist*, 234c).

The sophists, however, are not the only ones whose words enchant the young. Socrates', too, seem to have the same capacity. Meno: "Socrates, I used to be told, before I began to meet you, that yours was just a case of being in doubt yourself and making others doubt also; and so now I find you are merely bewitching me with your spells and incantations, which have reduced me to utter perplexity. . . . [I]f you went on like this as a stranger in any other city you would very likely be taken up for a wizard" (*Meno*, 79e–80b). Consider also Alcibiades' praise of Socrates in the *Symposium* (215e–16a): "When I hear him [Socrates] I am worse than any wild fanatic; I find my heart leaping and my tears gushing forth at the sound of his speech, and I see great numbers of other people having the same experience. When I listened to Pericles and other skilled orators I thought them eloquent, but I never felt anything like this; my spirit was not left in a tumult and had not to complain of my being in the condition of a common slave: whereas the influence of our Marsyas here has often thrown me into such a state that I thought my life not worth living on these terms."

29. See also the Stranger's suggestion that it is impossible for a person to know all things (*Sophist*, 233a, 235a).

30. Socrates warns the young Hippocrates:

And we must take care, my good friend, that the sophist, in commending his wares, does not deceive us, as both merchant and dealer do in the case of our bodily food. For among the provisions, you know, in which these men deal, not only are they themselves ignorant what is good or bad for the body, since in selling they commend them all, but the people who buy from them are so too, unless one happens to be a trainer or a doctor. And in the same way, those who take their doctrines the round of our cities, hawking them about to any odd purchaser who desires them, commend everything that they sell, and there may well be some of these too, my good sir, who are ignorant which of their wares is good or bad for the soul; and in just the same case are the people who buy from them, unless one happens to have a doctor's knowledge here also, but of the soul. So then, if you are well informed as to what is good or bad among these wares, it will be safe for you to buy doctrines from Protagoras or from anyone else you please: but if not, take care, my dear fellow, that you do not risk your greatest treasure on a toss of the dice. (*Protagoras*, 313d–e)

31. For the feeling of shame that generally goes with being a sophist, see *Phaedrus*, 257d and *Protagoras*, 312a.

32. See *Apology*, 29d–e.

33. See, for example, Brian Vickers, *In Defence of Rhetoric* (Oxford: Clarendon Press, 1988), 83–147; Nancy S. Struever, *The Language of History in the Renaissance* (Princeton: Princeton University Press, 1970), 5–39; Havelock, 155–294; Guthrie, passim.

34. George Henry Lewes, *The Biographical History of Philosophy From Its Origin in Greece Down to the Present Day* (New York: D. Appleton and Co., 1857), 103.

35. Ibid., 104.

36. Ibid., 103.

37. Ibid., 103–4.

38. George Grote, *A History of Greece From the Earliest Period to the Close of the Generation Contemporary with Alexander the Great* (London: John Murray, 1888), 38.

39. Ibid., 75.

40. Havelock, 163.

41. Vickers, 84.

42. Guthrie, 4.

43. For a view on Plato's philosophy as situated discourse, see Raphael Demos' "Introduction" to Jowett:

The public likes to paint for itself a picture of the philosopher as living in Olympian detachment from human affairs. But Plato's philosophy did not arise in a vacuum; it was occasioned by his contact with immediacy. And his ideal of a philosopher is that of a philosopher-king, that is to say, of thought as the focal centre of social life. In Plato, abstract thought is stimulated by immediate insight; his philosophy is born out of his criticism of the current Athenian scene. Here was Homer, the universally respected poet. Plato disliked Homer on account of his anthropomorphic conception of the gods; through his criticism of Homer Plato was led to frame a picture of God as above human weaknesses and vices. There were the vociferous Sophists, by attacking whom, Plato was led to formulate his doctrine of ideas. Plato was a member of the Athenian democracy; by his efforts to correct its faults, he was led to formulate his conception of the ideal state. Plato was confronted by the tremendous fact of Socrates. . . . And from the impact of the personality of the master upon the pupil, there emerged in the philosophy of Plato the doctrine of the supreme value of justice and virtue." (B. Jowett, *The Dialogues of Plato*, vol. 1 [New York: Random House, 1937], 11)

44. See *Protagoras*, 319a. For the shortcomings of the sophistic movement, see E. R. Dodds, "The Sophistic Movement and the Failure of Greek Liberalism" in *The Ancient Concept of Progress* (Oxford: Clarendon Press, 1973), 92–105.
45. See Isocrates' *Against the Sophists* and *Antidosis*.
46. In this regard, consider the brief exchange between Socrates and Alcibiades in *Alcibiades*, 2.145e–46b:

SOCRATES:   Then what sort of state do you suppose it would be, where the people were good bowmen and flute-players, together with athletes and artists in general, and mingled with these the men whom we have just mentioned as knowing war in itself and slaughter in itself, and orator wind-bags too with their political bluster, but all of them lacked this knowledge of the best, and none knew when or upon whom it was better to employ their respective arts?
ALCIBIADES:   A paltry one, I should call it, Socrates.
SOCRATES:   Yes, you would I expect, when you saw each one of them vying with the other and assigning the largest part in the conduct of the state to that
   *Wherein himself is found most excellent,*
I mean, what is done best by rule of his particular art—while he is generally off the track of what is best for the state and for himself, because, I conceive, he has put his trust in opinion apart from intelligence. In these circumstances, should we not be right in saying that such a state is one great mass of turmoil and lawlessness?
ALCIBIADES:   We should, upon my word.

47. Plato could have easily supported his point by making reference to the ways in which the orators and the Athenians had responded to the circumstances surrounding the Sicilian expedition or the insurrection of Mytilene.
48. For a relevant discussion on this point see Richard Weaver, "Edmund Burke and the Argument from Circumstance" and "Abraham Lincoln and the Argument from Definition" in Richard Weaver, *The Ethics of Rhetoric* (Chicago: Henry Regnery, 1953), 53–114.
49. For a discussion comparing the *Palamedes* and the *Apology*, see James A. Coulter, "The Relation of the 'Apology of Socrates' to Gorgias' 'Defense of

Palamedes' and Plato's Critique of Gorgianic Rhetoric," *Harvard Studies in Classical Philology* 68 (1964): 269–303; Guido Calogero, "Gorgias and the Socratic Principle 'Nemo Sua Sponte Peccat," *Journal of Hellenic Studies* 77 (1957): 12–17; and Kenneth Seeskin, "Is the Apology of Socrates a Parody?" *Philosophy and Literature* 6, nos. 1–2 (1982): 94–105.

50. For a discussion of the differences between eristic, disputation, and dialectic, see George B. Kerferd, *The Sophistic Movement* (Cambridge: Cambridge University Press, 1981), 59–67.

51. The cultural tensions Plato introduced, according to Havelock, are reflected in the general "drive towards the abstract" and in the "battles between concepts, categories, and principles," battles that had their antecedents in "the combats of Homeric heroes" and, as we have seen, the rhetorical contests of the sophists. See Eric A. Havelock, *Preface to Plato* (Cambridge, Mass.: Harvard University Press, 1982), 304.

52. According to Huntington Cairns, "The dialogue form permitted him [Plato] to lead men to this insight [the world is pervaded by Reason], it permitted the playfulness and the bitterness, the irony and the fairness, for which the dialogues are also famous. It allowed him almost the freedom of the contemporary novelist. As a form it imposed no limitations on his poetic imagery, and it allowed him also the utmost philosophical seriousness. But notwithstanding his unrivaled mastery of the dialogue he never subordinated meaning to form." See "Introduction" in *The Collected Dialogues of Plato*, Edith Hamilton and Huntington Cairns, eds., (Princeton: Princeton University Press, 1973), xiv.

Unlike Cairns, who looks at Plato's use of the form of dialogue from an aesthetical viewpoint, Jaeger takes a historical perspective. Plato, he says, knew "so well that his philosophy arose in a particular climate of thought and held a particular historical position in the whole development of the Greek mind, that he always made his dialectic take the dramatic form of dialogue, and begin with an argument between representatives of various types of contemporary opinion." See Werner Jaeger, *Paideia*, vol. 2, trans. Gilbert Highet (New York: Oxford University Press, 1976), x.

53. For a discussion of Platonic dialogue as an invitation to philosophy, see Arthur A. Krentz, "Dramatic Form and Philosophical Content in Plato's Dialogues," *Philosophy and Literature* 7, no. 1 (Spring 1983): 32–47; Drew A. Hyland, "Why Plato Wrote Dialogues," *Philosophy and Rhetoric* 1 (1968): 38–50.

54. As Socrates recounts in the *Apology*, 21b–22e, the same thing happens when Socrates enters into discussions with the artisans and politicians of Athens.

55. Consider, for example, Sophocles' Antigone.

56. See *Theaetetus*, 174b–75b.

57. Consider, for example, Thrasymachus' *On the Constitution*, 85B.1.

58. See *Seventh Letter*, 326a–b and *Republic*, 473c–d.

Chapter 4

# Isocrates' Reception
# of the Sophists

Compared to Plato's reception, Isocrates' is more complicated. Unlike Plato, who rejected sophistical rhetoric in its entirety and sought
to replace it with his dialectic, Isocrates denounced only some of the
sophists' rhetorical practices and approved others. The result of this
mixed response was not an alternative to but a new version of rhetoric, one that left several premises of the sophistical tradition intact
while challenging some of its methods and results. Accordingly, commentators who focus on Isocrates' approval of the sophists have un-
derstandably construed him as a second-generation sophist. This
construal is best reflected in Jaeger's portrayal of Isocrates as a notable
"representative of the sophistic and rhetorical culture which had
flourished in the Periclean period,"[1] and as "a genuine sophist . . .
who brought the sophistic movement in education to its culminating
point."[2]

According to this portrayal, Isocrates followed the sophists' tracks
and refined the tradition they had started. True enough, he adopted
their professional practice of teaching rhetoric for money, posited that
rhetoric in itself is neither beneficial nor harmful,[3] and sided with the
argument that responsibility for rhetoric's misuse or abuse lies with
the practitioner, not the teacher.[4] Like the sophists, he glorified rhetoric's capacity to bring and hold people together, to accomplish what
physical power cannot, and to invent and satisfy human desires.[5] In
the spirit of Protagoras, he committed himself to teaching students
ways in which they could manage their own affairs and the affairs of
the State effectively. In the manner of Gorgias, he composed epideictic orations, one of them on the same theme—Helen. And in the tradition of Antiphon, he wrote speeches for the courts. Like other
orators (e.g., Gorgias and Lysias) he addressed the theme of concord
among the Hellenes, although his treatment of it, so he thought, far

surpasses in thoughtfulness and elegance that of his predecessors.[6] Not to be outdone by the sophists in self-praise, Isocrates prided himself again and again that his rhetorical compositions are superior to theirs in eloquence, originality, and thoroughness.[7]

On the basis of these and other similarities, the perception of Isocrates as a second-generation sophist is justified. But Isocrates is also quite different from the older sophists; so much so, in fact, that he can be said to have contributed to the discourse of their vilification in the fourth century B.C. Accordingly, commentators who stress his denunciation of the sophists see him as departing from the sophistical tradition and instituting new rhetorical practices. Indeed, he shares none of their irreverence, playfulness with language, or rhetorical bravado. Their ways were cosmopolitan and nomadic; his were metropolitan and most characteristically Athenian. Their teaching was tutorial and apparently nonsystematic; his was institutional and seemingly more programmatic. Where they had no specific political vision, he envisioned a united Hellas spreading territorially and culturally beyond its boundaries; and where they saw no difference between Greek and barbarian, he asserted Greek superiority.

These differences are accentuated even more if we consider that the cultural milieu in which Isocrates practiced his rhetoric differs significantly from that of the sophists. Their world, as we have noted, was one of cultural exuberance, self-confidence, and intellectual experimentation; his was one of inwardness, self-reflection, and sociopolitical reconstruction. Not surprisingly, their rhetoric was daring, playful, even audacious; his was conservative, apologetic, even defensive. Their cultural charge as heirs of the mythopoetic tradition was to work out a new prose at a time when poetry was showing signs of collapse as the dominant discursive force in the culture—if the sophists faced any competition, it came from within their own circle. Isocrates' self-assigned charge, on the other hand, was considerably heavier. He not only had to make sense out of his sophistical heritage; he also had to compete with philosophy for cultural supremacy, battle against extreme forms of contemporary sophistry, and reshape public perceptions about sophistry, oratory, and philosophy.

The Isocratean reception of the sophists, then, is complicated because its disposition toward the sophistical tradition consists of an uneven mixture of affirmations and denials, approvals and denunciations. But what makes it even more complicated is its apparent disparagement and endorsement of Plato's reception. At times, Isocrates

views the sophists the way Plato does: combative pretenders, deceivers, and word-jugglers; other times, he considers them worthy predecessors or contemporaries whom he has outdone in his capacities
as a practitioner and teacher of rhetoric. Despite their commonalities,
however, the Platonic and Isocratean receptions of the sophists remain different. Whereas Plato's reception relies on the powers of the
intellect to discern the truth about rhetoric, Isocrates' depends heavily
on the lessons of history. Isocrates concentrates less on the philosophical integrity of the sophists' doctrines and more on their worldly
reputation and impact on contemporary society. When he critiques
them, the standard of his criticism is generally usefulness (ὠφέλεια),
not truth or exact knowledge. Time and again, his point is that many
of their lessons are simply not useful (χρήσιμα) to life;[8] and this explains why he often regards them as hyperintellectual acrobats in-
dulging in hair-splitting arguments about minute and inconsequential
subtleties. In his mind, their emphasis on training for combat in the
courts is myopic, narrow, and selfish—forensic rhetoric typically concerns the interests of too few people. Similarly, their artistically over-
done discourses may be fascinating, especially to the young, but they
help neither Athens nor Hellas to come to terms with their larger and
more urgent irresolutions.[9]

Once again, this is not surprising. As in the case with the older
sophists, there are as many similarities between Isocrates and Plato as
there are differences. Both he and Plato stayed away from active politics, although for apparently different reasons. Each headed a school,
although what they taught differed significantly. Both were Athenians of means, but their attitudes toward the age of Pericles and their
proposed solutions for Athens' problems were not exactly identical.
Both were concerned with the state of politics and education, although Plato's approach was more theoretical and Isocrates' more
practical. Both critiqued the sophists but from different angles and
with different criteria. Both espoused philosophy as a good way of
life, but their use and understanding of the meaning of the term *philosophy* differed considerably. Finally, both endeavored to influence
political leaders to see their respective visions of a new world—Plato,
a world ruled by uncompromised intelligence; Isocrates, a world
guided by practical wisdom.

Clearly, Isocrates is neither a pure sophist nor a pure philosopher.
Even a casual reading of his compositions shows that he sees merit
both in rhetoric and philosophy.[10] However, and this may be the big-

gest difficulty with the Isocratean reception, his uses of such terms as sophist, rhetoric, and philosophy throughout his works are neither unequivocal nor consistent. Although aware of the older sophists (he names Gorgias and Protagoras a few times), his uses of sophist are mostly generic, and generally refer to the sophists of his own generation.[11] Even more troublesome for us, used as we are to relying primarily on Plato's perspective, is his view that *sophist* refers not only to one who teaches rhetoric, political discourses, and disputation but also to one who trains students in dialectical philosophy, abstract ethical principles, and the truth of timeless propositions. Similarly, he often uses *philosophy* to mean rhetoric.[12] But even his attitude toward rhetoric is not uniform. Some kinds of rhetoric, especially his, are precisely as they ought to be: thoughtful, elegant, wise; other kinds, especially his competitors', are not even worthy of the name rhetoric.

Although posterity has, until recently, largely adopted Plato's meaning of these three terms, Isocrates cannot be faulted with erroneous or careless usage—the meaning of each term and the differences among them at the time were contested among intellectuals and confused in the mind of the public.[13] Fortunately for us, Isocrates pays some attention to the practices associated with each term; and this enables him to say that some sophists, orators, philosophers are admirable, others contemptible—it all depends on what they do. Some sophists, for example, teach students oratory and political discourses while others train them in disputation and winning lawsuits contrary to the spirit of the laws. Likewise, some orators have given Athens its greatest blessings while others have injured Athenian audiences by encouraging them to endorse only that which flatters them.[14] Finally, some philosophers truly care about the development of the mind and the improvement of conduct while others deal in worthless abstractions. In all three cases, Isocrates' point is the same: generalizations about sophists, orators, and philosophers are unbecoming to a discriminating mind and unfair to the exceptional person in any one class.

Its complications aside, Isocrates' reception makes one realize that Plato, however harsh, was not alone in his condemnation of sophistical rhetoric. At the same time, it obligates one to look beyond Plato and see that the same cultural phenomenon (the sophistic movement) can be perceived, even among contemporaries, in more ways than one. But if this is so, the Isocratean reception provides an alternative reading, one suggesting that Plato's judgment of the sophists may have been more severe and more extreme than necessary. This, how-ever, is not to say that Isocrates was entirely sympathetic to the sophists—as I have already noted, he was both their supporter and critic. Finally, because Isocrates' reception is tied to his own version of rhetoric, a thorough familiarity with Isocrates' sophists yields not only some understanding of the fate of sophistical rhetoric in the fourth century B.C. but also a view of the rhetoric of Isocrates himself.

In what follows, I attempt to negotiate the difficulties I have iden-tified in Isocrates' reception of the sophists. In the course of this ne-gotiation, I pay attention not only to what he says about sophists, orators, and philosophers but also to how he understands rhetoric. This is necessary because his own view of rhetoric helps explain why Isocrates both applauds and condemns the sophists, why he consid-ers some aspects of sophistical rhetoric important and others not, and why he carries on with some of its elements while leaving others be-hind. In the first part of the ensuing discussion I show that his treat-ment of sophists, orators, and philosophers goes hand in hand with his efforts to make distinctions and valuations within each class, and with his attempts to disassociate himself from those sophistical, rhetorical, and philosophical practices he disapproves of. I then turn to a consideration of his circumstances, paying particular attention to changes in sociopolitical conditions, education, and the growth of written rhetoric. In the course of this discussion, I show that Isocrates' reception of sophistical rhetoric constitutes not only a re-sponse to his situation but also a vehicle through which he advances a rhetoric that differs appreciably from that of his predecessors.

## Isocrates on Sophists, Orators, and Philosophers

Isocrates' sophists are a notorious and influential class of profes-sional educators whose general reputation in the society leaves much to be desired.[15] What accounts for their unbecoming reputa-tion is a variety of objectionable practices: claiming to know every-thing (πάντα φασκόντων εἰδέναι), discussing the poets of the past but saying nothing original about them,[16] magnifying little things by means of words (τὰ μικρὰ τοῖς λόγοις ὑπερβάλλεσθαι),[17] chattering empty nonsense (μάτην φλυαρεῖν),[18] neglecting their true inter-ests and pursuing pleasures (ἀμελήσαντες τοῦ συμφέροντος ἐπὶ τὰς ἡδονὰς ὁρμῶσιν),[19] "showing off their oratory (ἐπιδείξεις ποιουμένους) in the public assemblies or in private gatherings, contesting (διαγωνιζομένους) against each other, making extravagant promises (καθ' ὑπερβολὴν ὑπισχνουμένους),[20] disputing (ἐρίζοντας), reviling each other (λοιδορουμένους), [and] omitting nothing in the language of abuse (οὐδὲν ἀπολείποντας κακῶν)" (*Antidosis*, 147–8). However, Isocrates notes, neither their practices nor their reputation have always been so. Recalling the days when sophists enjoyed the respect and admiration of their contemporaries, he declares that "things were not like that in the time of our ancestors; on the contrary, they admired the sophists, as they called them, and envied the good fortune of their disciples" (*Antidosis*, 313).

Focusing more specifically on the contemporary sophists' discursive repertoire, Isocrates criticizes in his *Helen* their excessive and persistent interest in advancing what he considers absurd or paradoxical claims. Some, for example, assert that "it is impossible to say, or to gainsay, what is false, or to speak on both sides of the same questions." Others maintain that "courage and wisdom and justice are identical, and that we possess none of these as natural qualities, but that there is only one sort of knowledge concerned with them all." Still others "waste their time in captious disputations that are not only entirely useless, but are sure to make trouble for their disciples."[21] Isocrates responds that, to begin with, many of these claims and practices are not new—they can be traced back to such older sophists as Protagoras, Gorgias, Zeno, and Melissus. True, when these sophists first showed that it is easy to contrive false statements (ψευδῆ μηχανήσασθαι λόγον), they may have impressed their contemporaries with what was then a novel intellectual discovery.[22] But to continue along the path of proving things by verbal quibbles is to belabor a point long since refuted. Worse, it is to harm students, who, instead of learning to be versed on the practical affairs of their city, are trained to argue paradoxical and useless theses (i.e., the life of beggars and exiles is more enviable than that of the rest of mankind).[23] In addition to their paradoxical character, many of the discourses of contemporary sophists deal with trivial subjects.[24] Compositions addressing significant subjects like life in the polis, the welfare of the State, and the education of the young are difficult to compose for they require knowledge of the various forms and uses of discourse as well as a degree of seriousness and dignity. By contrast, trivial discourses, like the praise of bumble-bees, salt, and human misfortunes, are easy to compose as they are all written according to formulae whose mastery demands little effort. Isocrates attributes such bizarre compositions to

weakness (δι' ἀσθένειαν). Because they have nothing new or interesting to say about noble and elevated topics, topics on which
there is much competition among all citizens (ἐν οἷς ἅπαντές εἰσιν
ἀνταγωνισταί), some sophists resort to obscure subjects, subjects
which may be intriguing because they are unheard of but which nobody else cares about. These sophists can be said to resemble the
"athlete who, although pretending to be the best of all athletes, enters
a contest in which no one would condescend to meet him" (*Helen*,
10). Therefore, they should stop treating exotic or extraordinary topics and realize that "while it is easy by eloquence to overdo the trivial
themes, it is difficult to reach the heights of greatness of the others;
and while on famous subjects one rarely finds thoughts which no one
has previously uttered, yet on trifling and insignificant topics whatever the speaker may chance to say is entirely original" (*Helen*, 13). In
sum, Isocrates' charge is that artistic originality for its own sake cannot meet the criterion of sociopolitical utility.

By virtue of their love for paradoxical claims and trivial subjects,
much of what the sophists have to say does not help improve public
life. For Isocrates, educated citizens should be a richer source of practical insights than the uneducated. Their learning ought to translate
into workable arrangements in civic affairs, wise solutions of political
problems, and thoughtful settlements of societal issues. But when
learning amounts simply to techniques of sheer eloquence or captious
disputation, without a sense of purpose and without an eye to beneficial results, the vital functions and fate of the state are either neglected or left to the ignorant, the uncultivated, and the ignoble.
Therefore, sophists who are content to teach these techniques ought
to change their ways. Specifically, they ought "to pursue the truth, to
instruct their pupils in the practical affairs of our government and
train to expertness therein, bearing in mind that likely conjecture
(ἐπιεικῶς δοξάζειν) about useful things is far preferable to exact
knowledge (ἀκριβῶς ἐπίστασθαι) of the useless, and that to be a little superior in important things is of greater worth than to be preem-
inent in petty things that are without value for living (μηδὲν πρὸς τὸν
βίον ὠφελοῦσιν)" (*Helen*, 4–5).

In view of the above criticisms of the sophists, it should come as no
surprise that Isocrates is anxious to disassociate himself from them. In
this regard, he observes that many of the sophists' rhetorical practices
draw little praise and much ridicule or hatred from the general public.[25] What is worse, they harm decent sophists by giving them, too, a

bad name.[26] Himself a self-professed sophist, Isocrates complains that even though he does nothing of what typical sophists do, he shares their shady reputation just the same. His explanation of this phenomenon is twofold. First, lay people assume that a common professional label like sophist necessarily implies a set of common practices. As such, they "attribute the iniquities of those who profess to be sophists, but in practice are far different, to those whose ways have nothing in common with them" (*Antidosis*, 215). Second, some sophists are spreading the false rumor that Isocrates is merely a writer of speeches for the courts. But, he responds, this is as absurd as calling "Pheidias, who wrought our statue of Athena, a doll-maker" (*Antidosis*, 2). Aware that many people have been misled about him, he maintains that had people bothered to acquaint themselves with his work and practices, they would find that he is no ordinary sophist. But as it is, he acknowledges painfully, they malign him unfairly: "I am continually being misrepresented by obscure and worthless sophists (τῶν σοφιστῶν τῶν ἀδοκίμων καὶ πονηρῶν) and being judged by the general public not by what I really am, but by what they hear from others" (*Panathenaicus*, 5).

Because Isocrates had suspected that the public might confuse him with typical sophists, he says in *Antidosis* (193) that he took care to avoid the charge of making extravagant promises to prospective students: "when I entered upon my profession, I wrote and published a discourse in which you will find that I attack those who make pretensions which are unwarranted, and set forth my own ideas."[27] But his preemptive efforts were apparently in vain. Judging from the opening pages of *Antidosis*, Isocrates is a disillusioned man:

> I had always thought . . . that owing to this choice [to speak and write not on petty disputes in the manner of the sophists but on important and elevated subjects] and to my retired life in general, I stood fairly well in the opinion of all the lay public. Then when my career was near its close . . . I came to realize that even outside my profession there were those who were not disposed towards me as I had thought; nay, that some had been absolutely misled as to my pursuits and were inclined to listen to my detractors, while others, who were well aware of the nature of my work, were envious, feeling the same towards me as do the sophists, and rejoiced to see people hold false opinions of my character. (*Antidosis*, 4)

Yet another area in which Isocrates does not wish to be confused with the sophists is the area of monetary wealth. As we have seen, one of the factors responsible for the popular prejudice against the sophists was their reputed riches from teaching. In *Antidosis*, Isocrates finds it necessary to counter the public perception that he, too, had accumulated enormous riches as a teacher of rhetoric. His line of argument is twofold: first he challenges the common belief that sophists receive exorbitant pay;[28] second, he points out that of the money he himself has made over the years he has spent more on his public duties and less on himself:[29] "Generally speaking, you will find that no one of the so-called sophists has accumulated a great amount of money, but that some of them have lived in poor, others in moderate circumstances" (*Antidosis*, 155). Even if one were to inquire about Gorgias, the one sophist reputed to have devoted himself to making money (περὶ τὸν χρηματισμὸν γενόμενος), and remembered for having made more than any other sophist (ὁ πλεῖστα κτησάμενος), one would find that at his death he left only a thousand staters.[30]

In addition to his critique of some sophistical rhetorical practices and his efforts to disassociate himself from them, Isocrates has some kind words for the sophists. Like his critical words, his complimentary comments are made on the basis of his notion of the useful. In one of his most positive remarks, he suggests that some sophists are worth studying. Without naming anyone in particular, he advises Demonicus to practice eclectic polymathy, which entails taking from what the sophists have to offer those things that are useful: You should "not only abide by what I have said, but acquaint yourself with the best things (τὰ βέλτιστα) in the poets as well, and learn from the other wise men (τῶν ἄλλων σοφιστῶν) also any useful lessons they have taught (εἴ τι χρήσιμον εἰρήκασιν). For just as we see the bee settling on all the flowers, and sipping the best from each, so also those who aspire to culture ought not to leave anything untasted, but should gather useful knowledge from every source" (*To Demonicus*, 51–52).[31]

The mere suggestion that some sophists are worthy of study challenges the two most common charges against sophistry: that it is nothing but sham and chicane (φλυαρία καὶ φενακισμός), and that it corrupts its students. Those who make the first charge argue that rhetorical ability is inborn and, therefore, one either has it or does not—it simply cannot be taught. Those who make the second point maintain that once students become proficient in rhetoric they use it to scheme to acquire other people's property.[32] Isocrates takes both charges head on: "there is not a sound or true word in either complaint" (*Antidosis*, 198). To begin with, it is well known that some sophists have indeed helped students improve their rhetorical skills: "many of those who have sat under the sophists (πολλοὺς τῶν ὑπὸ τοῖς σοφισταῖς γενομένων) have not been duped nor affected . . . but some of them have been turned out competent champions [of oratorical contests] (ἱκανοὺς ἀγωνιστὰς) and others able teachers" (*Antidosis*, 203–4).[33] Second, it is neither pleasurable nor profitable nor honorable for a sophist to corrupt his students. Because a professional teacher depends for his livelihood and public esteem on the kinds of students he graduates, it behooves him to turn out nothing but the best.[34] Isocrates also discredits the second claim, that rhetorical proficiency is an instrument of scheming on other people's property; if this were so, he argues, then all accomplished speakers would be intriguers and sycophants. But the truth is that the best statesmen come from among those who study most the art of rhetoric (*Antidosis*, 230–31). This is evident not only in contemporary life but also in history. One should consider, for example, that "Solon was named one of the seven sophists and was given the title which is now dishonoured . . . ; and Pericles studied under two of the sophists, Anaxagoras of Clazomenae and Damon, the latter in his day reputed to be the wisest among the Athenians" (*Antidosis*, 235).

Clearly, Isocrates' remarks about the sophists combine two contradictory lines of reception—one endorsing, the other critical. Both lines depend on Isocrates' notion of rhetoric as a culturally necessary activity, an activity capable of addressing both significant and trivial subjects, pursuing both beneficial and harmful purposes, and enriching or impoverishing public life. Seen together, the two lines suggest that it is not safe to assume that all sophists are wealthy, teaching what cannot be taught, and corrupting their students. Some are financially well off, others poor; some teach useful, others useless, things; and some corrupt their students while others help them achieve distinguished careers in politics. Therefore, to concentrate only on their positive contributions would be as one-sided a practice as to focus only on their negative impact. Given the capacities of rhetoric for both good and evil, Isocrates must have concluded, a critical reception requires a mixed appraisal.

Broadly speaking, Isocrates' reception of the orators follows the same path as his reception of the sophists. In particular, he critiques some oratorical practices without dismissing all orators, and without disparaging the art of rhetoric on account of the dubious practices of some.[35] Next, he disassociates himself from orators in general and from those teachers of oratory whose program he considers unacceptable or unprofitable. Lastly, he speaks positively about rhetoric as he himself understands, practices, and teaches it.

The orators, for Isocrates, are quite influential in shaping public opinion.[36] Because of their ability to fix blame and advocate persuasively a particular course of action, they are often employed by the politicians at whose pleasure they serve.[37] But since they are usually under such compulsion, many of the things they say in public should not be believed.[38] By and large, they are known for haranguing the people "not for the good of the state, but for what they themselves expect to gain. . . . [T]hese orators are either wrangling (λοιδορουμένους) among themselves in the assemblies over deposits of money or insulting (λυμαινομένους) our allies or blackmailing (συκοφαντοῦντας) whosoever of the rest of the world chances to be the object of their attacks" (*Panathenaicus*, 13).

As a class, contemporary orators have not done much good for Athens; on the contrary, they have caused many of its misfortunes.[39] Abusing their power over the masses, the orators claim to love the people but in fact are the bane of the whole State. Ever since they became powerful, they have repeatedly misled the city, and are now reproaching it with doing violence to the Hellenes and extorting money from its allies. Moreover, they have managed to persuade the majority of the populace that meddlesomeness is preferable to tranquility, injustice to justice, and covetousness of the possessions of others to attention to one's affairs.[40] In doing so, they have caused many disturbances, the worst of which is war. Their typical tactic is to focus on the momentary gratifications of the crowds and to disregard the future of the state. Beyond the fact that they have risen from low beginnings to an enviable position, the orators have grown rich while impoverishing the well-to-do and keeping the needy dependent on public money for court service. In effect, the orators wish to keep their fellow citizens in a state of helplessness because they realize that only this way will they be able to maintain their power. For all these reasons, they deserve to be loathed: "no class is so inimical to the people as our depraved orators and demagogues."[41] But, amazingly, the public seems either pleased with or apathetic to their objectionable practices and questionable impact.[42]

The orators, Isocrates explains, owe their wickedness mainly to the public, which gathers to listen to them and usually approves of what they say. For their part, the orators flatter the public by appealing to its fears, vanity, and greed. The more the public approves of what the orators say, the more powerful they become in shaping the public's thoughts and actions. Conversely, the more the orators cater to the public, the more it tends to approve of what they say.[43] In a passage reminiscent of Cleon's dismay with his listeners' intoxication with rhetorical displays, Isocrates criticizes the audience of his *On the Peace* for corrupting the orators: "Indeed, you have caused the orators to practice and study (μελετᾶν καὶ φιλοσοφεῖν), not what will be advantageous to the state, but how they may discourse in a manner pleasing to you. And it is to this kind of discourse that the majority of them have resorted also at the same time, since it has become plain to all that you will be better pleased with those who summon you to war than those who counsel peace" (*On the Peace*, 5).

Another, more important, reason for the orators' influence on and success with the crowds is their participation in and affinity for the culture of rhetorical spectacles and contest. Here Isocrates' remarks can be seen as responses to the excessively exhibitive and competitive aspects of sophistical discourse as practiced in his time. In and through the eloquent words they stage in public gatherings, orators, Isocrates observes, please their listeners' senses of hearing and sight, not their intelligence. Himself a believer in the enormous power of pleasing discourse to persuade an audience, Isocrates advises the young king Nicocles to use not the most useful but the most mythical discourses when addressing his subjects. It is clear, he says,

> that those who aim to write anything in verse or prose which will make a popular appeal should seek out, not the most profitable discourses (τοὺς ὠφελιμωτάτους) but those which most abound in fictions (τοὺς μυθωδεστάτους); for the ear delights in these just as the eye delights in games and contests (τοὺς ἀγῶνας καὶ τὰς ἁμίλλας). Wherefore we may well admire the poet Homer and the first inventors of tragedy, seeing that they, with true insight into human nature, have embodied both kinds of pleasure in their poetry; for Homer has dressed the contests and battles (τοὺς ἀγῶνας καὶ τοὺς πολέμους) of the demigods in myths, while the tragic po-

ets have rendered the myths in the form of contests and action (εἰς ἀγῶνας καὶ πράξεις), so that they are presented, not to our ears alone, but to our eyes as well. With such models, then, before us, it is evident that those who desire to command the attention of their hearers must abstain from admonition and advice, and must say the kind of things which they see are most pleasing to the crowd. (To Nicocles, 48–49)[44]

Judging from this piece of advice, it would appear that Isocrates understood that those who attended rhetorical events were not only listeners but also spectators, and that the orators were staging and performing their rhetoric accordingly. It would also appear from his discussion in the Panegyricus (43–46) that the orators' techne had its roots in the ancient custom of public festivals (πανηγύρεις), a custom still thriving in Isocrates' time. In their present form, he notes approvingly, these institutionalized forms of public assembly include "contests not only of speed and strength, but of eloquence and wisdom (λόγων καὶ γνώμης) and of all the other arts" (45). Of the many visitors to these festivals, some come to exhibit (ἐπιδείξασθαι) their talents, others to watch (θεάσασθαι) the spectacle of contestants (ἀγωνιζομένους) competing against each other for grand prizes. One of the results of this interaction is that both spectators and contestants feel a sense of satisfaction and pride, the former from knowing that the spectacles are performed for their sake, the latter from knowing that the world has come to gaze upon them (44).

Isocrates must have also understood that orators, their natural talents for rhetorical performances aside, acquire their persuasive skills in and through much experience in actual competition. Although he nowhere portrays himself as a competitor,[45] he endorses, at least in principle, the idea of competition by observing that "honors and distinctions are wont to be gained, not by repose, but by struggles (οὐκ ἐκ τῆς ἡσυχίας ἀλλ᾽ ἐκ τῶν ἀγώνων)."[46] In the field of rhetoric, competition is nowhere more developed than in Athens, the school of and training grounds for all accomplished speakers:

Athens is looked upon as having become a school for the education of all able orators and teachers of oratory. And naturally so; for people observe that she holds forth the greatest prizes for those who have this ability, that she offers the greatest number and variety of fields of exercise (γυμνάσια) to those who have chosen to enter contests of this kind (τοῖς ἀγωνίζεσθαι περὶ τὰ τοιαῦτα) and want to train (γυμνάζασθαι) for them, and that, furthermore, everyone obtains here that practical experience which more than any other imparts ability to speak. (*Antidosis*, 295–96)

Clearly for Isocrates, the practices of his contemporary orators are driven by two impulses—the exhibitive and the competitive. The problem with most orators, however, lies not with the impulses themselves but with the way they manifest themselves. Many orators, that is, overemphasize the performative and agonistic aspects of their oratory. In so doing, they give the impression that display and combative discourses are the only two kinds. But the truth is that there are many more, including the Hellenic, political, and panegyrical kinds (λόγους Ἑλληνικοὺς καὶ πολιτικοὺς καὶ πανηγυρικοὺς).[47] What recommends these latter discourses is both their highly stylized character and their urgently significant themes: they are "more akin to works composed in rhythm and set to music than to the speeches which are made in court. For they set forth facts in a style more imaginative and more ornate; they employ thoughts which are more lofty and more original, and, besides, they use throughout figures of speech in greater number and more striking character" (*Antidosis*, 46–47). But despite the stylistic and topical excellence of these discourses, the ethic of competition in rhetoric is so prevalent that some people "judge the most ambitious oratory by the standard of the pleas made in the petty actions of the courts" (*Panegyricus*, 11).[48] Similarly, the aesthetic of exhibition is so dominant in contemporary oratorical practice that orators and listeners alike have lost sight of political topics—topics of cardinal importance to themselves and their fellow citizens.

For these reasons, Isocrates attempts to disassociate himself from most orators. As in the case with the sophists, this move seeks to underscore the distinction between trivial and significant topics, useless and useful discourses, beneficial and harmful rhetoric. On several occasions, he points out that, because of his physical make-up, he was never an orator in the ordinary sense of the term.[49] Even so, he lived and worked as if he were an orator: "I took refuge in study and work and writing down my thoughts, choosing as my field, not petty matters nor private contracts, nor the things about which the other orators prate, but the affairs of Hellas and of kings and of states" (*Panathenaicus*, 11).[50] During his long career, he tells us, most orators were busy fighting with one another, misleading the public, and making unwarranted promises; he, on the other hand, has been a tireless voice exorting "the Hellenes to concord among themselves and war against the barbarians" (*Panathenaicus*, 13).[51] On the issue of praising Athens, Isocrates recognizes no superior; of those who declaim Athens, some denounce it recklessly, others praise it too extravagantly, and still others not adequately enough.[52] Drawing what is arguably the biggest distinction between most orators and himself, he reiterates that while they produce orations for exhibitions (ἐπιδείξεις) and court battles (ἀγῶνας), he writes technically superior discourses for the purpose of instruction (διδασκαλικοὺς καὶ τεχνικοὺς); while they attempt to mislead their listeners, he writes discourses aiming at the truth; and while they speak to please and gratify, he writes to rebuke his listeners' faults and admonish them.[53]

For Isocrates, however, all these differences have gone largely unnoticed. As a result, most people confuse him with the orators "in spite of the fact that myself and these orators are so far apart in our ways of thinking and that I have chosen a field so much more worthy, the majority of the people estimate us, not in accordance with our merits, but in a confused and altogether irrational manner" (*Panathenaicus*, 15). As I have already suggested, Isocrates attributes this confusion to the public's inability to discriminate among sophists, orators, and philosophers; to say nothing about discriminating between worthy and unworthy figures within each category. The important question, however, is not so much why the public may have been confused as what Isocrates did with this confusion. Taking it as an undesirable given, he kept trying, seemingly for a lifetime, to dispel it and, in so doing, to explain his own actions as a teacher and practitioner of rhetoric.

In his mind, the fact that so many orators were practicing the kind of rhetoric he considered destructive or irrelevant did not mean that all rhetoric is a decadent enterprise. Likewise, the fact that so many teachers were teaching what he regarded as a form of distasteful rhetoric (how to win in the courts and how to dazzle audiences with paradoxical discourses) did not signify that rhetorical education had to be that way. The problem, for Isocrates, lay not with rhetoric itself but with the practices to which it was being put.[54] Still, most lay people could not make this distinction; and as a result, they were finding themselves ill-disposed towards all eloquence,[55] not realizing that, if taught properly and practiced responsibly, it could yield benefits of the highest order. In one of the most often quoted passages from

Isocrates, (*Nicocles*, 5–9), we read about the civilizing effects of rhetoric, its crucial function in building and maintaining societies, as well
as its necessary role in human thought and understanding. And in
the *Panegyricus* (48–49), we read that Athens has understood, more
than any other state, the centrality of rhetoric in all forms of intellectual culture. Whether a skill or a talent, eloquence for the Athenians
was an object of desire,[56] a sign of intelligence, a mark of liberal education, and a means to power and honor.

These instances of rhetoric's unqualified glorification notwithstanding, Isocrates' praises of rhetoric are mostly about his own version of
it, a version seeking to respond to the sociopolitical exigencies of the
present, to exhibit mastery of the artistic resources of language, and
to lead to beneficial outcomes. In his words, "the best (most beautiful)
kind of rhetoric [is] that which deals with the greatest things (themes,
affairs) and, while best displaying the ability of those who speak,
brings most benefit to those who hear" (*Panegyricus*, 4). Insofar as this
version acknowledges the exhibitive element of public rhetoric, it can
be said to preserve at least one aspect of the sophistical tradition. But
inasmuch as it insists on grand themes and beneficial results, it can be
said to deviate from the rhetorical practices of the sophists. This deviation becomes most apparent when we take a look at Isocrates' attempts to explain his rhetoric as a philosophical enterprise.

On several occasions, Isocrates gives the impression that his discourses can best be described as philosophy about rhetoric (τὴν περὶ τοὺς
λόγους φιλοσοφίαν).[57] Accordingly, he portrays himself as a director
of students of philosophy (ἐγὼ τοὺς φιλοσοφοῦντας ἐπανορθῶ),[58] refers to what he does as philosophy (φιλοσοφία),[59] and claims that
his students are occupied with philosophy (περὶ τὴν φιλοσοφίαν
διατρίβοντες).[60] Does this mean that his intellectual pursuits are identical to those of other philosophers (i.e., Plato)? No, not necessarily.
In one instance, he differentiates between the teachers of philosophy
and the teachers of rhetoric: the former are interested in their
students' moral conduct while the latter aim at their proficiency in
eloquence (*To Demonicus*, 3–4).[61] In another instance, he distinguishes
between orators (ῥητορικοὺς), those who can speak before a crowd,
and good thinkers (εὐβούλους), those who can best debate things
in their own minds.[62] But despite these distinctions, Isocrates' explanation of his rhetoric as philosophy seems to be motivated by the
wish to distance himself from the sophists' bad reputation and to create a new discursive space, a space in which philosophy and rhet-

oric coexist interdependently.[63] In his mind, philosophy is the means to sound judgment: "I hold those men to be wise (σοφοὺς) who are able by their powers of conjecture to arrive generally at the best course [of action or speech], and those men to be philosophers (φιλοσόφους) who occupy themselves with the studies from which they will most quickly gain that insight" (*Antidosis*, 271). Those studies, however, are nothing less than studies in rhetoric. As Isocrates explains it, the acquisition of wisdom has at least three requirements: the ambition to speak well, the desire to persuade others, and the wish to seize one's advantage.[64] The ambition to speak well will almost certainly lead one to address great subjects, the kind that concern the common good of humanity; and it will obligate one to choose as examples those human actions that are the most illustrious and edifying. The desire to persuade others will cause concern with being honorable and highly esteemed among one's fellow citizens. As for the wish to seize one's advantage, it will guide one to become righteous, faithful, and conscientious in dealing with other people. In all three cases, the principle observed by those seeking wisdom is that people are most persuaded by a good person. But if this is so, studies in rhetoric cannot help but improve one's sense of honesty and justice.[65]

Insofar as the philosophers of his time were also claiming the area of a person's moral development as their own, Isocrates must have been faced, once again, with the task of differentiating himself from yet another class of intellectuals. However, the distinctions he draws between himself and them are not as many, as explicit, or as sharp as those between himself and the sophists or the orators. Hardly in a position to argue against moral education, he instead tackles some philosophical claims. As we have already seen, he suggests that the notion that courage, wisdom, and justice are identical is as paradoxical and useless as the notion that there is only one sort of knowledge concerned with all the virtues.[66] Such discourse is utterly useless as it does not improve a person's moral conduct. Tackling philosophy's second claim, scientific knowledge, he observes that such disciplines as geometry and astronomy do not belong, properly speaking, in the field of philosophical studies; rather, they should be considered "gymnastic of the mind and a preparation for philosophy" (γυμνασίαν τῆς ψυχῆς καὶ παρασκευὴν φιλοσοφίας) (*Antidosis*, 266). Finally, he notes that many of those who have pursued philosophy (πολλοὶ τῶν φιλοσοφησάντων) have remained in private life (*Against the Sophists,* 14), suggesting that most of those who pursue rhetoric opt for a life in the public arena. Although this last observation may seem innocent, it is difficult not to see its critical tone, especially if we recall Isocrates' commitment to the improvement of public life.

Beyond the fact that these distinctions are left undeveloped, they are in conflict with other comments about philosophy, comments giving the impression that Isocrates simply appropriated what we generally regard as philosophical concerns. For example, he recognizes a division between body and soul (*To Demonicus,* 40), and asserts the superiority of the latter over the former (*Antidosis,* 250). Moreover, he acknowledges that philosophy has the capacity to establish laws and to inquire into the nature of things (καὶ νομοθετῆσαι καὶ τὴν φύσιν τῶν ὄντων ζητῆσαι) (*Busiris,* 22).[67] Further, he observes that there is a difference between those who truly philosophize (τοῖς ἀληθῶς φιλοσοφοῦσιν) and those who pretend to do so (τοῖς προσποιουμένοις) (*Panathenaicus,* 263).[68] Finally, he notes that "the cultivation of the mind is the noblest and worthiest of pursuits" (*Antidosis,* 304), and argues that when it comes to teaching rhetoric there is a big difference between those who make rash promises (τοῖς ῥαδίως ὑπισχνουμένοις) and those who know something about discourses (τοῖς εἰδόσι τι περὶ αὐτῶν) (*Against the Sophists,* 16). All of the above comments could easily have been Plato's.

Thus far we have seen that Isocrates' reception of the sophists affirms productive and beneficial while denouncing idle and harmful rhetorical practices. The main thrust of his comments directs us to the realization that all sophists are not the same—some are worthy of study and imitation, others deserve censure and contempt. Using the sophists now as a basis from which to advance his own educational program, now as a source of confusion about the conceptualization, practice, and effects of public discourse, Isocrates published many compositions in which he distinguishes his own rhetorical practices from those of his competitors. In so doing, he put into motion a qualitatively different rhetoric, one commonly associated with the tradition of civic eloquence.

According to the Isocratean reception, the sophists are commendable for sensitizing the public to the central role logos plays in every accomplishment and expression of human civilization. However, their discourses, typically too agonistic and too spectacular, have created the impression that rhetoric is either a means of winning legal battles or a disinterested form of artistic play with words. Because everyone wants to be a winner, and because all people have an affinity for entertainment, these discursive practices attract much public applause. But because the will to victory often disregards ethical conduct, and because entertainment often distracts attention from serious matters, these very same practices also constitute objects of suspicion. In effect, the public simultaneously admires and mistrusts, envies and detests those with facility in language. This is so because it realizes that orators, who are usually the sophists' students, are always ready to tell people what to think and do but they often put their own gain ahead of the welfare of their listeners and the State. Against this fundamental ambivalence, Isocrates articulates a rhetoric whose announced purpose is neither to win contests nor to perform discursive spectacles but to offer insightful advice on social and political issues. Because this rhetoric intersects philosophy at the point of practical wisdom, Isocrates considers it, at least in part, a philosophical pursuit.

### Isocratean Rhetoric and Its Circumstances

Combining Isocrates' affirmations and criticisms of the rhetorical tradition and the discourse of philosophy, I have placed him at the point where rhetoric and philosophy converge. At this precise point, I have argued, there emerged a new version of rhetoric, a version that sought to address the urgent needs of the times. Concentrating neither on display rhetoric (λόγους ἐπιδεικτικοὺς), competitive debates (λόγους ἀγωνιστικοὺς), nor on abstract knowledge (λόγους φιλοσοφικοὺς), this rhetoric turned its attention to the political life of Hellas, and produced instructive discourses (λόγους διδασκαλικοὺς) that attempted to teach students and statesmen alike ways in which they could address their circumstances insightfully. But why this turn? What could this rhetoric accomplish that the discourse of pure sophistry or pure philosophy could not? Answers to these questions can be had by examining some of the circumstances to which Isocratean rhetoric was tied.

Along with Plato, Isocrates belongs to the Hellenic period of introspection and reconstruction, a period whose meaning he obviously wanted to shape and whose direction he clearly wished to influence. Like Plato, he grew up in a time of cultural effervescence while his adult years coincided with an era of political decline. For all their differences, Isocrates and Plato were faced with common political and social conditions: wars between and strife within the city-states, one revolt after another, intellectual disorientation, lawlessness, social disorder, and political chaos. To a certain extent, Isocrates addressed these conditions the same way Plato did—by condemning political corruption, the frantic pursuit of personal gain, the lack of knowledge, pointless exhibitions, and destructive competitions. But Isocrates' responses also differ from Plato's. While Plato saw salvation in the hands of philosophically trained politicians or politically active philosophers, Isocrates saw it in a new generation of orators (*On the Peace*, 145). While Plato's new rulers would be driven by uncompromised intelligence, Isocrates' would possess sound judgment, which they could acquire through the study of (his version of) rhetoric and the lessons of history. Finally, while Plato's reforms would restrict rhetoric (*Statesman*, 304; *Phaedrus*, 259e–ff), Isocrates' would mobilize it for the good of Athens and the whole of Hellas. In short, where Plato saw the cure for rhetoric in dialectic, Isocrates saw it in rhetoric itself. Strictly speaking, Isocratean rhetoric turned neither to the individual's capacity for and susceptibility to language (in the manner of the sophists) nor to political or legal philosophy (in the manner of Plato). Rather, it turned to communities of people living in the polis amidst a deluge of unwieldy rhetorical forces and under a particular political and legal system. Accordingly, its focus was not on political or legal but on rhetorical reform. This reform was to be worked out in Isocrates' school and expressed in his appeals to living men of political affairs (i.e., Philip and Nicocles), not imaginary philosopher-kings or statesmen.

Like the older sophists, Isocrates taught rhetoric. But while they had traveled from city to city to teach the new *techne*, he opened a school in Athens and had students travel there to attend (*Antidosis*, 87–8, 224, 226). With this new arrangement, rhetoric stopped being solely a nomadic show, and was given for the first time an institutional base.[69] From the time of Pericles, Athens had been familiar with the rhetoric of the sophists; but wherever they were going they were taking their lessons and exhibits along.[70] This meant that students interested in a sustained study of rhetoric, but unable to follow the master's trail, had to wait for his next visit. While, then, itinerant teachers could only provide short-term, discontinuous instruction, the opening of Isocrates' school provided a permanent place where the art of discourse could be studied at length and without interruption.

However, the new institutional setting meant more than uninterrupted study in a central location. It meant, first, that the art the sophists had imported as a novelty had now entered the mainstream culture; as such it needed to concern itself more with the enhancement of its status and less with the initial search for visibility and legitimacy. Even before the opening of Isocrates' school, rhetorical education had overshadowed other kinds. But now it had an additional task: to clear the ambivalence the public felt about it by achieving high levels of excellence, and producing meaningful results. Second, it meant that "a prolonged and systematic course of instruction [could] be organized, instead of the cramming system to which itinerant teachers, however brilliant, necessarily tended."[71] Third, it meant that the student's relation to the school was more formal than the tutorial student/master relationship—there was less chance that a learned student would turn the tables on an institution in the way Tisias had turned them on Corax. Fourth, and perhaps most important, it meant that rhetoric had to attend to the affairs of the state. Insofar as the new school purported to prepare students for the trials of public life, it had to keep the State's pulse in mind. In all four cases, Isocrates can be said to have deviated from the sophistical tradition by initiating a new challenge: institutionalizing rhetorical instruction and specifying its future direction in accordance with the demands of political life.

Prior to this challenge, the sophists had promised to arm the interested individual with the rhetorical equipment necessary "to become a real power in the city" (*Protagoras*, 318e–19a). By contrast, Isocrates' own promise was to turn his students into insightful governors or responsible citizens. This difference is not to be attributed to two different philosophies of education—each program was a reaction to the prevailing conditions of its epoch. The sophistical program grew partly out of the need to fill the new seats of power created by the Periclean political reforms. It was a program driven by circumstantial demands and designed to satisfy personal ambition. By contrast, the Isocratean program sought to compensate for the lack of enlightened political leadership and mindful citizenship apparent throughout Hellas in the decades following the Peloponnesian Wars. Departing from the unregulated practices of the older sophists, Isocrates linked rhetoric to the articulation of wise governance and civic conscience. Clearly, each program sought to address a specific set of needs; but whereas the sophistical program had construed rhetoric as the key to social survival and political prominence, the Isocratean turned it into an expression of and a guide to pan-Hellenic welfare.

Although the sophists did not have a common approach to rhetorical education, their differences can be understood as variations of a central theme: the command of logos is the means par excellence to power.[72] This logocentric premise did not purport to spell out what one should do once in power.[73] It only asserted the potency of logos to influence people's thoughts and direct their actions. Accordingly, the sophists taught the properties of language, the rules of its operation, the possibilities of its structure, and the conditions of its impact.[74] Neither purpose nor subject-matter were part of their instruction. For them, rhetoric was a formal, not a moral, issue. Their chief task was to enable, not to enlighten.[75]

Naturally, these educational practices left the question of the proper uses of rhetoric unanswered (as we have seen, sophistical rhetoric escaped the *prepon-aprepes* opposition by means of the alternative of *kairos*). This question was tackled both by Plato and Isocrates. But unlike Plato's epistemological and moralistic response, Isocrates' took a pragmatic turn. Committed to the proposition that the art of persuasion must be put to beneficial uses, he introduced two new requirements to rhetorical education—the thematic and the pragmatic.[76] The thematic asked that rhetoric concentrate on significant matters while the pragmatic demanded that it make a positive contribution to the life of the audience (*Panegyricus*, 189; *Helen*, 12; *Nicocles*, 10). Apparently both requirements were introduced to counter two questionable rhetorical practices (supposedly the result of sophistical education)—disinterested verbal exhibitionism and the unscrupulous pursuit of personal gain. Isocrates seems to have reasoned that rhetoric could no longer be justified or function meaningfully on aesthetic or agonistic grounds alone. Eloquence for its own sake, he must have thought, was a misplaced priority in a culture striving to come to terms with its political urgencies and civic irresolutions. Similarly, a combative rhetoric may have been helpful in the development of strong individual egos but was often blind to the needs of a society searching for its center of gravity.

Even so, public rhetoric could hardly do without the elements of exhibition and competition. As we have seen, crowds were thought to be moved the most by brilliant spectacles of oratorical performance; and ideas were thought to be rising and falling in contest with counter-ideas. But if these two aspects of the sophistical tradition could not be eradicated entirely, they could at least be put in the service of sociopolitical coherence and order. Isocrates must have concluded that if the greatest affairs could somehow replace petty themes, and if communal benefits could replace private ones, rhetoric could demonstrate that its greatness lay in its capacity to repair the sociopolitical compass of a people and in its readiness to articulate their collective good.

All this could be done by means of a twofold realization: first, that the cultural ethic of competition had been brought to a point of crisis by the Peloponnesian Wars; and second, that cooperation was one of the main new and needed ideas in the fourth century B.C. But Isocrates' rhetorical reforms could hardly be introduced without some kind of challenge against the status quo. Thus in the domain of education, it is not simply a coincidence that he cast *Antidosis* in the form of a legal *agon* seeking to reverse public disfavor with the necessary evil of sophistical rhetoric and attempting to achieve victory over his competitors. Against the background of a presumed shortage of capable and loyal public servants, he could boast that his school was dedicated to educating pupils to see beyond their own interests and to serve Athens and Hellas selflessly. The proof of the superiority of his program was in the number and kind of pupils it had produced. In his mind, no other educator could produce as impressive a list of students who "had spent large sums of their private fortunes upon the city" (*Antidosis*, 93–94). As an educator, then, Isocrates not only set out to compete with other educators; he also declared himself a winner on account of the exemplary conduct of his students.

The paradox of denouncing the agonistic character of sophistical rhetoric agonistically is also evident in Isocrates' political discourses. As a self-styled pacifist, he had to battle against the blindness of greed, the thirst for power, and the will to victory—three liabilities in the political actions of his fellow Athenians and other Hellenes. But Isocratean pacifism was a limited program. Designed to stop several Hellenic states from draining each other's vital resources, inter-Hellenic cooperation was only half of the story. The other half was reopening the fronts of battle with the barbarians. Envisioning a united Hellas led by Athens to greatness, and believing in the repeatability of the glorious days of Marathon and Salamis, Isocrates advocated concord among the Hellenes but war between them and the barbarians. In doing so, he did not so much condemn as relocate the agonistic ethic of the sophistical tradition. Political competition among the Hellenes had produced disastrous results but, as history had taught, combat in the form of warfare between Hellenes and barbarians could yield profit.

If the ethic of competition had been brought to a crisis by the Peloponnesian Wars, the aesthetic of exhibition was checked by the growth of the new technology of writing. By the middle of the fourth century B.C., writing had taken firm roots in the soil of a predominately oral culture.[77] Even so, writing was regarded as an innovation and, as such, with suspicion.[78] Moreover, the primacy of the spoken word over its written counterpart was asserted again and again by prominent figures.[79] Himself at the center of this critical transition in the production and dissemination of logos, Isocrates had two burdens to face: his own vocal weakness on the one hand, and a popular sentiment against written rhetoric on the other. Addressing the latter, he acknowledges in *To Philip* (25) that there is much difference "in persuasiveness between discourses which are spoken and those which are to be read, and that all men have assumed that the former are delivered on subjects which are important and urgent, while the latter are composed for display and personal gain." After this allusion to his dilemma as a writing orator, he asks the Macedonian king to put "aside the prejudices . . . against speeches which are composed to be read" (29), and read his discourse with an open mind.[80]

The negative attitude against writing notwithstanding, rhetoric became increasingly written during Isocrates' lifetime.[81] Even before the fourth century B.C., the sophists had done some writing in the form of handbooks for rhetoric, model speeches for their students, and forensic orations for their clients' day in court. Still, the sophists owed much of their notoriety to their oral eloquence before small gatherings of interested spectators or larger audiences in public functions.[82] By contrast, Isocrates became famous for his written works (*Antidosis*, 87). Lacking the daring and the strong voice required in the public platform, he became a writing orator whose compositions served at least as arguments for producing, studying, and practicing rhetoric in the written mode.

Unlike its oral counterpart, written rhetoric could escape the ritualism of public performance, avoid the evanescence of orality, and transcend the demands of local audiences. To be sure, Pericles' democratic reforms had opened up public spaces where the citizens' voices could be heard. But judging from actual rhetorical events, it was the orators' voice that benefited most from these reforms. Specif-

ically, it was their voice that was most often heard to be moving people to action, making them think guilty or innocent, or telling them to
vote for war or peace. For their part, the masses seemed incapable of
resisting the power and charm of the orators' words. Effectively, the
orator became democracy's tyrant as his voice was not so much representing as shaping the will of the people. But insofar as oral rhetoric
had to adapt to the interests of local audiences, it was helping to perpetuate their provincial values, thereby maintaining differences and
hostilities between one city-state and an other.[83] Any changes result-
ing from the speaking orators' promptings were mostly confined
within the borders of a single state without any chance of bringing
several states together. But if this is so, oral rhetoric functioned so as
to keep each city-state isolated from the rest. While it is unlikely that
the orators intended this kind of isolation, their rhetoric nevertheless
had the effect of creating and maintaining division among city-states.

Seen in this light, the older sophists' declamations on the need for
pan-Hellenic concord could hardly have succeeded. Spoken rhetoric
was bound to the limitations of oral/aural communication.[84] Lacking
materiality, the spoken word was fated to vanish as soon as it was
uttered; and despite the mnemonic devices the orators had borrowed
from the poets (meter, rhyme, and highly formalized tropes and figures), oral rhetoric could mainly serve the purposes of immediacy.
What was said one day could not be trusted to hold the next. Likewise, the same orator could say now one thing, and then its opposite.
Consistency and noncontradiction in speech required, at the very least,
a strong memory—the kind popular audiences are not known for.

In contrast to its oral counterpart, written rhetoric was part of
what Havelock has called the silent revolution.[85] This revolution reversed the order of the experience of oral rhetoric by making the word
visible and its effects invisible.[86] The writer-orator could still turn out
poeticized phrases.[87] But these now amounted to phonic vestiges, in-
scribed signs of imagined sounds meant to arouse and affect audiences indirectly. If we are to rely on and generalize from Isocrates,
writing invited readers to follow arguments, not cadences; it solicited
their thoughtful responses, not their care-free indulgence in ritualized
public performances.[88] In so doing, it asked them to put aside their
localistic orientation and consider his texts, pondering the possibility
of a unified Hellenic world.

Spoken rhetoric could only address a small circle of people at a
time, a circle usually defined by the radius of the orator's vocal reach.

But since texts can travel further than the human voice, Isocrates' written addresses can be said to have aimed at a geographically broader audience, one that included distant readers throughout the Hellenic world.[89] Even so, the relatively low level of literacy at that time suggests that the number of people addressed by his written message must have been limited. Isocrates, however, seems less concerned with this limitation than with the fact that speaking to the masses is virtually useless when it comes to serious projects like pan-Hellenism. As he puts it in *To Philip* (12), "to burden our national assemblies with oratory and to address all the people there throng together is, in reality, to address no one at all." Although Isocrates had to take into account a greater diversity of opinion and sensibility than a strictly local orator, his written rhetoric seems to have been directed mainly to those few who could make a difference (*To Philip*, 13). Unlike a local audience of listeners, a national audience of readers required a rhetoric broad enough to encompass a wider range of political orientations; more importantly, it demanded a rhetoric focusing on matters of enduring interest. To the extent that such a rhetoric could be produced, it could go beyond the boundaries of the polis and turn many local assemblies into a single national audience. More precisely, it could change Athenians, Spartans, Thebans, and Argives into the Hellenes of Athens, Sparta, Thebes, and Argos. In other words, it could transcend provincial concerns and forge a truly Hellenic mentality. For Isocrates, this transformation could be accomplished through written rhetoric. Because writing did away with the requirements of presence, it could offer readers some detachment from local loyalties by addressing them privately, thus affording them time for contemplation and study (*Evagoras,* 76). In so doing, it could overcome the biggest obstacle against pan-Hellenism, "the particularism and authority of the polis."[90]

The above account of Isocrates' reception of the sophists points out that rhetoric, in addition to the hostile treatment it received in Plato's hands, was also affirmed so long as it would meet new criteria, and adapt to the new conditions. Practiced, taught, and applied in new ways and under different conditions, rhetoric was now beginning to depart from its sophistical forms and to expand its practical and conceptual horizons. At the practical level, it was moving from the stage to the page, a departure that turned spectators into readers, temporary circumstances into more or less permanent ideas, and improvisation into premeditated improvisation. Further, it was moving from the sound and the fury of oratorical contests or the free give-and-take of disputation to the regulated and insulated environment of the school, a departure that turned aspiring orators into industrious students and would-be public arguers into calculating thinkers. Moreover, it was moving from the logic of circumstances to the logic of principles, a departure that sought to turn dissensus into consensus, and the expressions of contrary alternatives into the search for the one master discourse that could effect a strong unity among a divided people.

At the conceptual level, rhetoric began to move away from its critical and towards a conserving function. This becomes apparent if we juxtapose two well-known passages with explicit remarks about logos: Gorgias' *Encomium of Helen* (8–14) and Isocrates' *Nicocles* (5–9).[91] In the former passage, logos is portrayed as a δυνάστης (lord, master, ruler), while in the latter as an ἡγεμὼν (leader, commander, chief). Both of these anthropomorphic characterizations acknowledge the authority of logos. But while Gorgias stresses its power to rule arbitrarily over people, Isocrates emphasizes its ability to lead them to worthwhile ends. Both rhetoricians recognize people's susceptibility to and capacity for persuasion. But while Gorgias dwells on logos' psychological impact on the individual, Isocrates underscores its civilizing influence on human communities.[92] In short, the former highlights the dynastic power of language to impose, to undermine, to violate, to deceive, and to distort;[93] the latter underlines its hegemonic capacity to collect, to unify, to lead, and to facilitate.

That these two conceptualizations should be so is not surprising if we consider them in their textual context. To prove Helen's innocence, Gorgias depicts logos as an overpowering force that Helen had no chance of resisting: "What cause then prevents the conclusion that Helen . . . against her will, might have come under the influence of speech, just as if ravished by the force of the mighty?" (12); and further, "if she was persuaded by speech she did not do wrong but was unfortunate" (15). For his part, Isocrates makes the case for monarchy by asserting that logos constitutes the foundation of its existence and the requirement of its continued prosperity: "I regard those [discourses] as the best and most worthy of a king . . . which teach how men in power should deal with the people, and how the rank and file should be disposed to their rulers. For I observe that it is through such discourses that states attain the highest prosperity and greatness" (10).

Beyond their textual context, these two conceptualizations of logos can be said to constitute appropriate responses to two corresponding sets of political circumstances. Before the advent of constitutional reforms in the Hellenic world, tyranny was a common form of government. Tyrants, typically self-appointed dictators seeking to further their own interests, generally rose to and fell from power by similar means: intrafamilial succession, overthrow, or assassination. While in power, they usually ruled by force, terrorizing communities, eliminating opponents, and suppressing personal rights.[94] For their ways, they were admired by some, despised by others, and feared by all. Within a tyrant's circumscribed turf, anyone could fall victim to his tempestuous temperament, and no one was beyond his reach and power. Eventually, tyranny as a form of government declined and was replaced with rule by representation.

But even after its decline, tyranny and its politics persisted, this time both between and within the Hellenic city-states. Athens, for example, had managed to become the strongest power of the Hellenic world largely because of its tyrannical policies: imposing its will on its allies, violating their sovereignty, enslaving their population, and controlling their affairs.[95] Inside Athens, reputedly the most democratic of the Hellenic states, there was no guarantee against tyranny. As the ruthless rule of the Thirty Tyrants in 404 B.C. attests, Athenians were not immune to tyrannical practices that included the closing of the rhetorical schools, the persecution of intellectuals, the confiscation of personal property, banishments, and executions. Clearly, the overthrow of tyranny had not signaled the end of tyrannical practices.

The above historical account suggests that from the exercise of tyrannical power to the dynastic conception of logos was only a short distance. This distance becomes even shorter if we recall that the "logos *dynastes*" formulation was advanced by Gorgias, who, like most Leontinians, must have been familiar with the tyrannical rule of Gelon and Hieron in nearby Syracuse. Basically, Gorgias argued that, like the typical tyrant, a logos rises to power by ousting its predecessor (*Helen*, 13). Once in power, it employs its ways of deceiving (8, 10), constraining (12), frightening (9, 14), and even killing its subjects (14) until it is overturned by a more powerful logos. As the case of Helen illustrates, logos is a tyrannical force that controls human destiny in decisive ways; and as the history of tyrannical regimes reveals, logos is a tyrant's worst enemy.

Beyond this interdependence of language and politics, the dynastic conception of logos finds further warrant and explanation in the pattern of the politics of thought during the latter half of the fifth century B.C. In that domain, the sophistic movement exposed the arbitrariness and exploited the vulnerability of the traditional legacies of the culture. Assuming the form of a rhetorical revolt, this movement victimized many notions of the past and imposed new ones. Under the new logocracy, man was declared the measure of all things (Protagoras), the gods were called clever human fabrications designed to serve the purposes of social control (Critias), being was shown to be on an equal footing with nonbeing (Gorgias), justice was defined as nothing but the interest of the stronger (Thrasymachus), and slavery was explained as a matter of convention, not natural law (Antiphon). By virtue of the force of these new understandings, logos emerged as a *dynastes* who could dethrone stronger arguments and install in their place weaker ones. In its new conceptual characterization, logos deposed the tyranny of the tradition and imposed the tyranny of innovation.

Naturally, these developments were not without consequences. As limited democracy gradually replaced tyranny, and as the sophistic movement shook the foundations of the mythopoetic tradition, a plurality of forces came to the front. Governing, no longer a one-man proposition, involved many people. In many states, propertied elites, merchants, workers, intellectuals, and alien residents represented political interests to be reckoned with. The same trend toward pluralization obtained in interstate politics as Athens, surrendering its claim to Hellenic supremacy after the end of the Peloponnesian Wars, was reduced to only one of several lesser powers. In the domain of economics, the once self-sufficient economy of the city-state yielded to the need for interstate and international commerce. As wealth, previously concentrated in one or two cities, became more evenly distributed, several states emerged as economic powers. Culture, too, once gathered primarily in Athens, was now being spread throughout Hellas by traveling sophists and book merchants.[96]

Not surprisingly, the consequences of pluralization included divisiveness and conflict. In the political sphere, several states attempted to assume the leadership of Hellas but all failed. Internally, they proved unable to unite the various factions within their borders. With each state and each faction looking after its own interests and disregarding the interests of others, the result was prolonged strife within and war between the states. On the social sphere, the chasm between the rich and the poor widened while litigation increased enormously. Unable to meet people's material and intellectual needs, the state could no longer command their loyalty. Not surprisingly, interest in the state declined while interest in the individual grew. In thought, the questioning of the intellectual tradition led to the emergence of so many perspectives on and explanations about the world that eventually nothing seemed universally valid.[97] Excessive pluralization in all departments of life had precipitated a crisis of disunity and disaffection with customary forms of political, social, and intellectual authority. Hence Isocrates' hegemonic conception of logos, a conception presupposed by and inspiring his vision of pan-Hellenic unity. Conceived hegemonically, logos could forge a new vision of cooperation and *omonoia* (like-mindedness), a vision that could send an unsettled culture in search of a new consensus and stability. More than a eulogy of logos, then, the section of *Nicocles* we have been considering (5–9) represents a stand against the outcomes of extreme pluralization and for the promise of reunification. Clearly, the political and intellectual turmoil of the times warranted a change from the dynastic to the hegemonic conceptualization of logos.

Which of the two conceptualizations is superior is not the issue here. Both are historically grounded formulations describing ways in which rhetoric functions. In the case of the sophists, the primary function of logos is critical. In this capacity, it often operates so as to create a crisis by casting doubt on and dissolving (καταλῦσαι) (*Helen,* 21) the established realities. Whenever logos does this successfully, it stimulates the impulse to undermine what is actual and thus create new possibilities (*Helen,* 13). In the case of Isocrates, the principal function of logos is constructive (κατασκευάσας) (*Nicocles,* 6). Insofar as it can shape reality, it works so as to build necessary institutions and create human communities held together by common beliefs. When successful in doing so, it articulates what eventually becomes accepted, and stimulates the impulse to affirm and stabilize.

In this chapter, we have considered Isocrates' reception of the sophists. What we have seen is a complex discourse at once affirming and negating sophistical rhetoric, a discourse critiquing without condemning his predecessors, and announcing a departure from the discursive practices of his contemporaries. Indebted to the tradition the sophists had initiated, Isocrates imitates their work but only up to a point; time and again, he follows their example but never entirely.

Convinced that public discourse must be useful to the audience's life, Isocrates attacks those sophists, orators, and philosophers who deal in paradoxes, trivialities, and abstractions. Likewise, he finds fault in discourses seeking narrow goals and disregarding broader, that is, communal or pan-Hellenic concerns. Aware of the ways in which popular orators interact with large crowds, he denounces competitive discourses for seeking to win at any cost and spectacular ones for seeking to please without teaching something useful.

In the midst of a culture dispersed in its social, political, and intellectual activities, Isocrates produced a rhetoric pointing away from the periphery and towards a center. At this center, there lay arguments for the necessity of properly functioning institutions, the importance of consensus and cooperation, the need for serious rhetorical education, the advantages of pan-Hellenism, and the benefits of political stability. Supported by Isocrates' hegemonic notion of logos, the opening of his school, and the growth of writing, these arguments provided the counterforce to the forces of dissociation and paved the way for Aristotle.

## Notes

1. Werner Jaeger, *Paideia: The Ideals of Greek Culture*, 3 vols., trans. Gilbert Highet (New York: Oxford University Press, 1939–1944)) vol. 3, 49.
2. Ibid., 48. For points of view agreeing with Jaeger's, see Henri I. Marrou, "Education and Rhetoric" in M. I. Finley, ed., *The Legacy of Greece: A New Appraisal* (Oxford: Clarendon Press, 1981), 189–90; George A. Kennedy, *The Art of Persuasion in Greece* (Princeton: Princeton University Press, 1963), 17, 178; R. C. Jebb, *The Attic Orators*, 2 vols. (London: MacMillan and Co., 1893), vol 2, 52; J. F. Dobson, *The Greek Orators* (London: Methuen, 1919), 12–13; Jacqueline de Romilly, *Magic and Rhetoric in Ancient Greece* (Cambridge, Mass.: Harvard University Press, 1975), 55, 57; Lorenzo Sears, *The History of Oratory from the Age of Pericles to the Present Time* (Chicago: Scott Foresman, 1897), 45; Charles S. Baldwin, *Medieval Rhetoric and Poetic* (New York: Macmillan and Co., 1928), 5.
3. As he puts it in the general case, "things do not of their own nature either help or harm us but the manner in which they are used and employed by men is the cause of all the things that befall us" (*Panathenaicus*, 223). The more particular case appears in *Nicocles*, 1–2: People should not "condemn these means by which one may gain advantage without sacrifice of virtue, but

rather those men who do wrong in their actions or *who deceive by their speech and put their eloquence to unjust uses"* (my emphasis).

4. Recall *Gorgias*, 456a–57c and compare with *Antidosis*, 251–53.

5. See *Nicocles* (5–9) and compare to Protagoras' "Great Speech" in *Protagoras* (320c–28d) and Gorgias' *Encomium of Helen* (8–14).

6. See *Panegyricus*, 3–6.

7. As proof of the superiority of his discourses, Isocrates points out that some people imitate them even though they dare find fault with them (*Letter*, 9, 15).

8. See *Helen*, 5–6.

9. See Ibid., 7 and *Antidosis*, 269.

10. This makes sense if we accept the tradition that he was a student of Gorgias and Socrates. See George Norlin's "Introduction" in *Isocrates*, vol. 1, xii–xviii.

11. Consider, for example, his reference to "the sophists who have lately sprang up" in *Against the Sophists*, 19.

12. According to George Norlin, Isocrates' use of φιλοσοφία "may be nothing more than a protest against the preposterous claims made by certain sophists for the omnipotence of their instruction." See his "Introduction" in *Isocrates*, vol. 1, xxvii.

13. Here we may recall the Socrates of the *Gorgias* (465c): "they [sophistic and rhetoric] are so nearly related that sophists and orators are jumbled up as having the same field and dealing with the same subjects, and neither can they tell what to make of each other, nor the world at large what to make of them." To this Socratic observation one could include that philosophy too is puzzling to "the world at large."

14. See *Antidosis*, 231 and *On the Peace*, 5.

15. For Isocrates' assertion of the public's prejudice against the sophists, see *To Philip*, 26 (τὰς δυσχερείας τὰς περὶ τοὺς σοφιστὰς) and *Antidosis*, 168 (τῆς περὶ τοὺς σοφιστὰς διαβολῆς).

16. See *Panathenaicus*, 18.

17. See *Helen*, 13 and *Panathenaicus*, 36.

18. See *To Philip*, 13.

19. See *Antidosis*, 221.

20. See *Against the Sophists*, 16.

21. See *Helen*, 1.

22. Compare with Gorgias' claim that those who persuade do so by "molding a false argument" (ψευδῆ λόγον πλάσαντες) *Encomium of Helen* (11).

23. Isocrates advances virtually the same line of thought in *Antidosis* (268–69) where he advises young men not "to be stranded on the speculations of the ancient sophists (τῶν παλαιῶν σοφιστῶν), who maintain, some of them, that the sum of things is made up of infinite elements; Empedocles that it is made up of four, with strife and love operating among them; Ion, of not more than three; Alcmaeon, of only two; Parmenides and Melissus, of one; and Gorgias,

of none at all. For I think that such curiosities of thought (περιττολογίας) are on a par with jugglers' tricks which, though they do not profit anyone, yet attract great crowds of the empty-minded, and I hold that men who want to do some good in the world must banish utterly from their interests all vain speculations and all activities which have no bearing on our lives."

24. For this criticism, see *Helen* (8–13).

25. See *Antidosis*, 148.

26. See *Against the Sophists*, 1, 11. For the way the lay mind works when it comes to sophistical promises and practices, see 7–8.

27. Of course, the reference here is to his *Against the Sophists*.

28. See *Antidosis* (156–57). See also *Against the Sophists* (3–5), where he takes the sophists to task for the incommensurability of the high value of their lessons and the low prices they charge: "although they set themselves up as masters and dispensers of goods so precious [happiness, virtue, prosperity wisdom], they are not ashamed of asking for them a price of three or four minae!"

29. See *Antidosis*, 158.

30. See Ibid., 155–56.

31. Isocrates makes virtually the same point in *To Nicocles*, 13.

32. See *Antidosis*, 197–98

33. Consider also Isocrates' argument that natural talent alone is not always enough; one also needs education. "Formal training . . . cannot fully fashion men who are without natural aptitude into good debaters or writers, although it is capable of leading them on to self-improvement and to a greater degree of intelligence on many subjects" (*Against the Sophists*, 15).

34. For the full argument on this issue, see *Antidosis*, 209–29.

35. See *To Nicocles*, 47.

36. See *Antidosis*, 136–39.

37. See *The Team of Horses*, 5–7 and *Plataicus*, 3.

38. See *Plataicus*, 38.

39. For a special class of evil orators, the sycophants, who have harmed Athens, see *Antidosis*, 312–20.

40. See *On the Peace*, 26.

41. See Ibid., 129.

42. This portrayal of the orators appears in Ibid., 121–31.

43. In *Antidosis* (133) Isocrates elaborates on his views on the multitude by way of reference to his advice to his student Timotheus: " 'You observe,' I would say to him, 'the nature of the multitude, how susceptible they are to flattery; that they like those who cultivate their favour better than those who seek their good; and that they prefer those who cheat them with beaming smiles and brotherly love to those who serve them with dignity and reserve.' "

44. See also *Panathenaicus*, 1.

45. On the contrary, he refers to himself as neither a public orator nor a general nor an otherwise powerful man (μήτε δημηγορῶν μήτε στρατηγῶν μήτ᾽ ἄλλως δυνάστης) (*Letter*, 1, 9).

46. See also *Helen*, 17 and *Evagoras*, 4.

47. Other kinds of prose discourse include genealogies of the demigods, studies in the poets, histories of wars, and dialogue (*Antidosis*, 45).

48. For Isocrates' comparison between his own rhetoric and the oratory of the courts, see *Antidosis*, 48–50.

49. See *To Philip*, 81; *Panathenaicus*, 9–10; *Epistle*, 1.9; and *Epistle*, 8.7.

50. Isocrates repeats this same point in his *Letter to the Rulers of the Mytilenaeans* (7): "It is true that I have abstained from political activity and from practicing oratory: for my voice was inadequate and I lacked assurance. I have not been altogether useless, however, and without repute; on the contrary, you will find that I have been the counsellor and coadjutor of those who have chosen to speak well of you and our other allies, and that I have myself composed more discourses on behalf of the freedom and independence of the Greeks than all those together who have worn smooth the floor of our platforms."

51. See his mention of his difference with the orators on the issue of war between Athens and Philip over Amphipolis (*To Philip*, 2).

52. See *Panathenaicus*, 37–38.

53. See Ibid., 271.

54. See *Nicocles*, 2–4.

55. See Ibid., 5 ff.

56. See also *Antidosis*, 246–48.

57. See *Panegyricus*, 10.

58. See *To Demonicus*, 3.

59. See *Antidosis*, 50. In the same passage, however, he also refers to it as power, faculty (δύναμις), or profession/occupation (διατριβή). See also his reference to *Antidosis* as partly a discussion about philosophy and expositions of its power (*Antidosis*, 10).

60. See *Antidosis*, 41.

61. In *Against the Sophists* (21), however, he notes that his philosophy, which includes the study of political discourses, is more likely to yield the benefit of an honest character than facility in oratory.

62. See *Nicocles*, 8.

63. See *Antidosis*, 270–80.

64. See Ibid., 275.

65. For a variation of the wise attributes or capacities reflected in the rhetorically educated person, see *Panathenaicus*, 30–31.

66. See *Helen*, 1. See also *Against the Sophists* (21), where Isocrates suggests that justice cannot be taught.

67. For the philosopher's interest in the nature of humans and things, see also (*Panathenaicus*, 240).

68. See also (*Letter*, 9, 15), where Isocrates refers to the disagreeable character of those who pretend to philosophize (προσποιούμενοι φιλοσοφεῖν).

69. For a more detailed discussion of this point, see G. C. Field, *Plato and His Contemporaries* (London: Methuen, 1930), 32–33; John W. H. Walden, *The Universities of Ancient Greece* (New York: Charles Scribner's Sons, 1909), 33.

70. Kenneth J. Freeman and M. J. Rendall, *Schools of Hellas: An Essay on the Practice and Theory of Ancient Greek Education from 600 to 300 B.C.* (New York: Kennikat Press, 1969), 163–64.

71. Field, 33.

72. See James Jarrett, *The Educational Theories of the Sophists* (New York: Columbia University Teachers' College Press, 1969), 16.

73. For two opposing views, see *Gorgias* (466b–69a) and *On the Peace*, 103–5.

74. For a detailed account of the sophists' concern with language, see C. J. Classen's "The Study of Language Amongst Socrates' Contemporaries" in Carl J. Classen, *Sophistik* (Darmstadt: Wissenschaftliche Buchgeselschaft, 1976), 215–47.

75. See Gunther Heilbrunn, "Isocrates on Rhetoric and Power," *Hermes* 103, no. 2 (1975): 166.

76. See Jaeger, vol. 3, 60–61.

77. For a background on the distinction between the spoken and the written word, see Freeman and Rendall, 208–9; Frederic G. Kenyon, *Books and Readers in Ancient Greece and Rome* (Oxford: Clarendon Press, 1951), 25; William C. Greene, "The Spoken and the Written Word," *Harvard Studies in Classical Philology* 60 (1951): 51; Eric A. Havelock, "The Oral and the Written Word: A Reappraisal" in Eric A. Havelock, ed., *The Literate Revolution and Its Cultural Consequences* (Princeton: Princeton University Press, 1982), 338; Eric A. Havelock, *The Muse Learns to Write* (New Haven: Yale University Press, 1986); Walter Ong, *The Presence of the Word* (New Haven: Yale University Press, 1967); Walter Ong, *Orality and Literacy* (New York: Methuen, 1982).

78. See S. H. Butcher, "The Spoken and the Written Word" in *Some Aspects of the Greek Genius* (London: MacMillan and Co., 1893), 178 ff; Tony Lentz, "Writing as Sophistry: From Preservation to Persuasion," *Quarterly Journal of Speech* 68, no. 1 (February 1982): 60–68.

79. See, for example, Alcidamas' argument that "written speeches do not deserve even to be called speeches, but as it were forms and figures and imitations of speeches." Likening spoken speeches to bodies and written speeches to statues, he continues: "the speech spoken straight from the mind on the spur of the moment is living and has a soul and follows circumstances and is like real bodies, but the written one, in nature like the image of a speech, is doomed to inanition" *On the Sophists* (27–28).

For Plato's well-known preference for spoken over written discourse, see *Phaedrus* (274c–75e) and *Letter* (7.344c).

Aristotle, too, reflects the bias against written speeches when he says (*Rhetoric*, 1404b) that "speeches of the written or the literary kind owe more of their effect to their diction than to their thought." One is tempted here to continue: by contrast, speeches of the spoken or the nonliterary kind owe more their effect to their thought than to their diction.

Of course, the irony in all three authors is that their remarks against writing are registered in writing.

80. See also *Letter*, 1.1–3.

81. The same happened with poetry. But while Isocrates wrote for readers, the poets "always wrote for listeners." Eric A. Havelock, *Preface to Plato* (Cambridge, Mass.: Harvard University Press, 1982), 46.

82. See *Gorgias*, 447a–b, *Protagoras*, 310e, and *Hippias Major*, 282b–d.

83. Hinting at this point, Plato remarks that while it is easy "to praise Athenians among Athenians" it is difficult "to praise Athenians among Peloponnesians or Peloponnesians among Athenians" (*Menexenus*, 235d–36a).

84. See Gorgias' *Encomium of Helen*, 8, 11, 13.

85. Havelock, *Preface*, 41.

86. Consider Gorgias' view that logos is invisible and its effects visible *Encomium of Helen* (8).

87. See *Antidosis*, 47. It is noteworthy that Isocrates conceded that poetry has greater impact than rhetoric, and complained that because the poets are granted the use of the aesthetic resources of language they are more effective than the prose orators, who are not permitted to use the same resources (*Evagoras*, 8–11).

88. Aware that the audiences of his time expected some degree of ornamentation in rhetoric, Isocrates defends the plane prose of two of his works, and calls the preoccupation with style a youthful concern (*To Philip*, 27–29; *Panathenaicus*, 1–4); R. C. Jebb (51–57) observes that stylistic graces in Isocrates' compositions are as elegant but not as plentiful as in the speeches of the sophists.

89. Contrasting statues to written speeches (monuments to documents), Isocrates notes in *Evagoras* (74): "I know that images must of necessity remain solely among those in whose cities they were set up, whereas portrayals in words may be published throughout Hellas."

90. Heilbrunn, 160.

91. For a discussion comparing these two passages, see de Romilly, 52–54.

92. For an excellent discussion of Gorgias' psychological understanding of logos, see Charles P. Segal, "Gorgias and the Psychology of the Logos," *Harvard Studies in Classical Philology* 66 (1962): 99–155.

93. See Roger Moss, "The Case for Sophistry," in Brian Vickers, ed., *Rhetoric*

*Revalued* (Binghampton, N.Y.: Center for Medieval and Early Renaissance Studies, 1982), 207–24.

94. N. G. L. Hammond, *A History of Greece to 322 B.C.* (Oxford: Clarendon Press, 1963), 145–52.

95. For a telling account of Athens' tyrannical policies, see Thucydides, "The Melian Dialogue," 5.17.

96. Hammond, 521–32.

97. Wilhelm Windelband, *A History of Philosophy*, 2 vols., trans. James H. Tufts (New York: Harper and Row, 1958), vol. 1, 68.

# Chapter 5

# Aristotle's Reception
of the Sophists

Aristotle's reception of the sophists resembles, in some respects, those of Plato and Isocrates; yet, it differs sufficiently from theirs to merit a separate treatment.[1] For the most part, the Aristotelian reception revolves around the axis of the critical attitude carved out by Plato and, to a lesser extent, Isocrates. That it should do so is hardly surprising given that Aristotle shared with his teacher (Plato) on the one hand and his pedagogical rival (Isocrates) on the other a common set of cultural realities and a similar sociopolitical horizon; and it is hardly surprising in the light of his lengthy studies in Plato's Academy as well as his familiarity with Isocrates' rhetorical compositions. But Aristotle had a mind of his own, a mind devoted neither to the articulation of universal forms nor to the expression of pan-Hellenic manifestos, but rather to the compilation and structuration of what was known in several areas of inquiry during his time.[2] In contrast to the Platonic and Isocratean receptions, which evaluated the sophists' notions and practices by the criteria of abiding truth and situated usefulness respectively, the Aristotelian relies more heavily on the standards of historical significance and logical correctness. Along with Aristotle's conceptualization of rhetoric as a distinct field of study (an art with its own rules and principles), the application of these two standards led to the following reception: because they contributed to the cultural reservoir of rhetorical insights, the sophists are historically important; but because their reasoning was often flawed, it needs to be corrected.

This twofold assessment rests on Aristotle's view that all discoveries are the result of either elaborations on previously worked matters or original inventions (*Sophistical Refutations*, 183b.17–20). By his own admission, a good part of his *Rhetoric* constitutes an elaboration of prior insights: "on the subject of rhetoric there already existed much material enunciated in the past" (*Sophistical Refutations*, 184a.10–84b.1). On the other hand, his *Topics* stands as an original invention: "regarding reasoning (συλλογίζεσθαι) we had absolutely no earlier work to quote" (*Sophistical Refutations*, 184b.2). These remarks suggest that, as a successor of the sophists, Aristotle responds to a twofold need. Insofar as the sophists had left some of the earlier materials of rhetoric in a state of confusion and incoherence, Aristotle set out to systematize (ὁδοποιεῖν) them and render them coherent;[3] but inasmuch as they had practiced argument and refutation without adhering to an explicit theory of dialectic, he undertook to discover a method of arguing any point without contradiction (*Topics*, 100a.18–20)[4] and defending any thesis consistently (*Sophistical Refutations*, 183b.5–6). The result was two treatises: the *Rhetoric* and the *Topics*.

Beyond the standards it employs and the assessment it advances, the Aristotelian reception of the sophists also differs from its Platonic and Isocratean counterparts in the way it is carried out. Whereas Plato and Isocrates had written rhetorical compositions seeking to imitate, mock, refute, or outdo the sophists,[5] Aristotle is content to theorize, to follow his newly devised rules of the arts of rhetoric and logic, and to judge sophistical rhetoric by them. Speeches as self-sufficient units of discourse addressing a particular issue are nowhere to be found in Aristotle. In his texts, oratory as a cultural practice is simply abandoned while the capacities for meta-rhetorical discussion and critical commentary are boosted. In the light of the above characteristics, Aristotle's reception affords us yet another view, a view from a historically informed perspective and a newly developed logical stance. By virtue of its historical sensitivity, his reception can be said to incorporate both Platonic and Isocratean views on the sophists. But by virtue of its presumed logical correctness, it can be said to stand more or less alone. But if this is so, Aristotle's perspective is partly tied to and partly independent of the perceptions of his two seniors.

Like Plato and Isocrates, Aristotle refers to the older as well as his contemporary sophists by name or, collectively, as a class.[6] Often abstracting from many particulars a general principle, he also discusses the sophist as a composite of several features—a type. Therefore, his remarks can be taken to refer to common rather than individualistic traits and practices, except, of course, when discussing a named individual. Following Plato, Aristotle defines the sophist as a practitioner of questionable rhetorical and argumentative practices. But whereas Plato had defined him with a dramatic sense of urgency, turning the act of defining into a venturesome expedition of hunting down a cunning beast, Aristotle defines him dispassionately, so as to fulfill his authorial obligation to his readers, to meet, that is, their expectations of informational clarity and intellectual decorum. In searching for the sophist, Plato, as we have seen, had encountered difficulties, now finding and now losing him along the blurred lines separating philosophy from nonphilosophy, statesmanship from nonstatesmanship, and rhetoric from nonrhetoric. But with Aristotle, the lines of demarcation are made sharper, and as a result the sophist is found more easily and defined with greater confidence.

Following Isocrates, Aristotle attempts to evaluate the practices of the sophists. But whereas Isocrates had judged them according to their impact on the culture at large, and had concluded that some are good while others wicked, Aristotle assesses them according to their contributions to Hellenic thought, concluding that while they had helped make the rhetorical tradition rich, their contribution to reasoning was virtually nil. As we have seen, Isocrates had tried to distinguish the sophists from the philosophers and the orators; and as we will see, Aristotle attempts to make similar distinctions. But while Isocrates' effort was meant to prevent the perception that he himself was a bad sophist, Aristotle's was designed to establish the superiority of philosophy over sophistry. Finally, while Isocrates had sought to appropriate sophistical rhetorical practices and put them into the service of what he regarded as an immensely urgent project (pan-Hellenism), Aristotle sought to technologize them and make them part of a more comprehensive system of rhetoric. The resemblances and differences between Aristotle and his two seniors aside, it appears that in the latter part of the fourth century B.C. the sophists had become a permanent part of the intellectual landscape of the Hellenic culture. It also appears that the Platonic and Isocratean efforts had not yielded a completed sophistical picture; the sophists' historical and contemporary identity still needed some details, and it took Aristotle to work them out.

While executing this task, Aristotle seems neither obsessed nor especially troubled by the sophists the way Plato does. Although he, too, adopts a critical stance toward them, his critique does not exhibit the Platonic elements of hostility and outright rejection. The sophists of Aristotle are more an object of study and less the mortal enemies of the investigator—at least, so it appears at first sight. Treating them as a part of early Hellenic intellectual history, Aristotle pays them some attention, seeks to overcome what he regards as their shortcomings in rhetoric, and to correct what he considers as their errors in logic. Yet in his overall project—a project encompassing a wide range of historical, critical, and theoretical inquiries—the sophists play only a minor role, the role of a peculiar intellectual phenomenon that somehow must be made intelligible and meaningful. Accordingly, Aristotle handles them as a given aspect of the Hellenic cultural heritage but does so without attaching to them the extraordinary significance they had been assigned in some Platonic dialogues. With Aristotle, the importance of the sophists begins to diminish. The older ones were not the sole culprits of the sociopolitical chaos of the fourth century B.C. that Plato had thought they were; rather, they represented an era of preliminary investigations in thought and language, investigations that now had to be rethought, straightened out, and brought to further completion. As for the second-generation sophists, they simply represented an extension of the earlier masters whose doctrines and practices they were perpetuating.[7] But in the context of the breadth and depth of Aristotelian intellectual inquiry, both the older and the younger sophists lose some of their prominence and weight. Once the principal intellectuals of the culture, the sophists of Aristotle are given the status of a single item in a large list of many entries.

Beyond its respect for the tradition and its commitment to a new conceptualization of rhetoric, Aristotle's reception of the sophists is also guided by distinctions he makes between rhetoric and other fields such as philosophy and politics.[8] Therefore, before looking more closely at his treatment of sophistical rhetoric, it is important to attend to these distinctions. Aristotle basically agrees with Plato's view that the sophists imitate the philosopher. However, Aristotle puts the matter slightly differently when he says that they practice apparent, but not real, wisdom.[9] Although it is difficult to say what exactly Aristotle means by apparent wisdom,[10] it is clear that real wisdom is what the philosopher possesses or practices.[11] On this matter, Aristotle and Plato agree. Now, if by apparent wisdom he generally means rhetoric, the art whose whole business is about appearances (πρὸς δόξαν), and by real wisdom dialectic, Aristotle can be said to depart from Plato and to rework the relationship of the two faculties by making the one a counterpart of the other.[12] But if by apparent wisdom he means fallacious argument, and real wisdom correct argument, then the sophists of Aristotle practice something that needs to be rectified by devising explicit rules of argumentation, not derided in the manner of Plato. On another vein, Aristotle refers to truth and action as the two aims that distinguish the philosopher from the orator and others like him: "philosophy is rightly called a knowledge of Truth (ἐπιστήμην τῆς ἀληθείας). The object of theoretic knowledge is truth, while that of practical knowledge is action; for even when they are investigating how a thing is so, practical men study not the eternal principles but the relative and immediate application" (*Metaphysics*, 993b.20–24). Similarly, while philosophy concerns itself with "the actual form of things," rhetoric is interested in the way things partake in these forms. "For instance, the philosopher asks what is injustice, the orator states that so-and-so is an unjust man: the former inquires into the nature of despotism, the latter what is a despot" (*Problems*, 956b.6–10).

Yet another point on which Aristotle converges with Plato regards the distinction between enlightened politics and rhetoric. Whereas Plato had argued that the sophists imitate the statesman and had subordinated rhetoric to knowledgeable political rule, or statesmanship (*Statesman*, 304), Aristotle claims that rhetoric, which the sophists do practice, resembles, but is not, political science. Aware that some sophists confuse rhetoric with political science while others rank rhetoric as the superior of the two (*Nicomachean Ethics*, 1181a.14–15), he asserts in no uncertain terms that these two areas of study differ at least in rank—rhetoric is subordinate to political science (*Nicomachean Ethics*, 1094b.2–3).[13] When considering the question of who should teach the science of legislation, Aristotle notes that in most other sciences it is the experts and the practitioners who do the teaching. However, in the case of politics, which includes legislation, "the sophists, who profess to teach the science [of politics] never practice it" (*Nicomachean Ethics*, 1180b.35–81a.1). Asserting that knowledge of politics requires both experience and study, Aristotle observes that "those sophists who profess to teach politics are found to be very far from doing so successfully. In fact, they are absolutely ignorant of the very nature of the science and of the subjects with which it deals" (*Nicomachean Ethics*, 1181a.12–14). As we move from Plato to Aristotle, the explicit change from statesmanship to political science, and the implicit change from practice to study should be obvious; but so should rhetoric's unchanged status. For both Plato and Aristotle, rhetoric is not simply different from politics; it is inferior to it.

Lastly, Aristotle departs from Plato's view that the sophists imitate the orator by suggesting that they, indeed, are orators.[14] In this capacity, they are said to have engaged in various practices some of which Aristotle regards as consistent with his own conception of the art of rhetoric, and some of which he does not approve. For example, he endorses Prodicus' way of waking up an audience dozing off (*Rhetoric*, 3.14.9), Gorgias' witty response to the bird that let fall her droppings upon him (*Rhetoric*, 3.3.4) and his advice to confound the opponents' earnest with jest and their jest with earnest (*Rhetoric*, 3.18.7), and Protagoras' contribution to the purity of style by using gender-specific nouns (*Rhetoric*, 3.5.5). By contrast, he disapproves of Protagoras' promise to make the weaker argument stronger and finds people's disgust with it justifiable (*Rhetoric*, 2.24.11). Likewise, he considers Gorgias' style too affected by poetry to serve adequately the purposes of prose (*Rhetoric*, 3.1.9).

Beyond his affinities with and departures from some Platonic views of the sophists, Aristotle also echoes some of Isocrates' sentiments about them as he attempts to distinguish them from other intellectuals (i.e., philosophers, dialecticians, eristics). But his remarks are marked neither by the anxiety nor the fear that the public might confuse him with ill-reputed sophists. Like Isocrates, he acknowledges that rhetoric can be used for a variety of purposes—some good, some wicked—an acknowledgement that would seem to support Isocrates' contention that all sophists are not the same. In contrast to Plato, who had seen in the art of persuasion a thoroughly corrupting force, Aristotle joins Isocrates in approving rhetorical know-how not only for its usefulness in advancing one's positions and defending oneself symbolically but also for its capacity to counteract rhetoric's unfair uses.[15] Lastly, he argues, like Isocrates, that the fact that some people misuse rhetoric does not constitute a grounds on which to denounce the art.[16] Beyond these commonalities, Aristotle differs from Isocrates in at least two important respects. First, he seeks neither to justify his own intellectual activities, nor to distance himself from inferior educators, nor to assess the sophists' overall impact on the Hellenic culture. Instead, he searches for what we would call disciplinary rules in several areas of study, and attempts to impose a sense of order on the existing materials of knowledge. Once he finds and organizes these rules, he then tries to determine the ways in which the sophists either observed them or did not. Second, he departs from Isocrates' view that there can be no foreknowledge of future circumstances (*Against the Sophists,* 2; *Antidosis,* 184) by asserting that future circumstances resemble past ones, an assertion that makes the future more or less knowable, if one has extensive knowledge of the past.[17] In this latter sense, he reasons that sophistical rhetoric and reasoning are not only historical data but also intellectual phenomena, which can resurface from time to time under certain conditions.

If, as we saw in the last two chapters, Plato rejected the sophists and Isocrates appropriated them, Aristotle sought to demonstrate where the sophists had erred or left matters more or less unfinished. This correcting and supplementing stance is not inconsistent with his treatment of most of his predecessors, whom, as Cope notes, he "hardly ever mentions . . . except for the purpose of finding fault."[18] The fault of the sophists in the field of rhetoric, Aristotle suggests, has been their tendency to disregard linguistic norms of proper usage and taste; in the field of argument it has been their proclivity to ignore or violate the rules of correct reasoning.[19] Their disregard of proper language and their transgressions against reason aside, the sophists did what they could, according to Aristotle, to advance the art of rhetoric; but they naturally left the task of its furtherance to their successors. Himself one of their successors, Aristotle seems to have reasoned that the sophists' rhetorical precepts needed neither to be dismissed and ridiculed, à la Plato, nor to be used selectively in order to address a set of new political realities, à la Isocrates; rather, they needed first to be taken into account as signposts of the rhetorical tradition, and second, to be elaborated and corrected.

Attempting to show how his rhetorical past had developed into the present, Aristotle situates the sophists at the early beginnings of the history of rhetoric and acknowledges his debt to them, in effect according them the kind of respect commonly due to the forefathers of a tradition. In so doing, he also places himself at the end of a long chain of development, a position carrying the obligation to extend and improve what one has inherited. This is how he puts the matter in his *Sophistical Refutations* (183b.17–34):

> In all discoveries, either the results of other people's work have been taken over and after having been first elaborated have been subsequently advanced step by step by those who took them over, or else they are original inventions which usually make progress which at first is small but of much greater utility than the later development which results from them. It is perhaps a true proverb

which says that the beginning of anything is the most important; hence it is also the most difficult. For as it is very powerful in its effects, so it is very small in size and therefore very difficult to see. When, however, the first beginning has been discovered, it is easier to add to it and develop the rest. This has happened, too, with rhetorical composition (περὶ τοὺς ῥητορικοὺς λόγους), and also practically with all the other arts. Those who discovered the beginnings of rhetoric carried them forward quite a little way, whereas the famous modern professors of the art, entering into the heritage, so to speak, of a long series of predecessors who had gradually advanced it, have brought it to its present perfection—Tisias following the first inventors, Thrasymachus following Tisias, Theodorus following Thrasymachus, while numerous others have made numerous contributions; hence it is no wonder that the art possesses a certain amplitude (πλῆθος).

Amplitude, however, does not mean completion or adequacy; rather, it means, at least in this case, a wide availability of materials from which to choose and many options to consider while rearticulating one's heritage and giving it a new direction. Cognizant of the tradition he had stepped into, and seemingly indebted to the sophists, Aristotle takes it upon himself to further the rhetorical art and thus make his own contribution to it. Generally embodied in his *Rhetoric*, his contribution consists of a new arrangement of the available precepts to date, and a bold step in a theoretical direction. But in addition to its novelty, Aristotle's elaboration is illustrated and given legitimacy by means of a multitude of citations from Homer, the tragedians, the sophists, and the orators—citations suggesting that his views about rhetoric are well grounded in the discursive practices of both his ancestors and his contemporaries.[20] However, what he has to say about sophistical rhetoric goes beyond his celebrated treatise, and finds itself in many of his other works including the *Topics*, especially Book Nine (*On Sophistical Refutations*), the *Ethics*, the *Politics*, and the *Poetics*.[21] The same holds about his comments on individual sophists—they are to be found not only in the *Rhetoric* but, as with Plato and Isocrates, dispersed throughout his corpus. Therefore, any study seeking to understand Aristotle's reception of sophistical rhetoric needs to examine Aristotle's works in their entirety.

Considered together, the above comments suggest that in Aristotle's mind the sophists' contributions to the art of discourse, however minimal or inadequate, must be valued because they at least stimulated further developments and shaped the understanding of subsequent thinkers and practitioners. Even if their views may seem somewhat odd or superficial to their successors, the sophists are not to be dismissed. Because early investigations are always problematic,[22] and because subsequent generations are usually the beneficiaries of such investigations, the proper attitude toward the early contributors to an art is gratitude:

> It is only fair to be grateful not only to those whose views we can share but also to those who have expressed rather superficial opinions. They too have contributed something; by their preliminary work they have formed our mental experience. If there had been no Timotheus, we should not possess much of our music; and if there had been no Phrynis, there would have been no Timotheus. It is just the same in the case of those who have theorized about reality (τῶν περὶ τῆς ἀληθείας ἀποφηναμένων): we have derived certain views from some of them, and they in turn are indebted to others. (*Metaphysics*, 993b.12–19)

Part of Aristotle's attitude toward the sophists can be discerned by two simple and warranted changes in this passage: first, substituting "those who have theorized about reality" with "those who have done work in rhetoric," and second, extending the logic of the Phrynis-Timotheus relation to read as follows: "If there had been no sophists, we should not possess much of our rhetoric; and if there had been no sophists, there would have been no Aristotle." Inasmuch, then, as the sophists were among the earliest practitioners and teachers of rhetoric, their initial observations are credited with having influenced the thinking of their successors, including that of Aristotle. But what sounds historically worthwhile to Aristotle the overviewer of the early days of rhetoric appears inferior to Aristotle the critic of discourse. Interestingly, what makes the sophists' views worthy and inferior at the same time is the same thing: their preliminariness. Preliminary discoveries, for Aristotle, are almost inherently tentative, incomplete, and inadequate. By contrast, subsequent ones (e.g., Aristotle's own) are more definitive, more complete, and more adequate. This is the Aristotelian system of development at work: successors generally outshine, outperform, and outdo their predecessors; or, the closer an idea or a practice is to its end, its *telos*, the better it is. Hence the general tendency of many traditional historians of rhetoric to regard Aristotle's *Rhetoric* as a refinement of previous versions of the art.

Beyond Aristotle's expressed gratitude to sophistical rhetoric, there lies the distant and impersonal discourse of a seemingly objective historian intent on describing the thinking and practices of the sophists. This discourse is complemented by that of a scientist (really, a knower) whose novel discoveries are invoked so as to straighten out the warped rules of the sophists' operations and to affirm the priority of the real over the apparent. In the *Rhetoric*, for example, Aristotle points out that the sophists had perverted the art of persuasion by relying too much on its inessential features (προσθῆκαι or τὰ ἔξω τοῦ πράγματος). As writers of technical handbooks (τέχναι), they emphasized inordinately emotional appeals, personal appearances, and stylistic techniques of delivery, but ignored enthymematic reasoning, which is the body (σῶμα) of persuasion (*Rhetoric*, 1.1.3). Further, they did not approach rhetoric methodically, that is, as an art with its own principles and rules. Because their main interest lay in practical matters and success in persuasion, they taught rhetoric not systematically but by relying on the various results of the art, not the art itself (*Sophistical Refutations*, 184a). In effect, they dealt mostly with rhetoric's countless particularities, not realizing that the totality of all these particularities does not amount to the essence of the art itself.

The same historical/critical tone is apparent in Aristotle's discussion of the sophists' studies and practices in the field of reasoning. Generally, Aristotle charges the sophists with espousing a fallacious logic and juggling with irrelevant arguments (τοῖς ἀλλοτρίοις λόγοις) (*Eudemian Ethics*, 1218b.23).[23] Like Isocrates, he notes that much of their argumentation is driven by their love of paradox. While discussing some of the difficulties arising out of the common opinions regarding virtuous behavior, Aristotle notes: "the sophists wish to show their cleverness by entrapping their adversary into a paradox, and when they are successful, the resultant chain of reasoning ends in a deadlock; the mind is fettered, being unwilling to stand still because it cannot approve the conclusion reached yet unable to go forward because it cannot untie the knot of the argument." To illustrate his point, Aristotle alludes to one of the sophists' familiar arguments, which seeks to prove that "Folly combined with Unrestraint is a virtue. It runs as follows: if a man is foolish and also unrestrained, owing to his unrestraint he does the opposite of what he believes he ought to do; but he believes that good things are bad, and that he ought not to do them; therefore he will do good things and not bad ones" (*Nicomachean Ethics*, 1146a.22–30). Aristotle refutes this argument by means of a lengthy discussion of the character of restraint and unrestraint (*Nicomachean Ethics*, 1146b.8–52a).

In addition to their paradoxical character, sophistical arguments are frequently contrary to generally held views. One such argument is that "not everything which is has come into being or is eternal" (*Topics*, 104b.25–26). Aristotle counters one part of this claim by maintaining that "everything which is generated is generated from something and by something; and by something formally identical with itself." On the basis of this thesis, which is part of his larger discussion of the priority of actuality over potentiality, he reasons that "it seems impossible that a man can be a builder if he has never built, or a harpist if he has never played a harp; because he who learns to play the harp learns by playing it, and similarly in all other cases. This was," he goes on to say, "the origin of the sophists' quibble that a man who does not know a given science will be doing that which is the object of that science, because the learner does not know the science." Aristotle responds to this sophistical quibble by observing that "since something of that which is being generated is already generated . . . presumably the learner too must possess something of that science" (*Metaphysics*, 1049b.28–50a.1). Aristotle refutes several other sophistical arguments but there is no need to list them all; nor is there any need to explore their nuances in detail. For our purpose, it suffices to say that in all his refutations the point is the same: when it comes to proper ways of reasoning, the sophists falter often.

Thus far we have seen some of the ways in which Aristotle's reception of the sophists resembles and differs from the receptions of Plato and Isocrates. We have also seen that Aristotle treats the sophists as worthy of consideration both for their early discoveries in rhetoric and their errors in reasoning. Convinced that their discoveries call for gratitude while their errors require rectitude, Aristotle attempts to redirect the rhetorical tradition and correct the sophistical mistakes in logic. In both cases, he searches for disciplinary rules whose observance promises to set both rhetoric and logic on the proper path to development. In what follows, I first present a version of Aristotle's portrait of the sophists, a portrait suggesting that they are less than philosophers. I then discuss Aristotle's *Rhetoric* as a treatise critiquing and preserving sophistical rhetoric. What I show in this discussion is

that Aristotle's modes of persuasion simultaneously criticize and preserve the sophists' rhetorical practices. At the same time, I show that
his three genres (deliberative, forensic, epideictic) perpetuate sophistical rhetoric by accommodating the logic of circumstances, the ethic
of competition, and the aesthetic of exhibition, respectively.

## Aristotle's Portrayal of the Sophists

Aristotle's portrait of the sophists is dull and uninspiring. It consists of a few definitions and several references to their epistemological claims, their rhetorical practices, their ways of reasoning, their
enterprising spirit, their motives, as well as various miscellaneous
items. Although more or less internally consistent, all these elements
of the larger picture lack brightness in color and fail to convey a vivid
impression of the sophists as men of splendor. On the other hand,
they outline with remarkable specificity and clarity the parameters
within which the sophists and their practices are to be found. In and
through his definitions of the sophist and sophistry, Aristotle manages to distinguish the sophist from other intellectuals, and sophistry
from the arts to which it bears a confusing resemblance. As we saw in
chapters 3 and 4, the public often confused rhetoric, sophistic, and
dialectic, and could not tell between sophists and philosophers or between good and bad sophists. Even so, it is doubtful that Aristotle's
comments were simply designed to put an end to public confusion
about sophistry. While such a goal cannot be precluded, his comments seem to be motivated by the wish to assert the primacy of philosophy. After all, Aristotle understands himself as a philosopher
intent on complementing and correcting the ways of the sophists.

To begin with, Aristotle notes that sophists and dialecticians resemble the philosopher but are, in fact, different from him. The main difference is as wide as that of appearance and reality: the sophists
appear to be as wise as the philosophers, and, along with the dialecticians, seem to be discussing the same subjects as the philosophers.
In Aristotle's words, "dialecticians and sophists wear the same appearance as the philosopher, for sophistry is Wisdom (σοφία) in appearance only, and dialecticians discuss all subjects, and Being is a
subject common to them all." Further distinguishing sophists and dialecticians from the philosopher, Aristotle observes that "sophistry
and dialectic are concerned with the same class of subjects as philosophy, but philosophy differs from the former in the nature of its ca-

pability and from the latter in its outlook on life. Dialectic treats as an exercise what philosophy tries to understand, and sophistry seems to be philosophy, but is not" (*Metaphysics*, 1004b.17–27).

In what seems to be an unmistakable reiteration of the Platonic separation of appearance from reality, the genuine from the counterfeit, Aristotle maintains that what the sophists do may appear to have all the features of what the philosopher does—their wisdom appears like philosophy and sounds like philosophy. But in reality sophistical and philosophical wisdom are worlds apart even though inexperienced thinkers cannot tell the difference. One of the better known practices of the sophists is refutation. Like dialecticians, they entertain their interlocutors' claims in the give-and-take of critical discussion only to refute them, thereby demonstrating their own expertise and superiority in argument. However, the principal problem with the sophistical kinds of refutation is that they are apparent, not real. In the opening lines of his *Sophistical Refutations* (164a.23–b.27), Aristotle takes the distinction between appearance and reality as a given, and then applies it to refutative arguments:

> That some reasonings are really reasonings, but that others seem to be, but are not really, reasonings, is obvious. For, as this happens in other spheres from a similarity between the true and the false, so it happens also in arguments. For some people possess good physical condition, while others have merely the appearance of it, by blowing themselves out and dressing themselves up like the tribal choruses; again some people are beautiful because of their beauty, while others have the appearance of beauty because they trick themselves out. . . . In the same way also reasoning and refutation are sometimes real and sometimes not, but appear to be real owing to men's inexperience.

Making yet another distinction between sophistry and philosophy, Aristotle points out that while the exclusive province of philosophy is to study the attributes of "Being qua Being," sophistry, like dialectic, "deal[s] with the attributes of existing things, but not of things qua Being, nor . . . of Being itself in so far as it is Being" (*Metaphysics*, 1061b.8–9). In other words, while philosophy studies what is substantive and essential, sophistry concerns itself with what is superficial and incidental. Unlike the philosopher, whose aim is to study "the whole of reality in its essential nature" (*Metaphysics*, 1005b.6–7),[24] Aristotle holds that the sophist is preoccupied with the accidental (τὸ συμβεβηκὸς), which "is only, as it were, a name." Instead of dealing with reality as it is (instead, that is, of addressing the necessity of what is), the sophist addresses the nonnecessity of what is not. Therefore, Aristotle concludes, "in a way Plato was not far from wrong in making sophistry deal with what is non-existent; because the sophists discuss the accident[al] more, perhaps, than any other people."[25] Because the accidental has no necessary connection to the essence of things, Aristotle regards it as "something closely akin to the non-existent" (*Metaphysics*, 1026b.15–22).[26] In effect, he suggests that if something happens neither always nor usually, if it is adventitious and outside the realm of necessity, we may treat it as though it did not happen at all. Alternatively, we may treat it as misleading because it resides at the surface of things whereas the essence is to be found in their core.[27]

In addition to defining the sophists by reference to their interest in appearances and their preoccupation with the accidental, Aristotle discusses them in terms of their purpose, which, he claims, distinguishes them from the dialecticians but not the rhetoricians. In the field of rhetoric, he notes, there is no distinction between one who speaks according to sound argument (κατὰ τὴν ἐπιστήμην) or to moral purpose (κατὰ τὴν προαίρεσιν). However, "in dialectic it is the moral purpose that makes the sophist, the dialectician being one whose arguments rest, not on moral purpose but on the faculty" (*Rhetoric*, 1.1.14).[28] The distinction between sophists and dialecticians is also made in *Sophistical Refutations* (171b.7–8), this time, however, in terms of the reality-appearance dichotomy: "The man who views general principles in the light of the particular case is a dialectician, while he who only apparently does this is a sophist." Again, the best a sophist can do is appear to be a dialectician.

Time and again, Aristotle claims that "the sophistic art consists in apparent and not real wisdom, and the sophist is one who makes money from apparent and not real wisdom." By contrast, the really wise man is one who tries "to refrain from fallacious arguments about the subjects of his knowledge and to be able to expose him who uses them." The wise man (the philosopher) can make money too, if he so wishes, by capitalizing on his knowledge; but generally a philosopher does not care about money.[29] What he does care about is giving sound reasons for his claims and trying to extract sound reasons from others. But if this is so, Aristotle argues, "it is essential for those who wish to play the sophist to seek out the kind of argument which we have mentioned [the kind that gives reasons or refutes]; for it is well worth his while, since the possession of such a faculty [the faculty of reason-giving and refuting] will cause him to appear to be wise, and this is the real purpose which sophists have in view" (*Sophistical Refutations*, 165a.22–32).

Clearly, Aristotle's wise man is not content simply to offer real proofs of what he claims; he also tries to expose the apparentness of the apparently wise, that is, the sophist. As we saw in the last chapter, this is precisely what Isocrates had tried to do, and thought that he had failed in more ways than one. This is also what Aristotle himself tries to accomplish in several of his works, especially in *Sophistical Refutations*. But rather than speak about his superiority over the sophists, something that Isocrates had done, Aristotle first works out a calculus of reasoning (i.e., *Analytics* and *Topics*) and then shows the ways in which they do not measure up to it.[30] In this sense, he may be judged wiser than Isocrates. But even Aristotle ultimately falls short of the goal of an air-tight distinction between the real and the apparent reasoner. For there is nothing to prevent the sophist from appearing to be doing for real all the things a wise thinker would be expected to do. Conversely, there is nothing to prevent the perception that a so-called wise thinker is only practicing another form of apparent wisdom. Finally, as Aristotle himself observes, "there is nothing to prevent a man [from] accepting what are not facts rather than the truth" (*Topics*, 161a.31). But if this is so, Aristotle can only be said to have taken refuge in the domain of a reality he considered superior to that of the sophists.

In this Aristotelian reality, reasoning and refutation are thought out well (without inconsistencies and contradictions) and carried out exactly.[31] By contrast, the kind of reasoning or refutation sophistry employs is not only apparent but also irrelevant: "By sophistical reasonings and refutations I mean not only the seeming but unreal reasoning or refutation but also one which, though real, only seems to be, but is not really, germane to the subject at hand."[32] Sophistry, in other words, often brings into a discussion irrelevant materials — materials not pertaining to the subject under consideration.[33] In doing so, it may succeed in contradicting the man under examination, but it does not "make clear whether he is ignorant." Aristotle maintains that a question-and-answer procedure should engage the ignorant and should seek to expose their ignorance. The sophists, however, do not limit themselves to the ignorant; they also try to en-trap (ἐμποδίζουσι) with sophistical arguments "even the man of sci-entific knowledge" (τὸν εἰδότα) (*Sophistical Refutations*, 169b.20–29).[34] Employing fallacies connected with the accidental (τὸ συμβεβηκὸς), they often succeed in creating the impression that they have refuted even the specialists and the experts: "they argue with the men of sci-ence with reasonings based on accident, and the latter, being incapa-ble of making distinctions, either give in when questioned, or think they have done so when they have not" (*Sophistical Refutations*, 169b.7–10).

Aristotle's attempts to specify as clearly as possible who the soph-ists are and what they do leads him to distinguish them from yet an-other class of pseudo-intellectuals: the eristics. While both classes are interested in semblances and winning intellectual contests through similar arguments, the eristics are after victory (νίκη) while the soph-ists are after an impressive reputation (δόξα). As Aristotle puts it, "those who behave like this (fighting unfairly in argument) merely to win a victory, are generally regarded as contentious and quarrelsome (ἐριστικοὶ ἄνθρωποι καὶ φιλέριδες), while those who do so to win a reputation which will help them to make money are regarded as sophistical." The difference between eristics and sophists, then, lies in their motives: "Quarrelsome people [eristics] and sophists use the same arguments, but not for the same reasons; and the same ar-gument will be sophistical and contentious but not from the same point of view. If the semblance of victory is the motive, it is conten-tious; if the semblance of wisdom, it is sophistical; for sophistry is an appearance of wisdom without the reality" (*Sophistical Refutations*, 171b.25–34).

Having distinguished the sophists from dialecticians, philosophers, and eristics, Aristotle gives several examples of their reasoning, which he generally finds erroneous. One of their argumentative prac-tices is to exaggerate the principle of identity and thus deny that "Ko-riscos" is the same as "good Koriscos" (*Eudemian Ethics*, 1240b.24–25). In effect, they argue that there is a difference between the individual thing and its essence, an argument which Aristotle disposes of by maintaining that at least "in the case of primary and self-subsistent terms, the individual thing and its essence are one and the same." Then he goes on: "It is obvious that the sophistical objections to this thesis [identity of the individual thing and its essence] are met in the same way as the question whether Socrates is the same as the essence of Socrates; for there is no difference either in the grounds of asking the question or in the means of meeting it successfully" (*Metaphysics*, 1032a.6–11).

Another argumentative practice the sophists engage in is to respond to questions demanding specificity by answering: "Partly yes and partly no," "Some are but some are not," "In one sense it is so, in another not." But when someone responds thus (that is, sophistically), Aristotle reports that "the hearers cry out against him as being in difficulty" (*Rhetoric*, 3.18.4). This may be an indirect criticism of the notion of *dissoi logoi*, a notion in whose spirit the sophists were making double and opposing responses even when the request was for a single answer. It may also suggest Aristotle's solution to the problem of the doubleness of discourse: of any two opposing answers, one is always superior to the other. In either case, it is noteworthy that Aristotle himself engages in the same sophistical practice when addressing the meaning of now in his discussion of time and motion: "the 'now,' which is identical everywhere, itself *retains its identity in one sense, but does not in another* [my emphasis]; for inasmuch as the point in the flux of time which it marks is changing (and so to mark it is its essential function) the 'now' too differs perpetually, but inasmuch as at every moment it is performing its essential function of dividing the past and future it retains its identity" (*Physics*, 219b.13–15). To support his point that a thing can retain its identity and also be different (in terms of its relations), Aristotle refers to the sophistical argument that distinguishes "between Koriscos in the Lyceum and Koriscos in the market-place" (*Physics*, 219b.21–22).

Yet another sophistical practice Aristotle mentions, in fact he calls it "the most sophistical of all frauds" (τὸ μάλιστα σοφιστικὸν συκοφάντημα), is the one which questioners use often and which "produces a striking appearance of refutation, when, though they have proved nothing, they do not put the final proposition in the form of a question but state conclusively, as though they had proved it, that 'such and such a thing, then, is not the case'" (*Sophistical Refutations*, 174b.9–12). This practice is labeled sophistical because it does not follow the proper procedure (instead of asking a question, it makes a statement) and because it does not meet the criteria of proof.

Having exposed the weaknesses of sophistical reasoning, Aristotle next questions the knowledge the sophists profess to possess and impart. In his estimation, the sophists can be said to know only accidentally (κατὰ τὸ συμβεβηκὸς); the true causation and necessity of things, the two things knowledge consists of, generally escape them. "We consider that we have unqualified knowledge of anything (as contrasted with the accidental knowledge of the sophist) when we believe that we know (i) that the cause from which the fact results is the cause of that fact, and (ii) that the fact cannot be otherwise" (*Posterior Analytics*, 71b.9–12). However, this conceptualization of knowledge is foreign to the sophists, who believe that to know is to have knowledge (τὸ ἐπίστασθαι τὸ ἐπιστήμην ἔχειν) (*Posterior Analytics*, 74b.23). Accordingly, they assume they know something if the premises of their starting point are generally accepted and true. However, Aristotle objects, "the starting-point is not that which is generally accepted or the reverse, but that which is primarily true of the genus with which the demonstration deals; and not every true fact is peculiar to a given genus" (*Posterior Analytics*, 74b.24–25). Because the sophists' knowledge is questionable, Aristotle observes, they demand their fees in advance; otherwise, "nobody would pay money for the knowledge which they possess" (*Nicomachean Ethics*, 1164a.32). The one exception to this financial arrangement, was Protagoras, who "used to tell his pupil to estimate the value he set upon his knowledge, and accepted a fee of that amount" (*Nicomachean Ethics*, 1164a.25–27). This way, he avoided facing complaints from students about not meeting his promises and not fulfilling his part of the educational bargain.

Finally, Aristotle critiques the sophists' use of language by charging them with using it improperly.[35] Their attempts to refute their opponents and create false illusions are characterized by such linguistic fallacies as "equivocation (ὁμωνυμία), ambiguity (ἀμφιβολία), combination (σύνθεσις), division (διαίρεσις), accent (προσῳδία), and form of expression (σχῆμα λέξεως)" (*Sophistical Refutations*, 165b.25–27). In and through these fallacious forms of language, the sophists succeed in creating the impression of refuting their opponents and in victimizing those inexperienced in the power of names (τῶν ὀνομάτων τῆς δυνάμεως) (*Sophistical Refutations*, 165a.17). In effect, the sophists exploit not only the malleability but also the inadequacy of language, the fact that it does not have a name for every single thing: "names and a quantity of terms are finite, whereas things are infinite in number; and so the same expression and the single name must necessarily signify a number of things" (*Sophistical Refutations*, 165a.11–14). Assuming that understanding requires that one know exactly which one thing out of a number is signified, Aristotle suggests that the sophists often frustrate their interlocutors' understanding by using names and expressions signifying more than one thing. In this regard, he notes that they often use homonyms (*Rhetoric*, 3.2.7; *Sophistical Refutations*, 165b.30–66a.6). Aristotle discusses the six fallacies that depend on language, offers examples of each, and proposes that the way to combat them is to advance "the opposite of that on which the argument [at hand] turns" (*Sophistical Refutations*, 179a.11–13).

On a more specific note, Aristotle takes issue with the claim of Bryson, the sophist, that "there is no such thing as foul language, because in whatever words you put a given thing your meaning is the same." Aristotle counters:

> This is untrue. One term may describe a thing more truly than another, may be more like it, and set it more intimately before our eyes. Besides, two different words will represent a thing in two different lights; so on this ground also one term must be held fairer or fouler than another. For both of two terms will indicate what *is* fair, or what *is* foul, but not simply their fairness or foulness, or if so, at any rate not in an equal degree. (*Rhetoric*, 3.2.13)

In this brief section, we have encountered Aristotle the philosopher and logician claiming that the sophists are mainly concerned with appearances, not reality. Their main subject of interest is neither the necessary nor the characteristic but the accidental. Their conception of knowledge is wrong, and much of their discourse contains linguistic as well as logical fallacies. Rather than address topics in their essence, they often discuss irrelevancies, matters beside the point. Interested more in apparent refutation than real proof, they seldom give reasons for their claims. Lastly, their love of paradox leads them to craft arguments against common sense and to disregard the proper uses of language.

### From Sophistical to Aristotelian Rhetoric

Thus far in this chapter, we have looked at Aristotle's historical/ critical treatment of the sophists and their discursive practices. What we have seen is two Aristotelian pictures: one sketching the sophists as early pioneers of and significant contributors to the rhetorical tradition, the other depicting them as philosophical pretenders whose pretenses can be exposed if one inquires into the logical structure of their argumentative practices. The attitudes behind these two pictures find further and more focused expression in Aristotle's *Rhetoric*, a work purporting to advance a new and superior version of rhetoric and to provide a theoretical ground for all rhetorical practices. In order, then, to get a more complete sense of Aristotle's understanding of the sophists, we turn our attention to the way in which he treats them in his *Rhetoric*. As we will see, Aristotle not only critiques sophistical rhetoric there; he also preserves and perpetuates it.

The *Rhetoric* has been hailed by many commentators as "the most admired monument of ancient rhetoric,"[36] a treatise with a great "deal of influence throughout the ages,"[37] a book that "stands apart and pre-eminent even where the predecessors and the successors are so numerous; it is the most philosophical (or, scientific) work ever produced on the subject."[38] While the praise heaped on the *Rhetoric* is nearly universal, its relation to the sophistical tradition is a contested issue. Some commentators have observed that Aristotle's treatise represents an attempt to break from the sophists. Cooper, for example, notes that the *Rhetoric* "is absolutely free from the Greek Sophistical tradition."[39] Similarly, Grimaldi points out that Aristotle's effort was "to free rhetoric from what is called the demagoguery of the Sophists with their crude appeal to the emotional (and irrational) in man and to dignify it as a discipline of the mind which is so much more becoming to the rational man."[40] Others, however, have suggested that these claims are unwarranted. Kennedy, for example, finds that the *Rhetoric* "draws heavily on sophistical rhetoric,"[41] something he attributes to Aristotle's "increased interest in the nature of existing practice and much less desire to impose an ideal system upon contemporary life."[42] Similarly, it is Solmsen's view that in some sections of the *Rhetoric* Aristotle "does little more than endorse the time-honored devices . . . which experts [sophistical or otherwise] 'use' to their own advantage."[43] The disparity of these two kinds of judgments about the *Rhetoric* is not difficult to explain: some of the commentators have paid attention only to Aristotle's sensitivity to tradition, others only to his commitment to innovation. But as we suggested earlier, Aristotle is both indebted to and critical of the sophists; he recognizes both their contributions to the rhetorical art as well as their shortcomings.

Aristotle's critical attitude toward his predecessors, including the sophists, is reflected in the opening lines of the *Rhetoric*: "previous compilers of 'Arts' of Rhetoric have provided us with only a small portion of this art," a portion that is neither technologically sound (ἔντεχνον) nor grounded in the essence (σῶμα) of the art. The things these compilers discuss constitute accessories (προσθῆκαι) that fall outside the subject proper (τὰ ἔξω τοῦ πράγματος). These rhetoricians, Aristotle goes on, fail to realize that the only artistic things in rhetoric are the modes of persuasion (πίστεις); moreover, they tell us nothing about enthymemes, the very substance (σῶμα) of the modes (*Rhetoric*, 1.1.3). These introductory remarks accomplish two goals: first, they identify a need which Aristotle's treatise promises to address, a gap which is about to be filled; second, they provide the reader with the expectation that what follows will concern itself with the modes of persuasion, which revolve around the enthymeme. But while the *Rhetoric* does meet the reader's expectations, it does so only partially. In what seems to be a deviation from its initially announced plan, the text as we have it also discusses some of the very things Aristotle locates outside the proper province of rhetoric (emotional appeals, style, delivery). Accordingly, his suggestion that his predecessors had missed rhetoric's core and had opted for its surface, that they had limited their instruction to its circumference leaving its center out of account, has puzzled readers who take his opening remarks at face value.[44]

Elaborating on the modes of persuasion, Aristotle notes that persuasion happens by virtue of *ethos* (the orator's moral character as exhibited by his speech), *pathos* (the hearers' emotional state as produced by the speech), and *logos* (the speech itself as it establishes what is true or apparently so) (*Rhetoric*, 1.2.4–6). These modes extend Aristotle's critique of the sophists' rhetorical practices by continuing his attack on their reasoning (logos) while adding to it two new elements — ethos and pathos. Since we have already dealt with some of the senses of Aristotle's understanding of logos as reasoning or proof, the following comments will mainly focus on the other two modes. About logos we need only mention here that it is the only mode that partakes of both philosophy and rhetoric; the other two belong to rhetoric only. Treating logos in its rhetorical sense, Aristotle notes that it consists of two elements — the enthymeme and the example. As one might expect from a philosopher writing about rhetoric, Aristotle explains these two elements in terms of their dialectical counterparts — the syllogism and induction (*Rhetoric*, 1.1.11; 2.8–11).

Because ethos comes out in the orator's speech, because one's character is reflected in what one utters, and because one is ultimately what one says, those who are perceived as dishonest, nonsensical, or selfish will generally fail to persuade their listeners. Clearly, the assumption here is that speech and character are closely related. It is an assumption Isocrates had stated explicitly in his *Nicocles* (7) when he said that "the power to speak well is taken as the surest index of a sound understanding, and discourse which is true and lawful and just is the outward image of a good and faithful soul." Stated negatively, this assumption would naturally indicate the exact opposite: bad speaking is an index of unsound understanding, and discourse which is untrue, unlawful, and unjust is the outward image of an evil and unfaithful soul. But stated in reverse, it would suggest that an evil and unfaithful soul (which is Aristotle's bad character) would express itself in untrue, unlawful, and unjust speech.

Aristotle's emphasis on ethos—which for him may be the most persuasive of the three modes (κυριωτάτην ἔχει πίστιν τὸ ἦθος) (*Rhetoric*, 1.2.4)—would seem to handicap the rhetorical practice of those who are generally perceived to be untrustworthy, ignorant, and duplicitous, that is, those whose character is questionable. Here it should be recalled that this was precisely the perception of the sophists by most people. As we saw earlier, they were viewed as untrustworthy on account of their foreign origin and itinerant status, ignorant of certain subjects requiring expertise, and dishonest in the light of their reputedly unkept promises. From this public perception to the dismissal of their rhetoric was only a small distance away. Because the sophists' character was questionable, the value of their rhetoric could not be far from being the same. Conversely, if their character was thought to be shady, it was because their rhetoric was not what it should have been. If we can generalize from Aristotle's comment on Protagoras (people were disgusted with his promise to make the weaker argument stronger) (*Rhetoric*, 2.24.11), the sophists' tainted reputation was formulated justly (δικαίως); they received the reputation they did because they deserved it.

To his credit, Aristotle insists that ethos should be acquired, not antecedent. We should judge an orator on the basis of his particular address, not his general reputation which precedes him (διὰ τὸν λόγον, ἀλλὰ μὴ διὰ τὸ προδεδοξάσθαι ποιόν τινα εἶναι τὸν λέγοντα) (*Rhetoric*, 1.2.4). The speaker's reputation, in other words, should be put aside when listening to a specific oration. In this regard, Aristotle maintains that any one orator should be given a fair hearing when speaking. Even so, he must have known quite well that reputation did play a significant role in the way a speaker was received and judged by his audience. Despite his theoretical position, then, he in effect puts before the sophists of his time a sizeable obstacle: to rehabilitate their bad reputation. But if one's bad reputation cannot be dispensed with entirely, rehabilitation is virtually impossible; and if it can, the sophists are being asked to practice Aristotle's version of rhetoric.

What complicates the discussion of reputation is the fact that most of our accounts represent the sophists as formidable speakers and successful persuaders. If we believe these accounts, we would have to conclude that their audiences were willing to suspend their doubts about them, or that the sophists could overcome their reputation by means of their performances, or that a bad reputation does not necessarily interfere with one's capacity to persuade. In Aristotelian terms, the sophists' success was, at least in part, due to their ability to manipulate language so as to create the impression in their listeners that they were honest, sensible, and well-disposed toward their audiences. By virtue of their linguistic dexterity, in other words, they were able to present themselves as meeting the three elements of rhetorical ethos, φρόνησις καὶ ἀρετὴ καὶ εὔνοια (good sense, virtue, and good will) (Rhetoric, 2.1.5). But if this is so, the sophists were not far from practicing what Aristotle was preaching. The only difference is that while he saw ethos reflected in and preceding language, they viewed ethos as a creation of language.[45] For his part, Aristotle, despite his effort to construct a rhetorical theory from which the sophistic types would be excluded, could not get away from their notion that it is one's speech which is responsible for the perception of one's character, not the other way around. Accordingly, he concedes that "it is not only necessary to consider how to make the speech itself demonstrative and convincing, but also that the speaker should show himself to be of a certain character" (Rhetoric, 2.1.2). This concession is of considerable magnitude because it grants, if only implicitly, that in rhetoric being a good character matters less than appearing to be so; or that unless one can produce time and again the appearance of being a good person, one will most likely fail in one's rhetorical endeavors. In the domain of rhetoric, being a good person is simply not sufficient; one must also create the appearance of being good. However, and this is where the sophists cannot be dismissed easily, the creation of such an appearance is largely an accomplishment of language, which, as we have seen, can work by representing not only that which is but also that which is not.

But if this is so, language can represent an ignorant, immoral, and self-centered orator as a knowledgeable, moral, and altruistic one. In other words, polished orators can speak so as to misrepresent their true character. Conversely, poor orators may fail to represent their character accurately. In both cases, the language of a speaker can fail: in the first instance, the listeners, and in the second, the speaker. Aristotle, who must have been aware of this issue, has no solution to offer except faith—faith that "things that are true and things that are better are, by their nature, practically always easier to believe in" (*Rhetoric*, 1.1.12). In an Aristotelian world, the orator's true character, be it good or wicked, will sooner or later surface and be seen as that which it is.

The case of pathos as the second mode of persuasion is also problematic, but for different reasons. To begin with, Aristotle charges in his opening polemic against his predecessors that much of their energy was directed at the techniques of arousing emotions such as prejudice, pity, and anger (*Rhetoric*, 1.1.4 and 9). The objection to such an emphasis on emotional appeals, according to Aristotle, is that it is misplaced. Properly speaking, one should focus on the particular issue itself, and disregard everything extrinsic to it. Accordingly, in the case of forensic rhetoric "the only business of the litigant is to prove that the fact in question is or is not so, that it has happened or not" (*Rhetoric*, 1.1.6). Similarly, in political rhetoric "the only thing necessary is to prove the truth of the statement of one who recommends a measure" (*Rhetoric*, 1.1.10). Worse than falling outside the proper domain of rhetoric, emotional appeals inevitably tend to skew the judge's judgment. Aristotle recognizes that people's emotional frame of mind affects the way they make decisions: "opinions vary, according as men love or hate, are wrathful or mild, and things appear altogether different, or different in degree; for when a person is favorably disposed towards one on whom he is passing judgement, he either thinks that the accused has committed no wrong at all or that his offense is trifling; but if he hates him, the reverse is the case" (*Rhetoric*, 2.1.4). But despite this acknowledgement, he insists that judgment, especially in legal matters, should be made with a cool and fully rational mind. For this to happen, the litigants should stay with the facts of the case. Whether these facts are "important or unimportant, just or unjust . . . is a matter for the dicast himself to decide; it is not the business of the litigants to instruct him" (*Rhetoric*, 1.1.6).

Seemingly going against his own objections about the orators' common practice of manipulating the feelings of their listeners, Aristotle also maintains that "the speaker should know how to put the judge into a certain frame of mind" (τὸν κριτὴν κατασκευάζειν) (*Rhetoric*,

2.1.2). This is so because the way the listeners are disposed toward the speaker himself makes a great difference when it comes to rhetorical persuasion (*Rhetoric*, 2.1.3); so much so, in fact, that Aristotle deems it necessary to devote ten chapters of his *Rhetoric* to a discussion of the emotions. At this point one might wonder: Does Aristotle have a double attitude regarding the role the emotions play in rhetorical discourse? If emotional appeals are outside the proper sphere of rhetoric, and if they pervert the judgment of the listeners, why does he spend so much time and space discussing their nature, objects, and grounds? In what way is he being critical of the sophists? Is he adding anything new to their thinking on passionate appeals in rhetoric or is he simply rephrasing it? Last, is there such a thing as a language devoid of all emotional content?

Before answering these questions, we should recall here that long before Aristotle, Gorgias had advanced an elaborate view of the impact of logos on the emotionality of its listeners. In his *Encomium of Helen*, Gorgias had observed that when listeners are charmed and bewitched by the orator's logos they lose their rational faculties and act in irrational ways. According to this view, emotions oppose reason and compel people who feel them intensely to act as if they were insane. In addition to this Gorgianic view, Aristotle must have known something of the precepts that Thrasymachus had articulated in his treatise on pathos, Eleoi (*Rhetoric*, 3.1.7); and he also must have known Plato's view of Thrasymachus as a master of emotional speech: "For tearful speeches, to arouse pity for old age and poverty, I think the precepts of the mighty Chalcedonian hold the palm, and he is also a genius . . . at rousing large companies to wrath, and soothing them again by his charms when they are angry, and most powerful in devising and abolishing calumnies on any grounds whatsoever" (*Phaedrus*, 267c–d).

Together, these two sophistical views suggest that to be an orator means to realize that human beings are roused by certain linguistic utterances and calmed by others. By extension, a successful orator is one who can manipulate language so as to make audiences feel in ways that render a given message more acceptable. Gorgias and Thrasymachus, then, privilege speech and the orator, respectively, while putting the audience at the mercy of two powerful forces against which it cannot resist. Aristotle, however, sought to subject the emotions to reason thereby turning them into a cognitive matter. There are reasons, he argued, why people feel the emotions they do, and knowledge of these reasons enables them to think rationally about their feelings or the orator's rhetoric seeking to excite or pacify them. In this regard, Fortenbaugh is correct when he observes that

> Aristotle developed a view of emotion that made clear the necessary involvement of cognition in emotional response. . . . Far from being hostile to reason, emotions are amenable to reason so that an orator can arouse and allay emotion while presenting reasoned arguments. . . . It is to Aristotle's credit that he pointed out the occurrence of judgment in emotional response and promoted persuasion "through the hearers" to a position coordinate with persuasion "through demonstration."[46]

While, then, Aristotle can be said to have criticized the sophists by subordinating human emotions to reason, he nevertheless preserves their realization that emotional response plays a significant role in rhetorical persuasion.

Even so, he still insists, in his discussion of delivery, that the orator's language should ideally be rational and strive only to prove his point: "as a matter of right, one should aim at nothing more in a speech than how to avoid exciting pain or pleasure. For justice should consist in fighting the case with the facts alone, so that everything else that is beside demonstration is superfluous" (τἆλλα ἔξω τοῦ ἀποδεῖξαι περίεργα ἐστίν) (Rhetoric, 3.1.5). According to this line of thinking, such things as style, delivery, and acting, necessary as they might be, are simply accessory to the rhetorical act for they are meant to charm the listeners. To support his claim, Aristotle, in one of the least convincing lines of the Rhetoric, observes that no one teaches geometry by using an ornate style or dramatic delivery (Rhetoric, 3.1.6). Therefore, those who put a premium on stylistic and performative considerations demonstrate their disregard of the language of rational proof.

As we have seen, Aristotle's modes of persuasion constitute, at least in part, a critique of sophistical rhetoric, a rhetoric that, according to him, paid no attention to the logical integrity of the oration, neglected the role of the orator's character in persuasion, and focused mainly on the manipulation of the listeners' emotions, which it treated as irrational forces. However, Aristotle's critique could go only so far for he ultimately had to acknowledge that all three modes are a function of language.[47] Language, that is, can be spoken so as to give the impression of proof, create the image of personal goodness, and produce the desired emotional state in one's listeners. Such an acknowledgement, however, amounts to a preservation of the very thing critiqued. Insofar as Aristotle accounts for success in persuasion, and insofar as the sophists were successful in their rhetorical practices, they must have been practicing a rhetoric akin to the one he prescribes. Aristotle, then, preserves sophistical rhetoric not only by illustrating several of his principles with examples from the sophists, but also—since, as he says, this is not an ideal world—by incorporating part of the circumstantial logic of their practice into the discourse of the *Rhetoric*. This is even more pronounced in his classification of rhetoric according to its genres.

Aristotle's division of rhetorical discourse into three kinds (deliberative, forensic, epideictic) is predicated on his observation that there are three kinds of listeners: critics, judges, and spectators (*Rhetoric*, 1.3.1–3). But to say that there are three kinds of listeners is to recognize, if only tacitly, that people learn how to be listeners of public discourse by frequenting the places and attending the occasions in which rhetoric typically takes place: the Assembly, the courts, and festivals. On the assumption that these human institutions were more or less permanent and that situations calling for a specific kind of rhetoric recurred frequently, Aristotle's three rhetorical genres are not simply categories in an abstract system of classification of rhetorical discourse but a restatement of the sophists' earlier realization that rhetoric shapes and is shaped by people's responses to circumstances (deliberative), their engagement in symbolic competition (forensic), and their participation in verbal exhibitions (epideictic). Even so, Aristotle does not join the sophists all the way. Circumstances, competitions, and exhibitions do shape rhetoric but they turn it into an open-ended proposition and a matter of happenstance without preventing it from being practiced randomly or habitually. If, however, rhetoric is conceptualized as a *techne* and treated systematically, it becomes obvious that rhetoric is determined by the audiences it addresses, which also means the places in which it happens and the purposes it serves. Thus the Assembly and an audience assembled to deliberate demand a rhetoric different from the one expected by a court and an audience gathered to adjudicate, and still different from the one anticipated by a festival and an audience brought together to celebrate. But if this is so, orators need to go beyond the sophistries of charming language, intriguing words, and clever phrases meant to please—these sophistries disregard the formal demands of the forums in which they are uttered. What they need to do is master the topics inherent to the particular kinds of rhetoric they practice. More specifically, deliberative orators should know the main topics of deliberation (ways and means, war and peace, the defense of the country, imports and exports, and legislation) (*Rhetoric*, 1.6.7–13), the components of happiness (1.5.1–17; the commonly held views regarding the expedient, the good, and the pleasant as well as the different forms of government (1.4–8). By extension, forensic orators should know about the human motives behind unjust actions, the mental states of those who act unjustly, and the dispositions of victims of injustice (1.10.2). Finally, epideictic orators should know about virtue and vice, the noble and the disgraceful (1.9). But regardless of their specialty, all orators should take into account the two main factors of human motivation — necessity and the desire for pleasure. This is so because each factor can be said to constitute one of the two poles of a continuum that characterizes all rhetorical discourse. Deliberative rhetoric is closest to necessity because people are driven by the imperative to action to respond to the particular circumstances they face. Epideictic is closest to pleasure because people listen to it in order to be diverted and entertained by the rhetorical performance of the orator. As for forensic, it occupies a middle position between necessity and pleasure. It is necessary because a society needs to adjudicate conflicts between its people and enforce its version of justice; and it is pleasant because a trial often resembles a competitive event in which the jurors participate by "listening merely for their own pleasure" (*Rhetoric*, 1.1.10).

Clearly, then, Aristotle departs from sophistical thinking by arguing that it is not enough to be informally attuned to the larger cultural currents or the more specific societal and political issues facing the citizenry; nor is it enough to treat every rhetorical utterance in the manner of the sophists, as a temporary and unique phenomenon. What orators need to do is address issues in their topicality and typicality. We have already suggested the case for rhetoric's topicality by mentioning some of the topics inherent in the three genres of rhetoric. What makes the case for its typicality is the fact that instances of deliberation, adjudication, and celebration occur time and again. People's life in the polis demands that they deliberate, adjudicate, and celebrate repeatedly. But if this is so, rhetoricians should attend to the typical features of these repeated situations. What this will enable them to do is address a variety of occasions and circumstances intelligently, and defend against the circumstantial exigencies and situational vagaries that may characterize an unprecedented occurrence. Put another way, a theoretically informed orator is able to place a single case within a larger context, a context that helps render the case meaningful. By contrast, an orator who approaches a case in its uniqueness and particularity runs the risk of getting entangled in a myriad of details and uttering an unintelligible message.

Regardless of an orator's approach to a particular case, public rhetoric concerns itself with deliberation. In his discussion of listeners and types of discourse, Aristotle explains that members of the Assembly deliberate about matters pertaining to the future, court judges about matters of the past, and spectators about the rhetorical ability of the orator. In all three instances, people deliberate because certain things "admit of issuing in two ways" (ἐνδέχεσθαι ἀμφοτέρως ἔχειν) (Rhetoric, 1.2.12).[48] In and through this observation, Aristotle can be said to be endorsing, at least partially, the doubleness of discourse as expounded by Protagoras' doctrine of *dissoi logoi*. If something can be both this way and that, and if only one of these two options can be exercised, one needs to weigh the two alternatives against one another—this is the essence of deliberation. But if among the things that "admit of issuing in two ways" we include language itself, it follows that people deliberate not only about the things language represents but also about the very language to which they are exposed, that is, whether it is appropriate, fitting, clear, telling, rich, plain, elegant, forceful. Aristotle's discussion of the duality of some things can also be said to be identifying the difficulties of deliberation as illustrated in Prodicus' story of *Heracles at the Crossroads*. If one is shown at least two ways of getting to a goal, one has to decide which of the two to take. Similarly, in the case of forensic and epideictic rhetoric, if the available options are reduced to two—guilty or not guilty, praiseworthy or blameworthy—one has to choose the one and not the other. But if deliberation takes place across rhetorical genres, and if people must deliberate about language, deliberation always amounts to an issue of choice among at least two alternatives. But to choose one alternative of two or more is to opt for one kind of language over another.

Generally for Aristotle, people listen to the orators because it helps them deliberate about things for which they have no systematic rules (*Rhetoric*, 1.2.12). Insofar as the circumstances at hand are the result of necessity or regularity, the orator has some prior knowledge of their characteristics and can therefore recommend reasonable courses of action, courses consistent with the past; but insofar as they are accidental or unprecedented, the orator has no guidelines to go by. In this regard, it is at least noteworthy that in his discussion of deliberation, Aristotle treats only those circumstances that happen necessarily or regularly (hence his formulation of rhetorical genres). The rest he assigns to the category of the accidental (τὸ συμβεβηκὸς), a category that, because it is infinite, cannot be treated systematically. Accordingly, he confines himself to the most usual and important subjects over which people deliberate, subjects which the orator must command. By contrast, the sophists had asserted that there are no limits to the orator's capacity for address.[49]

The fact that Aristotle restates sophistical rhetoric, even as he reformulates it to fit his own intellectual orientation, does not mean that he endorses the sophistical criteria of rhetorical discourse (opportunity, playfulness, possibility). On the contrary, he works out his own criteria of propriety, superiority, and actuality. Rhetoric for Aristotle is not so much a matter of kairotic opportunity as of propriety dictated by the rules of logic, communal norms of linguistic usage, and the essential nature of institutions and audiences. As such, the orator needs to say things appropriate for the Assembly, a court, or a festival and their respective audiences; and the best help for what to say in these forums comes from precedent, what others in similar circumstances have said in the past. Second, rhetoric's aim is not playfulness in itself but victory. This means that the orator should speak so as to be judged victorious over his opponent. The only guide here is speaking about things that are true and just not only because they have the tendency to prevail over their opposites (φύσει εἶναι κρείττω τἀληθῆ καὶ τὰ δίκαια τῶν ἐναντίων), but also because they are easier to prove and easier to believe in (εὐσυλλογιστότερα καὶ πιθανώτερα) (*Rhetoric*, 1.1.12). Lastly, rhetoric is not so much concerned with the possibility of something (although the possible does enter into rhetorical deliberation by way of one of the general lines of argument) (*Rhetoric*, 2.19), as with its grounding in actuality. Before the orator can venture to express future possibilities, he ought to discover how things are now and how they have been in the past. In other words, the best guide for the articulation of possibilities is actuality.

An important feature of actuality as adapted to the domain of rhetoric is probability, or that which is plausible (εἰκὸς). If there is a point where Aristotle and the sophists converge, that point is probability as a solution to the indeterminacy of public discourse and the contingency of human action. Because in the domain of rhetoric truth is not always available, the next best thing is probability. On this point, Aristotle's remarks continue his line of thinking that explains deliberation (people deliberate because certain things admit of issuing in two ways) (*Rhetoric*, 1.2.12): "most of the things about which we make decisions . . . present us with alternative possibilities (ἐνδέχεται καὶ ἄλλως ἔχειν). For it is about our actions that we deliberate and inquire, and all our actions have a contingent character; hardly any of them are determined by necessity" (*Rhetoric*, 1.2.14). Therefore, making decisions requires that we attend not to what happens always or necessarily or randomly but to what happens generally or usually. This is the province of probability, a province whose headquarters, so to speak, are located in actuality. For Aristotle, "A Probability is a thing that happens for the most part (ἐπὶ τὸ πολύ); not, however, as some define it, anything whatever but only if it belongs to the class of things that present us with alternative possibilities" (*Rhetoric*, 1.2.15).

But if people must deliberate about their actions, and if their actions are determined neither by necessity nor randomness, how does probability help the orator advocate a particular course of action or urge a specific judgment? As noted earlier, Aristotle's thinking on the three rhetorical genres is based on his view that certain things calling for rhetoric tend to happen repeatedly; and even though these things may vary amongst themselves, their variation happens within the parameters of regularity. In other words, if there is variation in the sociopolitical world, it is variation within limits. The orator, then, who understands that the limits of sociopolitical phenomena are furnished by their repetition and regularity, understands rhetorical probability. More precisely, the orator understands that most people are likely to behave in certain ways under certain conditions. Probability, then, requires a broad knowledge of human nature as well as a keen sense of how similar events in the past turned out. By extension, rhetorical discourse based on probability depends on historical knowledge, which forms the base upon which one can predict the outcome of an issue. In short, probability demands coming to terms with certain aspects of actuality and projecting or predicting the future from those aspects.

In sum, Aristotelian rhetoric issues from and supports the regularity and reliability of the sociopolitical world, the recurrence of human situations within it, and the cognitive character of the emotions. Further, it acknowledges the capacity of language to defend the integrity of the self, to make suggestions on the basis of a calculus of necessity and pleasure, and to propose choices on the grounds of a theory of human happiness turning on the axes of the good and the expedient. Moreover, it recognizes the malleability of language but insists on the obligation of the orator to strive and make it clear and appropriate, to prove claims by relying on the facts of the case and leaving irrelevant considerations aside. Going beyond the facts of each case, the orator's obligation includes the larger facts of normative uses of language, acceptable patterns of thought, and established parameters of action. This is a rhetoric that seeks to tame chance by working out a taxonomy based on probability and by providing a blueprint for political stability, societal coherence, and intellectual order.

There are good reasons why Aristotle's rhetoric turned out this way. Like the sophists, Aristotle was a non-Athenian intellectual who traveled extensively. His life's itinerary found him going from his native Stageira to Plato's Academy in Athens, to Asia Minor for teaching and research, to Macedonia as a tutor to the young Alexander the Great, back to Athens to teach at the Lyceum, and to self-imposed exile in Chalkis for his final days, in order to save the Athenians from sinning against philosophy for a second time. But unlike the sophists, who had attempted to make do with the available resources in their path, Aristotle seems to have taken with him wherever he went the same method of observation and analysis. As such, he can be said to have confronted his circumstances with a more or less fixed attitude—that of the scientist, the analyzer, the classifier. Like them, he was a polymath. As his many treatises attest, he was learned in politics, ethics, physics, metaphysics, logic, rhetoric, natural phenomena, biology, and geometry. But unlike the sophists, who had practiced rhetoric as they went along, that is, unsystematically, Aristotle sought to turn it into a distinct field of study. In so doing, he can be said to have focused on its theoretical underpinnings as suggested by the *pisteis* (ethos, logos, pathos). If this focus had a purpose, that purpose must have been to make rhetoric less dependent on the vagaries of chance and contingency. Further, he can be said to have transformed the cultural impulses of sophistical rhetoric (competition, spectacles, circumstances) into corresponding rhetorical genres (forensic, epideictic, deliberative). One way to account for this transformation is to say that rhetorical genres of one's own invention are easier to control than events and circumstances. Lastly, he can be said to have moved away from the performative orientation of the sophists and closer to a theoretical one. Once again, the explanation for this change is that the outcomes of theory are more predictable than those of performance.

While Aristotle's citizenship and travels can be treated as matters of chance, and while his polymathy may be attributed to his natural curiosity and intelligence, his thinking on rhetoric should be seen as a function of the character of his times. Earlier in this chapter, we noted that one of the reasons Aristotle's reception of the sophists resembles those of Plato and Isocrates is that he, much like them, participated in an epoch of sociopolitical turbulence, withdrawal, and inwardness. Writing about that epoch, Jaeger observes that

> This was precisely the age in which the self began to be emancipated from the objective side of life, when it felt more consciously than ever before that it could not be satisfied with external creation alone. At this time the private side of life withdrew from the turmoil of action into its quiet corner and made itself at home there. The private side of individuals also awoke and locked the door against uninvited guests. The absolute objective form in which Aristotle always presented himself to the outside world was already based on a conscious separation of personal from externalized activities.[50]

Aristotle's inwardness appears more pronounced than that of Plato and Isocrates if we consider that in his works oratorical practice, even for the purposes of illustration, is brought to an end. A public activity par excellence, sophistical rhetoric under Aristotle's stewardship was turned into an object of study. Judging from the contents of his *Rhetoric*, the only thing left there of the rhetorical tradition is some dim reminders in the form of choice extracts from orations cited to illustrate, even if negatively, a particular Aristotelian principle or generalization. Once the honored guests in the houses of prominent citizens like Callias, the sophists of Aristotle were turned into illustrative material in his treatises expounding new doctrines. Even so, Aristotle seems to have appreciated, much like Isocrates, the significance of rhetoric in shaping the thinking of a culture. The fact that his own *Rhetoric* sought to impose on the art of persuasion a taxonomical grid betrays his larger concern with *taxis* (order) and *nomos*

(law) as two responses to the disorder and lawlessness that characterized the discursive practices of the sophists.

## Notes

1. Regarding the relationship of the Platonic and Aristotelian representations
of the sophists, Carl J. Classen has observed that it is easy to "assume that
throughout his life Aristotle adhered to one stereotype, an unreflected picture of the sophists, which he inherited from his master. But this is an unwarranted oversimplification." See "Aristotle's Picture of the Sophists" in
George B. Kerferd, ed., *The Sophists and Their Legacy* (Wiesbaden: Franz
Steiner Verlag GMBH, 1981), 11.
2. Consider, for example, his compilation (with the help of his students) and
study of the constitutions of one hundred and fifty-eight states as a preparation for his Athenian Constitution.
3. See *Rhetoric*, 1.1.1.
4. See also *Sophistical Refutations*, 183a.37–38.
5. Consider, for example, the speeches in Plato's *Apology, Phaedrus, Symposium,* and *Menexenus,* as well as Isocrates' *Helen, Antidosis,* and *Against the
Sophists.*
6. Concerning Aristotle's views on both the older and the second generation
sophists as well as his overall assessment of both groups, see Classen, 23–24.
7. Consider, for example, Bryson's claim that "no one ever uses foul language" (*Rhetoric*, 3.2.13), a variation of Antisthenes' famous dictum that no
one can contradict himself or another. Also consider Lycophron's notion that
the law is "a guarantee of men's just claims on one another, but it is not designed to make the citizens virtuous and just" (*Politics*, 1280b.11–13).
8. For Aristotle, philosophy and politics are two areas of activity that attract
those rich enough to avoid the troubles of ordering their own household or
managing their slaves (*Politics*, 1255b.35–38).
9. See *Metaphysics*, 1004b.15–27. See also *Protrepticus* (45), where Aristotle differentiates between exactitude (as a form of real wisdom) and imitation: "The
philosopher alone, of all men, imitates that which among all things is the
most exact; for, what he looks at is originality and exactness itself, not merely
imitation." See Anton-Hermann Chroust, *Aristotle: Protrepticus: A Reconstruction* (Great Bend, Ind.: University of Notre Dame Press, 1964), 20–21.
10. It is not clear, in other words, whether apparent wisdom is apparent because the beholder perceives it to be so, or because the one professing it
knows that it is not real, or because it does not appear the way the philoso-

pher (i.e., Aristotle) thinks it should. Moreover, to say that $x$ is not $y$ does not say what $x$ is.

11. For Aristotle's understanding of the philosopher's preoccupation with truth and falsehood, see *Metaphysics*, 997a.14–15; for his interest in first principles and causes, see *Metaphysics*, 1003b.18–19; and for his capacity to theorize on all subjects, see *Metaphysics*, 1004a.33–34.

12. See *Rhetoric*, 3.1.5 and 1.1.1.

13. Even so, Aristotle acknowledges that rhetoric is not entirely foreign to political science. On the contrary, knowledge of political science is a constitutive part of rhetoric: "Rhetoric is composed of analytical science and of that branch of political science which is concerned with Ethics" (*Rhetoric*, 1.4.8).

14. However, recall Plato's view in the *Gorgias* (465c) that sophists and orators appear to be in the same class.

15. See *Rhetoric*, 1.1.1 and 1.1.12.

16. See *Rhetoric*, 1.1.13,

17. See *Rhetoric*, 2.20.8.

18. E. M. Cope, *An Introduction to Aristotle's Rhetoric* (Cambridge: MacMillan and Co., 1867), 43. Addressing Aristotle's attitude toward his predecessors, Cherniss has identified many references in Aristotle's works that "demonstrate in an uncontroversial manner his tendency to accommodate to his own doctrines every possible early statement by a reinterpretation of its obvious meaning." See Harold Cherniss, *Aristotle's Criticism of Presocratic Philosophy* (Baltimore: Johns Hopkins University Press, 1935), 339.

19. Of course, Aristotle is relying on the linguistic uses and taste of his time, and on the rules of logic he himself articulates in his *Analytics*.

20. The overview and synthesis of the rhetorical tradition in Aristotle's hands was apparently more pronounced in his now lost Συναγωγὴ Τεχνῶν. In an apparent reference to this treatise, Cicero observes: "Aristotle brought together in a single compilation the ancient writers on the art of rhetoric, going right back to their founder and inventor, Tisias; with great care he sought out the main tenets of each author name by name, wrote them down clearly, and meticulously expounded the difficult passages. And with the charm and brevity of his diction he so excelled the inventors themselves that no-one looks to learn their precepts from the original books, but everyone who wants to understand what they were resorts to Aristotle as a far more convenient expositor. Thus Aristotle published his own views and also those of his predecessors, so that from this work we become acquainted both with his own views and with the others." Jonathan Barnes, ed., *The Complete Works of Aristotle*, 2 vols. (Princeton: Princeton University Press, 1984), vol. 1, 2430.

Regarding the ways in which Aristotle changed the rhetorical tradition, see Friedrich Solmsen, "The Aristotelian Tradition in Ancient Rhetoric," in Keith V. Erickson, ed., *Aristotle: The Classical Heritage of Rhetoric* (Metuchen, N.J.: Scarecrow Press, Inc., 1974), 278–309.

On the impact of Aristotle's move from the practical to the theoretical level, E. M. Cope has observed: "The effect of this modification . . . is to withdraw the notion of the art in some degree from the exclusively practical application of it encouraged by the sophistical school, and to fix the attention rather upon its theory and method; in short, it tends to a more scientific treatment of the subject." *An Introduction to Aristotle's Rhetoric*, 34. To Cope's observation we can add that Aristotle's attention to rhetorical theory and method also changed rhetoric's function from persuading to knowing or discovering the available means of persuasion (οὐ τὸ πεῖσαι ἔργον αὐτῆς, ἀλλὰ τὸ ἰδεῖν τὰ ὑπάρχοντα πιθανὰ) (*Rhetoric*, 1.1.14).

21. For the connection between *Rhetoric* and *Poetics* see Friedrich Solmsen, "Introduction" in *Aristotle: Rhetoric and Poetics*, trans. W. Rhys Roberts and Igram Bywater (New York: Modern Library, 1954), 11–14. For the connection between the *Rhetoric*, the *Ethics*, and the *Politics*, see Christoper L. Johnstone, "An Aristotelian Trilogy: Ethics, Rhetoric, Politics, and the Search for Moral Truth," *Philosophy and Rhetoric* 13 (Winter 1980): 1–24.

22. See also *Metaphysics*, 993a.15, where Aristotle notes that "the earliest philosophy speaks falteringly, as it were, on all subjects; being new and in its infancy."

23. See also *Sophistical Refutations*, 169b.21–25.

24. See also *Metaphysics*, 993b.20–24, 997a.14–15, 1003b.18–19, and 1004a.33–34.

25. See also *Metaphysics*, 1064b.27–29.

26. For Aristotle's definition of the accidental, see *Metaphysics*, 1025a.14ff.

27. For a discussion of the relationship between surface and core in Aristotle's *Rhetoric*, see John Poulakos, "Aristotle's Indebtedness to the Sophists" in David Zarefsky, Malcolm O. Sillars, and Jack Rhodes, eds., *Argument in Transition: Proceedings of the Third Summer Conference on Argumentation* (Annandale, Va.: Speech Communication Association, 1983), 27–42.

28. In his explanation of this passage, J. H. Freese, the translator of the *Rhetoric*, states (14): "The essence of sophistry consists in the moral purpose, the deliberate use of fallacious arguments. In Dialectic, the dialectician has the power or faculty of making use of them when he pleases; when he does so deliberately, he is called a sophist."

For Aristotle's additional comments on the distinction between capacity and deliberate purpose (*proairesis*), see *Topics*, 126a.30–26b.3; *Nicomachean Ethics*, 1127b.15; and *Rhetoric*, 1.13.10.

29. In this regard, Aristotle recounts a story about Thales, who made a large sum of money by relying on his knowledge of astronomy to predict a rich crop of olives, "proving that it is easy for philosophers to be rich if they choose, but this is not what they care about" (*Politics*, 1259a.6–19).

30. On this point, Classen (14) has argued that "Aristotle is not concerned merely to refute, let alone ridicule fallacious arguments of the sophists, but again and again to reveal the reasons for their fallacies and the basis for their errors."

31. See *Metaphysics*, 1004b.15–27 and *Protrepticus*, 45.

32. See also *Eudemian Ethics*, 1218b.23.

33. This critical observation coincides with Aristotle's complaint in the *Rhetoric* (1.1.4) that litigants often talk about things that have nothing to do with the case, and his wish that all courts would adopt Areopagos' policy of restricting speech to what has a direct bearing on the case at hand.

34. Insofar as the men of knowledge were men of authority in Aristotle's culture, this sophistical practice was obviously undermining epistemological authority.

35. For an extended discussion of Aristotle's views on language, see Richard McKeon, "Aristotle's Conception of Language and the Arts of Language," *Classical Philology*, 41, no. 4 (October 1946): 193–206 and 42 (January 1947): 21–50.

36. George Kennedy, *The Art of Persuasion in Greece* (Princeton: Princeton University Press, 1963), 81.

37. Lane Cooper, "The *Rhetoric* of Aristotle," *Quarterly Journal of Speech*, 21 (February 1935), 11.

38. Rhys Roberts, *Greek Rhetoric and Literary Criticism* (New York: Longmans, Green, and Co., 1928), 18.

39. Cooper, 15.

40. William M. A. Grimaldi, *Studies in the Philosophy of Aristotle's Rhetoric* (Wiesbaden: Franz Steiner Verlag GMBH, 1972), 19.

41. Kennedy, 81.

42. Ibid., 85.

43. Solmsen, xxi.

44. However, see Grimaldi's view that the *Rhetoric* is a unified text, a text whose unity is due to the notion of the enthymeme.

45. Aristotle notes that some of his predecessors believed that the orator's worth (ἐπιείκεια) contributes nothing to persuasion (*Rhetoric*, 1.1.4). Along this vein, we should note that several extant speeches by the sophists lack references to the orator's character. However, Gorgias' *Palamedes* would seem to support Aristotle's emphasis on ethos. Consider, for example, Palamedes' appeals in 15–16, 29–30, and 32.

46. William W. Fortenbaugh, "Aristotle's *Rhetoric* on Emotions" *Archiv fur Geschichte der Philosophie* 52 (1970): 64.

47. However, see *Sophistical Refutations* (165b 23–24), where he argues that of the two modes of refutation one is unconnected with the language of the refutative act.

48. See also *On Interpretation*, 19a.17–39.

49. Consider Gorgias' and Hippias' claim that they could speak on any topic whatsoever (82A.1a; 26) and (86A.8).

50. See Werner Jaeger, *Aristotle: Fundamentals of the History of His Development*, trans. Richard Robinson (Oxford: Clarendon Press, 1934), 321.

# Conclusion

To this point, we have characterized the sophists as traveling intellectuals, nomadic bricoleurs, and cosmopolitan thinkers visiting Athens and other cities on numerous occasions. At the same time, we have considered their discursive practices in the light of the emergence of the city-state, the rise of the middle class, and the political change from the few to the many. Looking at the relationship between their sociocultural predicament and their intellectual formulations, we have encountered a rhetoric born out of the logic of circumstances, the ethic of competition, and the aesthetic of exhibition. We have also touched upon the senses in which this rhetoric can be said to be derived from and revolve around the notions of opportunity, playfulness, and possibility. Lastly, we have seen some of the ways in which this rhetoric was received by Plato, Isocrates, and Aristotle.

Our argument throughout has been that the sophists' rhetoric cannot be divorced from their social status, their political environs, or the cultural climate of their age. This means that their rhetoric was shaped by and, in turn, shaped the world around it. The same argument also applies to the three receptions they occasioned. What Plato, Isocrates, and Aristotle had to say about the sophists was to a large measure a response to a particular state of affairs—affairs thought to have been caused or supported by the sophists as a class of individualistic intellectuals unattached to the civic traditions and political arrangements of the cities they visited. In short, there are good reasons why these three receptions turned out the way they did. Our purpose, then, has been twofold: first to account for the shape sophistical rhetoric assumed, and second, to explain why it was rejected, qualified, or compromised in the fourth century B.C. On the basis of the accounts and explanations we have advanced, we are now in a position to elaborate both on our characterization of the rhetoric of the sophists as well as its critical receptions.

187

In the past, for the meaning of sophistical rhetoric we have generally relied on historians of philosophy. But their well-known contempt for rhetoric has mostly yielded unsatisfactory results—results essentially reiterating the moralistic and epistemological critiques of the ancient philosophers. Steeped in the Platonic and Aristotelian ways of thought, yet openly uninterested in rhetoric as the antagonistic other of philosophy, most historians of philosophy have treated sophistical rhetoric as an easily dismissible instance of mundane busy-work or an offense against decency and reason. But as we have suggested, a sound understanding of rhetoric can hardly be acquired by relying on those who know, before anything else, their own aversion to rhetoric. However, turning to those whose understanding of sophistical rhetoric amounts to nothing more than a warrant for their own attitude that anything goes would be equally unwise. One way to navigate through the waters of hostility and self-justification is to insist on meeting self-imposed demands of historical explanation. Having acknowledged our biases at the outset, and having attempted to satisfy the bidding of the dialectic of past and present, we briefly review in this concluding section our previous remarks, and take this discussion one step further.

Sophistical rhetoric maintains that the world of discourse consists not of a singular, real logos awaiting to be discovered and distinguished from its apparent counterpart, but of *dissoi logoi*—human linguistic creations in unceasing contest with one another. This means that any instance of rhetoric constitutes only one side of a two-sided issue, one utterance without its counter-utterance. When confronted by a one-sided discourse, sophistical rhetoric gives expression to an other, an unuttered side, in effect attempting to engage a seemingly victorious discourse into yet another contest in which victory for the same side is not guaranteed. In this sense, sophistical rhetoric is oppositional or, if its adversaries would have their way, eristic, contentious, argumentative, and combative. Even when confronted by a two-sided discourse, usually in the form of a binary opposition, sophistical rhetoric sides with neither pole; rather, it sidesteps both poles by means of a third alternative. In this sense, sophistical rhetoric is a rhetoric of third alternatives or, as its critics would have it, elusive, tricky, and slippery. In both senses, however, its aim is to displace or overcome an uttered logos temporarily, not to eliminate it once and for all. Such elimination would short-circuit its claim to make the weaker argument stronger, and negate its faith in the un-ending flow and constant circulation of discourse.

But, one may wonder, does not this characteristic of sophistical rhetoric apply also to the Platonic, Isocratean, and Aristotelian rhet-orics? Did Plato not portray in his dialogues two sides of discourse in opposition to one another? Did he not himself oppose the sophistical lines of thought? And did Isocrates and Aristotle, too, not counter in some measure the utterances of the sophists? And did they not pro-duce hybrid rhetorics, rhetorics of a third alternative, rhetorics in nei-ther the sophistical nor the Platonic traditions? To a certain extent, the answer to all these questions is yes. However, there is an important difference between the sophistical and the other three rhetorics. While the rhetoric of the sophists has no end-point, those of Plato, Isocrates, and Aristotle do. Plato's rhetoric ends with the arrival at the truth, Isocrates' with the accomplishment of political unification, and Aristotle's with the discovery of the possible means of persuasion or with the fulfillment of the internal designs of his teleological scheme. When Plato opposes the sophists, the idea is to point the way to the truth and the silence that goes with it. The main reason why Socrates and the sophists are engaged in dialectically designed talk is not to exchange views and learn from each other; rather, it is that the soph-ists' thoughtlessness needs to be eradicated or rectified. Therefore, the idea is to turn their rhetorical practices and notions upside down dialectically and thus portray them as losers in the game of truth-seeking, a game they are made to agree to play with Socrates. A dia-lectical discussion between Socrates and a like-minded interlocutor would have been nonsensical. Dialogue for Plato makes sense only between one who knows and one who does not. As for the Isocratean and Aristotelian critiques of the sophists, they are outcomes of com-plicated negotiations and compromises between the sophistical and Platonic extremes. But these critiques, too, arrive and stop at a partic-ular point—Isocrates at the point of sociopolitical harmony and Aris-totle at the point of intellectual orderliness. In short, the philosophers drive to, push for, or invite closure, completion, and culmination. By contrast, with the sophists there is no truth, no unity, no *telos*. When presented with a given proposition, the sophists respond with chal-lenges. For them, rhetorical contests are never finished. In a word, the distinction we have made holds because the philosophers articu-lated positions while the sophists provided only *op*-positions.

Inasmuch as counter-utterances and third alternatives are not already part of the familiar, and therefore *appropriate* phraseology of the past, sophistical rhetoric labors to utter novel words, fresh insights, and original thoughts.[1] As such, it can be said to intervene in the world of discourse tactically, with surprising utterances (παραδοξολογίας),[2] the kind that do not add to but disrupt established norms of linguistic action. As interventional discourse, sophistical rhetoric shatters aspects of conventional wisdom and unsettles the sensibilities of the accepted tradition. Its starting point is not so much the doxical positions (the commonly held views) of its audiences as the awareness that language itself is paradoxical,[3] and hence able to negate the affirmations or affirm the negations of a given tradition of linguistic constructs.[4] That is why the enemies of sophistical rhetoric have generally regarded it as strange, peculiar, eccentric, odd, ridiculous, or deviant. And that is also why it places a high premium on novelty.

Sophistical rhetoric regards prior discursive formulations as unable to accommodate the radical novelty of an ever-unfolding present. At any one moment, what is needed is not typical sayings but timely utterances, utterances treating the occasion they address as unprecedented and demanding countless adjustments, adaptations, and reconstitutions. Naturally, such utterances bet on the chance of the moment to make new disclosures apparent, and manifest themselves in a new vocabulary whose primary limitations and oppositions issue from another vocabulary—the vocabulary of custom and convention. Insofar, then, as sophistical rhetoric capitalizes on and creates situational *opportunities*, it can be said to be ahistorical. For the sophist, the accumulated linguistic wisdom from the past carries little, if any, weight, and has no inherent value or necessary relevance on matters of the present moment. That something was once believed does not mean that it still should be; nor that it must be believed in the future. But even as it ministers to the requirements of the present, sophistical rhetoric is interested in the past, but only inasmuch as it exemplifies ways of discarding the formulations of its anterior past. At the same time, it is concerned with the future, but only insofar as it promises to appear in the form of *possibilities* that have yet to be formulated.

In all of these capacities, sophistical rhetoric portrays the seemingly necessary (the actual) as otherwise. In so doing, it points out that the established order of things does not represent the manifestation of *a priori* truths but rather reflects human choices that people have forgotten were choices. In this sense, rhetoric suggests that if a given order is at all legitimate, it is so not inherently or permanently but only for as long as its heirs reaffirm the choices that have gone into its making. At any time, the existing order can be changed. In fact, it must be changed because the forms of human experience are so variegated that they call for renewed choices and renewed arrangements every step of the way. Briefly, then, sophistical rhetoric calls into question the received language, habitual ways of perception, and traditional modes of thought by challenging what other rhetorics take for granted. Accordingly, it cultivates skeptical attitudes—the kind that introduce elements of ambiguity and instability into the established order.

But because a given order always seeks its own perpetuation, and because it knows that downfalls begin with doubts, it labels those who challenge it symbolically as sophists, deceivers, beasts, radical skeptics, dissidents, anarchists, revolutionaries; and calls their discourses imprudent, nihilistic, subjective, nonserious, irreverent, immoral, pretentious, untrue, weaker and weakening (*to hetton*). This is its way of attempting to eliminate forms of opposition that may lead to its demise. Because the established order has on its side the authority and weight of tradition, an elaborate machinery of propagating one-sided discourses, and the means of enforcing its will, it always operates from a position of relative strength (*to kreitton*). Even so, its constant efforts to neutralize, diffuse, or appropriate sophistical discourses attest to its fear that logos, the very medium that under one form accounts for the order's own existence in the first place, can, under a different form, displace or overthrow it. But if this so, censorship is nothing more than a preference for some kinds of speech and an aversion to others.

Sophistical rhetoric wages symbolic war against all claims of immutability and fixity. Acknowledging the power of words over human beings and the self-referentiality of language,[5] it seeks to decodify or fracture the assumed verities of and about the world through new linguistic idioms, usually in the form of unusual combinations of heterogeneous elements or even simple reversals.[6] This is done by playing with the reasoning of discursive authority,[7] satirizing its incompetence,[8] exposing its contradictions, and laughing at its seriousness.[9] Always restless with what has already been said and accepted, it battles discursive actualities or impossible ideals, and seeks to cultivate the desire for actualizable possibilities.

Although driven by the senses of the opportune, the playful, and the possible, what sophistical rhetoric says can often acquire the status of the proper, the stronger, and the actual. In the event such a transformation does materialize, sophistical rhetoric does not hasten to galvanize and consolidate its newly acquired status. Rather, it resumes its assault on what in effect was its own discourse. This is so because it considers any rhetorical endeavor, including its own, to be standing on insecure grounds.[10] In the light of this awareness, sophistical rhetoric has no unchanging commitment to any one position, including what it itself has uttered—and that is why it has often been condemned for being inconsistent, unreliable, and unpredictable. In other words, it does not offer once and for all an alternative better than the ones already adopted or practiced. It can only offer, by way of the example of its own practices, several linguistic approaches to human experience—approaches that can only yield provisional, ephemeral, and ultimately disposable understandings.

As we moved from the sophists to Plato to Isocrates to Aristotle, we noted rhetoric's emphasis changing from the circumstantially determined, the competitively driven, and the aesthetically pleasing, to the ethically upstanding, the sociopolitically useful, and the theoretically sound. These changes, we also noted, happened against the background of two uneasy constancies: unexpected circumstantial exigencies in the theater of sociopolitical affairs, and the will to survive or succeed discursively in that theater. If these changes and constancies can be said to inform the Hellenic experience of rhetoric, the genius of the Greeks lies not in their capacity to articulate four different rhetorical perspectives; nor does it lie in some internal principle of development from the one perspective to the next. Rather, it lies in their ability to address varying circumstances variously, and in so doing mitigate the totalizing tendencies of each rhetorical perspective by the claims of the other three. Put another way, the three receptions of sophistical rhetoric constitute three attempts to interrogate a rhetoric born out of circumstances, contests, and spectacles along three different lines—the ethical, the useful, and the theoretical. Had the earliest rhetoric been Plato's, it too would have had to answer the questions posed by the aesthetic, the useful, and the theoretical perspectives. This is so not only because different times call for different rhetorics, or because each rhetorician holds onto his own perspective, but also because rhetoric itself constitutes a polymorphic art, an art of many characteristics and uses.

Despite their differences, the three receptions we have considered share more or less a common preference—the preference for the one over the many. One way to explain this preference of singularism over pluralism is by reference to the conditions that made its articulation possible. If it is granted that the sociopolitical manifests itself in the rhetorics of a given culture, Plato's universalism, Isocrates' pan-Hellenism, and Aristotle's developmentalism are but different ways of pointing to the unworkability of a loose collection of states, each following its own particular direction without regard to the whole. Consequently, all three receptions of sophistry recognize the failure of the Hellenic culture to work coherently for its own preservation and well-being. Accordingly, they exalt consensus—a goal demanding restraint, obedience, and discipline from its people—and affirm sociopolitical arrangements that favor cooperation over competitions, submission to universal versions of law and ethical behavior, knowledge over opinions, dialogue over debates, and introspection over exhibitions; in short, oligarchy over democracy.[11]

This preference, however, was far from arbitrary or pure. Commentators who have read Plato, Isocrates, and Aristotle apart from the tribulations of their age have managed to see only doctrines-in-themselves pitting one notion against another in a historical vacuum. But from what we have seen, it makes more sense that all three philosophers rejected sophistry as an item of luxury that could not be afforded during the lean times of reconstruction following the Peloponnesian Wars. In this sense, the age of Pericles, in all its exuberance and enthusiasm, was short-lived; and what succeeded it was an age of inwardness and sobriety, an age in which the extravagant impulses that sophistical rhetoric had expressed were tempered by means of conservative edicts designed to save the culture from its own excesses. Twenty-three centuries later, Nietzsche suggested in *The Birth of Tragedy* that in every tragedy Apollo would have to prevail every time over Dionysus.[12] If we cast the sophists as Dionysian spirits opposed by the Apollonian forces of Plato, Isocrates, and Aristotle in a drama entitled *The Birth of Rhetoric*, we would have to say that Nietzsche was right.

Even so, the philosophers' reaffirmation of the Apollonian vision during the fourth century B.C. cannot be said to have eradicated the sophistical doctrines of the fifth century. What this vision did accomplish was to provide three perspectives through which to reread these doctrines and evaluate their contribution to the culture from which they had sprung. According to these perspectives, Prodicus' Heracles would have had no difficulty deciding that Virtue was the better, if not the only, choice. Similarly, Protagoras' notion of *dissoi logoi* could be maintained, but only after agreeing to name the one logos genuine or real and the other counterfeit or apparent. And Gorgias' Helen would have had to accept some responsibility for her actions or defend them, à la Isocrates, as motivating the unification of the Hellenes against the barbarians. Under the weight of the newly articulated desires for a morally decent, intellectually reasonable, and sociopolitically responsible subject, the ethic of competition was to be denounced on account of the incontestability of the truth, the self-evident advantages of expediency, and the undeniability of reason. Similarly, the aesthetic of exhibition and spectacles was to be abandoned on account of the reality of things, a reality forged and displayed in the pages of books, not the stages of theaters. Last, the logic of circumstances was to yield to the logic of consistency and non-contradiction—two logics meant to grant correctness or truthfulness to only one of two or more options.

As Plato and Aristotle worked out their receptions of sophistical rhetoric, they moved from *legein* and *antilegein* to some form of *dialegesthai*. In several of his dialogues, Plato showed dialectic in action while Aristotle defined it as that which rhetoric can be said to resemble and that which has its counterpart (ἀντίστροφος) in rhetoric. In both instances, however, dialectic failed to make a compelling case for cooperation among interlocutors with competing perspectives and interests. In Plato's hands, the sophists were trounced because their persuasive tactics lacked the concern for the moral improvement of the citizens. In Aristotle's works, the syllogism and induction replaced charming language or emotional appeals and became the regulating principles of all discourse seeking to persuade by means of proof. In both cases, dialectic emerged as a form not of cooperating with but of overpowering the unknowing or unreasonable other. Unlike Plato or Aristotle, Isocrates did not follow the path of dialectic. Steeped in the rhetorical tradition of his predecessors, he nevertheless opted for what seems to many a reformed rhetoric. But as we have observed, the standards of rhetorical reform suggested themselves to Isocrates through the urgencies of political division and his vision of a pan-Hellenic union.

As intellectual proprietors heading three different educational institutions devoted to the rearticulation of the good life in Hellas, Plato,

Isocrates, and Aristotle sought to arrest and tame the beast that was the sophist, to call in the roaming nomads and normalize them. But how were they to combat the sophists' ambiguities, paradoxes, pretensions, exaggerations, and their disregard of the tradition-bound understandings of proper discursive conduct? How were they to make the case that an intellectual should work both for the welfare of the polis and the individual's soul? Because the emergence and success of the traveling sophists were unprecedented, the means to apprehend and comprehend them were simply unavailable. The cultural instrumentalities of poetic inspiration and religious superstition proved grossly inadequate when it came to dealing with a group of intellectuals seizing the opportunities for change and capitalizing on the readiness of the culture to find its way to its undisclosed future in an altogether novel manner. Still, the philosophers seem to have been committed to the proposition that the sophists' rhetorical practices had to be tempered or brought to a halt. From what we have seen, the philosophers tried to expel the sophists, and in so doing cleanse the culture of its impure elements. But if this is so, it is no surprise that the philosophers have been associated with conservative politics (Popper), while the sophists have been perceived as liberal (Havelock) or radical (Nietzsche) spirits intent on freeing people from the bondage of dysfunctional or inadequate institutions, or eradicating the premises of pre-Socratic morality, science, and philosophy.

As we have said, Plato, Isocrates, and Aristotle were grappling with the problems of their time, problems that included constant warfare between the city-states, strife between the classes, and legal, political, and educational reform. In the midst of all these problems lay the issue of logos and the ways in which it could move people to action. All three sought to address rhetoric in all its manifestations and consequences. Looking at it as taught or understood, and treating it as a pervasive and ever-present practice, they were seeking to come to terms with the unavoidable ambiguities of language, its relationship to the orators and their publics, and the problems these ambiguities posed to the societies and the political systems in place. In doing so, they were laboring to stabilize the instability of words, and by extension the instability of sociopolitical arrangements. If they could show that the world was governed by principles of order, logic, and history, they could drive home the point that rhetoric ought to reflect and uphold those principles or risk one disaster after another. Not surprisingly, the evidence that Plato, Isocrates, and Aristotle marshaled to illustrate their principles supported their side.

This is, then, how the philosophers argued the case against sophistical rhetoric, and it is on account of this case that they emerged victorious in the eyes of posterity. But as we have noted, if the philosophers' receptions managed to make sense, they did so thanks to the weight of unwieldy sociopolitical circumstances: all three argued that something had to be done to reinstitute a sense of order and to restore confidence in the interdependence of polis and citizen. With this imperative in mind, the philosophers rejected sophistical rhetoric because they saw it as part of a declining cultural guard of overasserted freedoms promoting licentiousness and anarchy, deliberate ambiguities fueling doubts and confusion, and personal ambition endangering the viability and functionality of the collective. As the guard changed, the philosophers tolerated rhetoric but only on the condition that it be supervised by the philosopher-overseer, who was to make sure that the players played by, not with, the new rules. Under the proposed regime of intellectual austerity and oligarchic politics, one could pursue rhetorical opportunities, but only so long as such pursuit would be regulated by the knowers, who were to maintain, uphold, and enforce the standards of normative versions of propriety. Likewise, rhetorical possibilities could be expressed but only with the proviso that their expression would fall within the parameters of logical integrity, sociopolitical unity, communal stability, collective responsibility, and the knowledge of the regularities of human nature in the social and political domains.

In the doctrines of the philosophers of the fourth century B.C., one finds idealistic as well as pragmatistic expressions of reform motivated by fear, disgust, and indignation. Presuming their own self-enlightenment, these expressions in effect were saying: "For the love of Hellas! Consider what we are proposing, and do as we ask." As could be expected, these pleas were not made without supporting documentation. Just as the Zeus of Protagoras' myth (*Protagoras*, 322a–d) had given people the political art and a sense of justice and respect for others in order to help them coexist, Plato, Isocrates, and Aristotle gave to a new generation of intellectuals the *Republic*, the *Panegyricus*, and the *Politics* for the same reason. But the philosophical trio went further by supplying people with the *Laws*, the *Antidosis*, and the *Ethics*—three discourses designed to keep them on the right side of virtue. Finally, they furnished them with the *Sophist*, the *Against the*

*Sophists*, and the *Sophistical Refutations* to help them identify what had to be expelled from the minds of the masses if they were to bring their march of folly to an end. This last contribution was but another version of the early ritual of scapegoating, a ritual meant to cleanse a community from all kinds of impurities and to restore its spiritual health.

But despite their offerings, the intellectuals of the fourth century B.C. never quite managed to escape the insights of the sophists. Plato, Isocrates, and Aristotle did compete in an open field with the sophists; but the presumption afforded by the urgent need for political reform was in their favor. Therefore, if they did win the minds of most thinkers of posterity, they did so not on account of the brilliance of their doctrines, but on account of their comprehensive approaches to a host of vexing problems and their disciplined plans for the correction of these problems. If it is granted that intellectuals turn to history in times of turmoil and irresolution, posterity has found Plato, Isocrates, and Aristotle engaging not because their thinking has timeless value but because posterity, too, has been searching for ways to battle its own troubles and realize its own aspirations. In other words, the appeal of the philosophers of the fourth century B.C. to later thinkers is to be traced to the relevance of their thinking to subsequent times. If they proved to be a constant source of enlightenment to their successors, the explanation is that the issues of political disintegration, social conflict, and legal and educational reform have always been constant. Posterity then seems to have adopted the doctrines of the philosophers not because they were more systematic or more comprehensive than those of the sophists, but because it too has always needed a starting place from which to address its own dilemmas.

But there is another, less appealing side to the story of the philosophical doctrines of the fourth century B.C. In Plato's pages, the common people of the time could read that they were mostly ignorant and unruly, and therefore doomed. In more ways than one, they were told that unless they opted for Plato's version of sociopolitical reform, they could not be saved except from an act of divine providence. Rhetoric, as the people had known it, was no longer a practice in which they could simply delight without considering its impact on them and, by extension, on the well-being of the state. Rather, it was a poison administered by unscrupulous orators to linguistically lulled masses and unsuspecting youths. In Isocrates' oratorical compositions, the same people could read about the grandeur of the good old days and the inferiority of their modern ways of thinking and acting. In so many words, they were told that political unity was the precious lesson that the Trojan War and the Persian Wars had taught, a lesson that had to be retaught, relearned, and relived. As for Aristotle's treatises, they too served a didactic function. His *Rhetoric* and *Poetics,* for example, urged listeners and spectators to leave oratorical and dramatic performances and go home to read treatises on rhetoric and drama. By extension, they asked their readers to stay away from public competitions and try to enter into a cooperative exchange not with their fellow citizens but with the authors of the texts his school of thought had produced. In all three cases, the public was given the news that the sophistical party was over and that a new age of regrouping was dawning.

Thus the story comes to an end. The lesson of the fourth century B.C. for the onlookers of posterity has been amply clear: it is dangerous and unbecoming to think sophistical thoughts and practice sophistical practices; sophistry spells danger; unexamined opinions lead to calamities; untamed utterances cause unruliness; and unmuffled speeches incite lawlessness. But despite its clarity and its many adherents, this lesson has never managed to put sophistry entirely out of mind. Two thousand and two hundred years of intense efforts to ban sophistry from the pantheon of Western thought have yet to succeed. Perhaps this has been so because the name philosophy, no matter how privileged and venerated, still contains within it the "soph-" of sophistry; or because, as Aristotle notes, "that which is shedding any quality retains something of that which is being shed" (*Metaphysics,* 1010a.18).

To be sure, the philosophers of the fourth century B.C. were right, but only partly so—one cannot build a sound sociopolitical structure on a foundation of sophistical doctrines and practices. If it is to function well, a state needs more stability and restraint than the sophists could promise or deliver. However, neither value by itself nor the two together can stand alone. If the principle of proportion in a society means anything, it means that stability and restraint must coexist with their opposites—instability and freedom. The philosophers were right, then, insofar as their efforts were aiming to temper excessive instability and irresponsible freedom; but they were wrong insofar as they sought to dismiss the doctrines of the sophists. The outcome of such a dismissal, more elaborate and more apparent in posterity than in antiquity, can in principle only be a servile and silent people, a people whose servility and silence makes a mockery of democracy. In this regard, Aristotle told one half of the story when he said that "all [men] begin . . . by wondering that things should be as they are" (*Metaphysics*, 1.2.15). The other half, which he left untold, is that some people begin by seeing how things are and wondering why they are not otherwise.

In the final analysis, it seems that sophistry was too lavish and too exorbitant an item to be afforded in the fourth century B.C. Sociopolitical as well as intellectual reform was an immense task, a task that required a turn from the belief in unlimited possibilities to an acceptance of the new conditions of austerity and limits. With this task came the realization that the need to reorganize public life went hand in hand with a twofold construal: sophistry as a multifaceted problem, and philosophy as a unitary solution. Insofar as sophistry had taught orators to unleash awesome discursive forces onto a citizenry too vulnerable to the charms of rhetoric, the philosophical solution was to produce a discourse maligning the orators, inoculating the citizens against the epidemic of sophistry, and reshaping their sensibilities along the straight lines of rational verities. If the problem was that the language of rhetoric played dubious games, the solution was to devise a new linguistic game, one that could redefine the rules of fair linguistic play and interrogate rhetorical games; alternatively, it was to point away from language altogether and toward immaterial essences (Plato), historical or immanent realities (Isocrates), or formal actualities (Aristotle). If the sophists had succeeded in persuading people to think that the world consisted of conflicting appearances, a case had to be made for the perennial lessons of history or the truths that resided in the inner core of the same world; by extension, the primacy of perception had to be discredited and supplanted by a new primacy—that of conception. In short, the senses had to be shown as unreliable and inadequate means of apprehending the world while mental intelligence had to be portrayed as the superior alternative.

In effect, this twofold proposition was an attempt to subordinate a rhetorical culture to a philosophical one. Such subordination could be effected by juxtaposing two sets of promises. Against rhetoric's promises to address particular events, philosophy promised general principles explaining most if not all occurrences. While rhetoric could offer only temporary solutions, philosophy promised lasting truths. And whereas rhetoric could deal only with the effects of things, philosophy promised a thorough understanding of their causes. In short, philosophy promised a sense of ideational control, the security of constancy, and the safety of permanence. At a time of incessant changes and undesirable consequences, philosophy's promises could not have been without some appeal. And even though they were made too late to save Hellas from itself, these promises found sympathetic audiences in subsequent centuries, including ours. During the last few decades, however, the promises of the philosophers have been shunned for those of the sophists. Why this may be so is the subject of another study.

## Notes

1. Consider, for example, Philostratus' report that Gorgias laughed at Prodicus "for speaking what was old-fashioned and had often been said before" (ἑωλά τε καὶ πολλάκις εἰρημένα) (82A.24). Also consider the conversation between Hippias and Socrates as reported by Xenophon (86A.14.5–7).
2. See 82A.1.2.
3. For an insightful discussion of the sophists' paradoxical uses of language, see Roger Moss, "The Case for Sophistry," in Brian Vickers, ed., *Rhetoric Revalued* (Binghamton, N.Y.: Center for Medieval and Early Renaissance Studies, 1982), 207–24.
4. In this regard, consider the paradoxical maxim "one cannot contradict" (οὐκ ἔστιν ἀντιλέγειν) attributed to Protagoras. See H. D. Rankin, "Ouk Estin Antilegein," in George B. Kerferd, ed., *The Sophists and Their Legacy* (Wiesbaden: Franz Steiner Verlag GMBH, 1981), 25–37.
5. Consider, for example, 82B.11.8–14 and 82B.3.84.
6. Consider, for example, Gorgias' reported reference to Xerxes as "the Persian's Zeus" and to vultures as "living tombs" (82B.5a).
7. See, for example, Gorgias' *On Non-being or On Nature* (82B.3), a discourse that several commentators have read as a parody of the Eleatic reasoning of Parmenides.
8. See, for example, Callicles' treatment of Socrates in Plato's *Gorgias*.
9. Consider, for example, Gorgias' reported claim that "the opposition's seriousness is to be demolished by laughter, and laughter by seriousness" (82B.12). For a discussion of this fragment, see Victor J. Vitanza, "What's 'at stake' in the Gorgian Fragment on Seriousness/Laughter?" *Pre/text* 10, 1–2 (1989): 107–14.
10. Consider, for example, Gorgias' view that "on most subjects most men take opinion as counselor to their soul, but since opinion is slippery and in-

secure it casts those employing it into slippery and insecure successes"
(82B.11.11).
11. However, see Aristotle's following critique of Socrates:

> The cause of Socrates' error must be deemed to be that his fundamental
> assumption (of perfect unity in the state) was incorrect. It is certain that in
> a way both the household and the state should be a unit, but they should
> not be so in every way. For in one way the state as its unification proceeds
> will cease to be a state, and in another way, though it continues a state, yet
> by coming near to ceasing to be one it will be a worse state, just as if one
> turned harmony into unison or a rhythm into a single foot. The proper
> thing is for the state, while being a multitude, to be made a partnership and
> a unity by means of education . . . ; and it is strange that the very philos-
> opher who intends to introduce a system of education and thinks that this
> will make the city morally good should fancy that he can regulate society by
> such measures as have been mentioned instead of by manners and culture
> (φιλοσοφία) and laws, just as the legislator introduced community of prop-
> erty in Sparta and Crete by the institution of public messes. (*Politics*,
> 1263b.30–64a.1)

12. See Peter Sloterdijk, *Thinker On Stage: Nietzsche's Materialism*, trans. Jamie
Owen Daniel (Minneapolis: University of Minnesota Press, 1989).

# Selected Bibliography

Adams, Charles D. "Recent Views on the Political Influence of Isocrates." *Classical Philology* 7 (1912): 343–50.

Adkins, Arthur W. H. "ἀρετή, τέχνη, Democracy and Sophists: *Protagoras* 316b–328d." *Journal of Hellenic Studies* 93 (1973): 3–12.

_____. "Form and Content in Gorgias' *Helen* and *Palamedes*: Rhetoric, Philosophy, Inconsistency and Invalid Argument in Some Greek Thinkers." In *Essays in Ancient Greek Philosophy*, ed. John P. Anton and Anthony Preus. Vol. 2. Albany: State University of New York Press, 1983.

Albury, William. "Hunting the Sophist." *Apeiron* 5 (1971): 1–12.

Ardley, Gavin. "The Role of Play in the Philosophy of Plato." *Philosophy* 32 (1967): 226–44.

Aristotle. *The Art of Rhetoric*. Trans. J. H. Freese. Cambridge, Mass.: Harvard University Press, 1982.

_____. *Politics*. Trans. H. Rackham. Cambridge, Mass.: Harvard University Press, 1977.

_____. *Nicomachean Ethics*. Trans. H. Rackham. Cambridge, Mass.: Harvard University Press, 1968.

_____. *Eudemian Ethics*. Trans. H. Rackham. Cambridge, Mass.: Harvard University Press, 1981.

_____. *Metaphysics*. Trans. H. Tredennick. Cambridge, Mass.: Harvard University Press, 1980.

_____. *On Sophistical Refutations*. Trans. E. S. Forster. Cambridge, Mass.: Harvard University Press, 1978.

_____. *The Poetics*. Trans. W. Hamilton Fyfe. Cambridge, Mass.: Harvard University Press, 1991.

_____. *On Interpretation*. Trans. H. P. Cooke. Cambridge, Mass.: Harvard University Press, 1973.

_____. *Physics*. Trans. P. H. Wicksteed and F. M. Cornford. Cambridge, Mass.: Harvard University Press, 1980.

_____. *Rhetoric and Poetics*. Trans. Rhys Roberts and Ingram Bywater. New York: Modern Library, 1954.

_____. *Topics*. Trans. E. S. Forster. Cambridge, Mass.: Harvard University Press, 1976.

———. *Minor Works*. Trans. W. S. Hett. Cambridge, Mass.: Harvard University Press, 1980.

Astrene, Thomas. "An Analysis of Thrasymachus' True Definition of Rhetoric." *Dialogue* 20 (April 1978): 57–63.

Backman, Mark. *Sophistication: Rhetoric and the Rise of Self-Consciousness*. New York: Ox Bow Press, 1991.

Baldry, H. C. *The Greek Tragic Theatre*. New York: W. W. Norton & Co., 1971.

Baldwin, Charles S. *Medieval Rhetoric and Poetic*. New York: MacMillan, 1928.

Barnes, Johnathan. *The Complete Works of Aristotle*. 2 vols. Princeton: Princeton University Press, 1984.

Barrett, Harold. *The Sophists: Rhetoric, Democracy, and Plato's Idea of Sophistry*. Novato, Calif.: Chandler & Sharp Publishers, 1987.

Beck, Frederick A. G. *Greek Education*. London: Methuen & Co., 1962.

Bestor, Thomas Wheaton. "Plato on Language and Falsehood." *Southwestern Journal of Philosophy* 9 (Fall 1978): 23–37.

Biesecker, Susan. "Rhetorical Discourse and the Constitution of the Subject: Prodicus' *Choice of Heracles*." *Argumentation* 5 (1991): 159–69.

Blank, David L. "Socratics Versus Sophists on Payment for Teaching." *Classical Antiquity* 4 (1985): 1–49.

Blass, Fredericus. *Antiphontis Orationes et Fragmenta*. Lipsiae: Aedibus B. G. Teubneri, 1892.

Bondeson, William. "Plato's *Sophist* and the Significance of Truth-Value Statements." *Apeiron* 8 (1972): 41–47.

Brake, Robert J. "Pedants, Professors and the Law of the Excluded Middle: On Sophists and Sophistry." *Central States Speech Journal* 20 (Summer 1969): 122–29.

Brown, Hazel L. *Extemporary Speech in Antiquity*. Menasha, Wis.: George Banta Publishing Co., 1914.

Brownstein, Oscar L. "Plato's *Phaedrus*: Dialectic as the Genuine Art of Speaking." *Quarterly Journal of Speech* 51 (December 1965): 392–98.

Bury, J. B., S. A. Cook, and F. E. Adcock, eds. *The Cambridge Ancient History*. Vol. 5. New York: Macmillan Co., 1927.

Butcher, S. H. *Some Aspects of the Greek Genius*. London: MacMillan and Co., 1893.

Butler, William Archer. *Lectures on the History of Ancient Philosophy*. London: MacMillan and Co., 1874.

Buxton, R. G. A. *Persuasion in Greek Tragedy*. Cambridge: Cambridge University Press, 1982.

Calogero, Guido. "Gorgias and the Socratic Principle *Nemo Sua Sponte Peccat. Journal of Hellenic Studies* 77 (1957): 12–17.

Carse, James P. *Finite and Infinite Games: A Vision of Life as Play and Possibility*. New York: Ballantine Books, 1986.

de Certeau, Michel. *The Practice of Everyday Life*. Trans. Steven F. Rendall. Berkeley: University of California Press, 1984.

Cherniss, Harold. *Aristotle's Criticism of Presocratic Philosophy*. Baltimore: Johns Hopkins University Press, 1935.

Chroust, Anton-Hermann. "Aristotle's Earliest 'Course of Lectures on Rhetoric,'" *L'Antiquite Classique* 33 (1964): 58–72.

_____. *Aristotle Protrepticus: A Reconstruction*. Great Bend, Ind.: University of Notre Dame Press, 1964.

Classen, Carl J. *Sophistik*. Darmstadt: Wissenschaftliche Buchgesellschaft, 1976.

_____. "Aristotle's Picture of the Sophists." In *The Sophists and Their Legacy*, ed. George B. Kerferd, 7–24. Wiesbaden: Franz Steiner Verlag GMBH, 1981.

Cole, Thomas A. *The Origins of Rhetoric in Ancient Greece*. Baltimore: Johns Hopkins University Press, 1991.

_____. "The Apology of Protagoras." *Yale Classical Studies* 19 (1966): 101–18.

_____. "The Relativism of Protagoras." *Yale Classical Studies* 22 (1972): 19–45.

_____. "Who was Corax?" *Illinois Classical Studies* 16 (1992): 65–84.

Cooper, Lane. "The *Rhetoric* of Aristotle." *Quarterly Journal of Speech* 21 (February 1935): 10–19.

Cope, E. M. *An Introduction to Aristotle's Rhetoric*. Cambridge: MacMillan and Co., 1867.

_____. "The Sophists." *Journal of Classical and Sacred Philology* 1 (June 1854): 145–88.

_____. "On the Sophistical Rhetoric I." *Journal of Classical and Sacred Philology* 2 (May 1855): 129–69.

_____. "On the Sophistical Rhetoric II." *Journal of Classical and Sacred Philology* 3 (March 1856): 34–80.

_____. "On the Sophistical Rhetoric III." *Journal of Classical and Sacred Philology* 3 (December 1856): 252–88.

Coulter, James A. "The Relation of the *Apology of Socrates* to Gorgias' *Defense of Palamedes* and Plato's Critique of Gorgianic Rhetoric." *Harvard Studies in Classical Philology* 68 (1964): 269–303.

Crawley, Sharon. "A Plea for the Revival of Sophistry" *Rhetoric Review* 7, no. 2 (1989): 318–37.

Deleuze, Gilles. "Nomad Thought." In *The New Nietzsche: Contemporary Styles of Interpretation*, ed. David B. Allison. Cambridge, Mass.: MIT Press, 1988.

Diels, Hermann, and Walther Kranz. *Die Fragmente der Vorsokratiker*. 3 vols. Berlin: Weidmannsche Verlagsbuchhandlung, 1952.

Dodds, E. R. *The Greeks and the Irrational.* Berkeley: University of California Press, 1951.

_____. *The Ancient Concept of Progress and Other Essays on Greek Literature and Belief.* Oxford: Clarendon Press, 1973.

Duncan, Thomas S. "Gorgias' Theories of Art." *Classical Journal* 33 (1938): 402–13.

Dupréel, Eugene. *Les Sophistes.* Neuchatel: Editions du Grifon, 1948.

Edelstein, Ludwig. "The Function of Myth in Plato's Philosophy." *Journal of the History of Ideas* 10, no. 4 (October 1949): 463–81.

Ehrenberg, Victor. *From Solon to Socrates: Greek History and Civilization during the Sixth and Fifth Centuries b.c.* London: Methuen & Co., 1970.

Epps, P. H. "Protagoras' Famous Statement." *Classical Journal* 59 (1964): 223–26.

Erickson, Keith V. *Aristotle: The Classical Heritage of Rhetoric.* Metuchen, N.J.: Scarecrow Press, 1974.

Field, G. C. *Plato and His Contemporaries.* London: Methuen, 1930.

Finley, Sir Moses I. *The Legacy of Greece: A New Appraisal.* Oxford: Clarendon Press, 1981.

Fisher, John. "Plato on Writing and Doing Philosophy." *Journal of the History of Ideas* 27 (April–June 1966): 163–72.

Fortenbaugh, William W. "Aristotle's *Rhetoric* on Emotions." *Archiv fur Geschichte der Philosophie* 52 (1970): 40–70.

Freeman, Kenneth J., and M. J. Rendall. *Schools of Hellas: An Essasy on the Practice and Theory of Ancient Greek Education from 600 to 300 b.c.* New York: Kennikat Press, 1969.

Fuks, A. "Isocrates and the Social-Economic Situation in Greece." *Ancient Society* 3 (1972): 17–44.

Garner, Richard. *Law and Society in Classical Athens.* London: Croom Helm, 1987.

Gerhard, W. A. "Plato's Theory of Dialectic." *New Scholasticism* 21 (1947): 192–211.

Gillespie, C. M. "The Truth of Protagoras." *Mind* 19 (1910): 470–92.

Glidden, David K. "Protagorean Relativism and Physis." *Phronesis* 22 (1977): 209–27.

Greene, William C. "The Spoken and the Written Word." *Harvard Studies in Classical Philology* 60 (1951): 23–59.

Grimaldi, William M. A. *Studies in the Philosophy of Aristotle's Rhetoric.* Wiesbaden: Franz Steiner Verlag GMBH, 1972.

Griswold, Charles. "Style and Philosophy: The Case of Plato's Dialogues." *Monist* 63 (January 1980): 530–46.

Grote, George. *A History of Greece From the Earliest Period to the Close of the Generation Contemporary with Alexander the Great.* 12 vols. London: John Murray, 1888.

Guthrie, W. K. C. *The Sophists*. Cambridge: Cambridge University Press, 1971.

Hagdopoulos, Demetrius. "Thrasymachus and Legalism." *Phronesis* 18 (1973): 204–8.

Hamilton, Edith, and Huntington Cairns, eds. *Collected Dialogues of Plato*. Princeton: Princeton University Press, 1973.

Hammond, Nicolas G. L. *A History of Greece to 322 B.C.* Oxford: Clarendon Press, 1963.

Harlap, Samuel. "Thrasymachus' Justice." *Political Theory* 7 (August 1979): 347–70.

Havelock, Eric A. *Preface to Plato*. Cambridge, Mass.: Harvard University Press, 1982.

_____. *The Liberal Temper in Greek Politics*. London: Jonathan Cape, 1957.

_____. *The Muse Learns to Write*. New Haven: Yale University Press, 1986.

_____. *The Literate Revolution and Its Cultural Consequences*. Princeton: Princeton University Press, 1982.

Hegel, G. F. *Lectures on the History of Philosophy*. 4 vols. Trans. E. S. Haldane. New York: Humanities Press, 1963.

Heilbrunn, Gunther. "Isocrates on Rhetoric and Power." *Hermes* 103, no. 2 (1975): 154–78.

Holland, R. F. "On Making Sense of a Philosophical Fragment." *Classical Quarterly* 6 (1956): 215–20.

Hudson-Williams, H. LL. "Political Speeches in Athens." *Classical Quarterly* 1 (1951): 68–73.

Hyland, Drew. "Why Plato Wrote Dialogues." *Philosophy and Rhetoric* 1 (1968): 38–50.

Isocrates. *Isocrates*. 3 vols. Trans. George Norlin and LaRue Van Hook. Cambridge, Mass.: Harvard University Press, 1968.

Jaeger, Werner. *Aristotle: Fundamentals of the History of His Development*. Trans. Richard Robinson. Oxford: Clarendon Press, 1934.

_____. *Paideia: The Ideals of Greek Culture*. 3 vols. Trans. Gilbert Highet. New York: Oxford University Press, 1970.

Jarratt, Susan C. *Rereading the Sophists: Classical Rhetoric Refigured*. Carbondale, Ill.: Southern Illinois University Press, 1991.

Jarrett, James. *The Educational Theories of the Sophists*. New York: Columbia University Teacher's College Press, 1969.

Jauss, Hans Robert. *Toward an Aesthetic of Reception*. Minneapolis: University of Minnesota Press, 1982.

Jebb, R. C. *The Attic Orators*. 2 vols. London: Macmillan, 1893.

Johnson, E. "Isocrates' Methods of Teaching." *American Journal of Philology* 80 (1953): 25–36.

Johnson, W. R. "Isocrates Flowering: The Rhetoric of Augustine." *Philosophy and Rhetoric* 9, no. 4 (1976): 217–31.

Johnstone, Christopher L. "An Aristotelian Trilogy: Ethics, Rhetoric, Politics, and the Search for Moral Truth." *Philosophy and Rhetoric* 13 (Winter 1980): 1–24.

Jowett, Benjamin. *The Dialogues of Plato.* New York: Random House, 1937.

Kelley, William G. "Rhetoric as Seduction." *Philosophy and Rhetoric* 6, no. 2 (Spring 1973): 69–80.

Kennedy, George A. "Isocrates' *Encomium of Helen:* A Panhellenic Document." *Transactions and Proceedings of the American Philological Association* 89 (1958): 77–83.

_____. "The Earliest Rhetorical Handbooks." *American Journal of Philology* 80 (1959): 169–78

_____. *The Art of Persuasion in Greece.* Princeton: Princeton University Press, 1963.

Kennyon, Frederic G. *Books and Readers in Ancient Greece and Rome.* Oxford: Clarendon Press, 1951.

Kerferd, George B. "Plato's Noble Art of Sophistry." *Classical Quarterly* 4 (1954): 84–90.

_____. "The Relativism of Prodicus." *Bulletin of John Rylands Library* 37 (1954–55): 249–58.

_____. "Plato's Account of the Relativism of Protagoras." *Durham University Journal* 42, no. 11 (1949): 20–26.

_____. "Protagoras' Doctrine of Justice and Virtue in the Protagoras of Plato." *Journal of Hellenic Studies* 73 (1953): 42–45.

_____. "Gorgias on Nature or That Which Is Not." *Phronesis* 1 (1955): 3–25.

_____. "The Moral and Political Doctrines of Antiphon the Sophist: A Reconsideration." *Proceedings of the Cambridge Philological Society* 184 (1956–1957): 26–32.

_____. "The Doctrine of Thrasymachus in Plato's *Republic.*" *Durham University Journal* 40 (1947): 19–27.

_____. "The First Greek Sophists." *Classical Review* 64 (1950): 8–10.

_____. *The Sophistic Movement.* Cambridge: Cambridge University Press, 1981.

_____. *The Sophists and Their Legacy.* Wiesbaden: Franz Steiner Verlag GMBH, 1981.

Krentz, Arthur A. "Dramatic Form and Philosophical Content in Plato's Dialogues." *Philosophy and Literature* 7, no. 1 (Spring 1983): 32–47.

Laistner, M. L. W. "The Influence of Isocrates' Political Doctrines on Fourth Century Men of Affairs." *Classical World* 23 (1930): 129–31.

Lang, Berel. "Presentation and Representation in Plato's Dialogues." *Philosophical Forum* 4 (Winter 1972–1973): 224–40.

Lentz, Tony M. "Writing as Sophistry: From Preservation to Persuasion." *Quarterly Journal of Speech* 68, no. 1 (February 1982): 60–68.

_____. *Orality and Literacy in Hellenic Greece*. Carbondale, Ill.: Southern Illinois University Press, 1989.

Levi, Adolfo. "The Ethical and Social Thought of Protagoras." *Mind* (1940): 284–302.

_____. "The Man-Measure Principle: Its Meaning and Applications." *Philosophy* 15 (1940): 147–67.

Lewes, George Henry. *The Biographical History of Philosophy From Its Origin in Greece Down to the Present Day*. New York: D. Appleton and Co., 1857.

Lienhard, Joseph T. "A Note on the Meaning of Pistis in Aristotle's Rhetoric." *American Journal of Philology* 87 (1966): 446–54.

Loenen, Dirk. *Protagoras and the Greek Community*. Amsterdam: N. V. Noord-Hollandsche Uitgevers Maatschappij, 1949.

Loreaux, Nicole. *The Invention of Athens: The Funeral Oration in the Classical City*. Trans. Alan Sheridan. Cambridge, Mass.: Harvard University Press, 1986.

MacDowell, Douglas M. *The Law in Classical Athens*. Ithaca, N.Y.: Cornell University Press, 1986.

Maguire, Joseph P. "Thrasymachus Or Plato?" *Phronesis* 16 (1971): 142–63.

_____. "Protagoras Or Plato?" *Phronesis* 18 (1973): 115–38.

_____. "Protagoras Or Plato? II." *Phronesis* 22 (1977): 103–22.

Marrou, Henri I. *A History of Education in Antiquity*. Trans. George Lamb. New York: Sheed and Ward, 1956.

McKeon, Richard. "Aristotle's Conception of Language and the Arts of Language." *Classical Philology* 41, no. 4 (October 1946): 193–206; and 42 (January 1947): 21–50.

Merlan, Philip. "Isocrates, Aristotle, and Alexander the Great." *Historica* 3 (1954–1955): 60–81.

Milne, Marjorie J. *A Study in Alcidamas and His Relation to Contemporary Sophistic*. Philadelphia: Westbrook Publishing Co., 1924.

Moore, J. M. *Aristotle and Xenophon on Democracy and Oligarchy*. Berkeley: University of California Press, 1975.

Morrison, J. S. "The Place of Protagoras in Athenian Public Life (460–415 B.C.)." *Classical Quarterly* 35 (1941): 1–16.

_____. "Antiphon." *Proceedings of the Cambridge Philological Society* 187 (1961): 49–58.

_____. "The Truth of Antiphon." *Phronesis* 8 (1963): 35–49.

Mortley, R. J. "Plato and the Sophistic Heritage of Protagoras." *Eranos* 67 (1969): 25–32.

Moss, Roger. "The Case for Sophistry." In *Rhetoric Revalued*, ed. Brian Vickers, 207–24. Binghampton, N.Y.: Center for Medieval and Early Renaissance Studies, 1982.

Moulton, Carroll. "Antiphon the Sophist *On Truth*." *Transactions and Proceedings of the American Philological Association* 103 (1972): 329–36.

Mulgan, R. G. "Lycophron and Greek Theories of Social Contract." *Journal of the History of Ideas* 40, no. 1 (1979): 121–28.

Murphy, Charles T. "Aristophanes and the Art of Rhetoric." *Harvard Studies in Classical Philology* 49 (1938): 69–113.

Navarre, Octave. *Essai sur la Rhétorique Grecque avant Aristote*. Paris: Librairie Hachette et Cie, 1900.

Nehamas, Alexander. "Eristic, Antilogic, Sophistic, Dialectic: Plato's Demarcation of Philosophy from Sophistry." *History of Philosophy Quarterly* 7, no. 1 (January 1990): 3–16.

Neserius, Philip George. "Isocrates' Political and Social Ideas." *International Journal of Ethics* 43 (1932): 307–28.

Nestle, Wilhelm. *Von Mythos zum Logos*. Aalen: Scientia Verlag, 1966.

Nietzsche, Friedrich. "Homer's Contest." In *Early Greek Philosophy and Other Essays*, trans. Maximillian A. Mugge. New York: Gordon Press, 1974.

_____. *The Gay Science*. Trans. Walter Kaufmann. New York: Random House, 1974.

_____. "Nietzsche Contra Wagner." In *The Portable Nietzsche*, trans. Walter Kaufmann. New York: Viking Press, 1971.

_____. *The Will to Power*. Trans. Walter Kaufmann and R. J. Hollingdale. New York: Vintage Books, 1968.

Ong, Walter. *Orality and Literacy*. New York: Methuen, 1982.

_____. *The Presence of the Word*. New Haven: Yale University Press, 1967.

Oscanyan, Frederick S. "On Six Definitions of the Sophist: Sophist 221c–231e." *Philosophical Forum* 4 (1973): 241–59.

Parker, Robert. "Greek States and Greek Oracles." In *CRUX: Essays in Greek History Presented to G. E. M. de Ste. Croix*, ed. P. A. Cartledge and F. D. Harvey. London: Duckworth and Co., 1985.

Partee, Morriss Henry. "Plato on the Rhetoric of Poetry." *Journal of Aesthetics Art Criticism* 33 (Winter 1974): 203–12.

Perleman, S. "Panhellenism, the Polis and Imperialism." *Historia* 15 (1976): 1–30.

Pfeiffer, Rudolf. *History of Classical Scholarship*. Oxford: Clarendon Press, 1968.

Picard, Charles. "Representations Antiques de l' Apologue dit de Prodicos." *Comptes Rendues de l' Academie des Inscriptions et Belles Lettres*. Paris: Librairies C. Klincksieck, 1951.

_____. "Nouvelles Remarques sur l' Apologue dit de Prodicos: Heracles entre le Vice et la Virtu." *Revue Archeologique* 42 (1953): 10–41.

Plato. *Statesman, Philebus*. Trans. H. N. Fowler. Cambridge, Mass.: Harvard University Press, 1925.

_____. *Lysis, Symposium, Gorgias*. Trans. W. R. M. Lamb. Cambridge, Mass.: Harvard University Press, 1975.

_____. *Euthyphro, Apology, Crito, Phaedo, Phaedrus*. Trans. H. N. Fowler. Cambridge, Mass.: Harvard University Press, 1933.

_____. *Republic*. Trans. Paul Shorey. Cambridge, Mass.: Harvard University Press, 1982.

_____. *Laws*. Trans. R. G. Bury. Cambridge, Mass.: Harvard University Press, 1967.

_____. *Theaetetus, Sophist*. Trans. H. N. Fowler. Cambridge, Mass.: Harvard University Press, 1961.

_____. *Laches, Protagoras, Meno, Euthydemus*. Trans. W. R. M. Lamb. Cambridge, Mass.: Harvard University Press, 1977.

_____. *Cratylus, Parmenides, Hippias Major, Hippias Minor*. Trans. H. N. Fowler. Cambridge, Mass.: Harvard University Press, 1926.

_____. *Charmides, Alcibiades I, II, Hipparchus, The Lovers, Theages, Minos, Epinomis*. Trans. W. R. M. Lamb. Cambridge, Mass.: Harvard University Press, 1964.

_____. *Timaeus, Critias, Cleitophon, Menexenus, Epistles*. Trans. R. G. Bury. Cambridge, Mass.: Harvard University Press, 1989.

Pohlenz, Max. "Tò πρέπον: ein Beitrag zur Geschichte des griechischen Geistes." *Nachrichten von der königlichen Gesellschaft der Wissenschaft zu Göttingen, Philologische-historische Klasse* (1933): 53–92.

Popper, Sir Karl R. *The Open Society and Its Enemies*. Vol. 1. Princeton: Princeton University Press, 1971.

Poulakos, John. "Toward a Sophistic Definition of Rhetoric." *Philosophy and Rhetoric* 16, no. 1 (February 1983): 35–48.

_____. "Rhetoric, the Sophists, and the Possible." *Communication Monographs* 51, no. 3 (September 1984): 215–26.

_____. "Gorgias' *Encomium to Helen* and the Defense of Rhetoric." *Rhetorica* 1, no. 2 (Autumn 1983): 1–16.

_____. "Aristotle's Indebtedness to the Sophists." In *Argument in Transition: Proceedings of the Third Summer Conference on Argumentation*, ed. David Zarefsky, Malcolm O. Sillars, and Jack Rhodes, 27–43. Annandale, Va.: Speech Communication Association, 1983.

_____. "Argument, Practicality, and Eloquence in Isocrates' *Helen*." *Rhetorica* 4, no. 1 (Winter 1986): 1–19.

_____. "Early Changes in Rhetorical Practice and Understanding: From the Sophists to Isocrates." *Texte: Revue de Critique et de Théorie Litteraire* 8/9 (1989): 307–24.

_____. "Interpreting Sophistical Rhetoric: A Response to Schiappa." *Philosophy and Rhetoric* 23, no. 3 (1990): 218–28.

Quimby, Rollin W. "The Growth of Plato's Perception of Rhetoric." *Philosophy and Rhetoric* 7 (1974): 71–79.

Rankin, H. D. *Sophists, Socratics and Cynics*. Totowa, N.J.: Barnes and Noble Books, 1983.

Reimer, Milton K. "The Subjectivism of the Sophists: A Problem of Identity." *Journal of Thought* 13 (January 1978): 50–54.

Rendall, Steven. "Dialogue, Philosophy and Rhetoric: The Example of Plato's *Gorgias.*" *Philosophy and Rhetoric* 10, no. 3 (Summer 1977): 165–79.

Ritter Michelle R. "In Search of the Real Protagoras." *Dialogue* 23 (April 1981): 58–65.

Robinson, Rachel Sargent. *Sources for the History of Greek Athletics.* Chicago: Ares Publishers, 1955.

de Romilly, Jacqueline. *Magic and Rhetoric in Ancient Greece.* Cambridge, Mass.: Harvard University Press, 1975.

Roseman, Norman. "Protagoras and the Foundations of His Educational Thought." *Pedagogica Historica* 11 (1971): 75–89.

Rosenmeyer, Thomas G. "Gorgias, Aeschylus, and *Apate.*" *Americal Journal of Philology* 76 (1955): 225–60.

Said, Edward W. *Beginnings: Invention and Method.* Baltimore: Johns Hopkins University Press, 1975.

Saunders, Trevor J. "Antiphon the Sophist on Natural Laws." *Proceedings of the Aristotelian Society* 78 (1977–1978): 215–36.

Schiller, F. C. S. *Studies in Humanism.* London: MacMillan and Co., 1912.

Sears, Lorenzo. *The History of Oratory from the Age of Pericles to the Present Time.* Chicago: Scott Foresman, 1897.

Seeskin, Kenneth. "Is the Apology of Socrates a Parody?" *Philosophy and Literature* 6, nos. 1–2 (1982): 94–105.

Segal, Charles P. "Gorgias and the Psychology of the Logos." *Harvard Studies in Classical Philology* 66 (1962): 99–155.

Sesonske, Alexander. "To Make the Weaker Argument Defeat the Stronger." *Journal of the Philosophy of History* 6, no. 3 (July 1968): 217–32.

Sheeks, Wayne. "Isocrates, Plato, and Xenophon Against the Sophists." *Personalist* 56 (1975): 250–53.

Sidgwick, Henry. "The Sophists." *Journal of Philology* 4 (1872): 288–307.

_____. "The Sophists—II." *Journal of Philology* 5 (1874): 66–80.

Sloterdijk, Peter. *Thinker on Stage: Nietzsche's Materialism.* Trans. Jamie Owen Daniel. Minneapolis: University of Minnesota Press, 1989.

Smith, Bromley. "Prodicus of Ceos: The Sire of Synonymy." *Quarterly Journal of Speech Education* 6 (1920): 51–68.

Solmsen, Friedrich. "The Aristotelian Tradition in Ancient Rhetoric." *American Journal of Philology* 62 (1941): 35–50.

_____. *Intellectual Experiments in the Greek Enlightenment.* Princeton: Princeton University Press, 1975.

Sprague, Rosamond K. *The Older Sophists.* Columbia, S.C.: University of South Carolina Press, 1972.

Stewart, M. A., and R. K. Sprague, "Plato's Sophistry I and II." *Aristotelian Society Proceedings* 51 (1977): 21–44 and 45–61.

Struever, Nancy. *The Language of History in the Renaissance*. Princeton: Princeton University Press, 1970.

Tarrant, Dorothy. "Plato as Dramatist." *Journal of Hellenic Studies* 75 (1955): 82–89.

Thomson, George. *Aeschylus and Athens: A Study in the Social Origins of Drama*. London: Lawrence & Wishart, 1980.

Thucydides. *History of the Peloponnesian War*. 4 vols. Trans. C. F. Smith. Cambridge, Mass.: Harvard University Press, 1969.

Untersteiner, Mario. *The Sophists*. Trans. Kathleen Freeman. New York: Philosophical Library, 1954.

Van Hook, LaRue. "Alcidamas versus Isocrates: The Spoken versus the Written Word." *Classical Weekly* 12 (1919): 89–94.

Vatai, Frank L. *Intellectuals in Politics in the Greek World*. London: Croom Helm, 1984.

Vernant, Jean-Pierre, and Pierre Vidal Naquet. *Myth and Tragedy in Ancient Greece*. Trans. Janet Lloyd. New York: Zone Books, 1990.

Vickers, Brian. *Rhetoric Revalued*. Binghampton, N.Y.: Center for Medieval and Early Renaissance Studies, 1982.

_____. *In Defence of Rhetoric*. Oxford: Clarendon Press, 1988.

Vollgraff, W. *L' Oraison Funèbre de Gorgias*. Leiden: E. J. Brill, 1952.

Weaver, Richard. *The Ethics of Rhetoric*. Chicago: Henry Regnery, 1953.

Walden, John W. H. *The Universities of Ancient Greece*. New York: Charles Scribner's Sons, 1909.

Welles, Bradford. "Isocrates' View of History." In *Classical Tradition: Literary and Historical Studies in Honor of Harry Caplan*, ed. L. Wallach, 3–25. Ithaca, N.Y.: Cornell University Press, 1966.

White, Eric C. *Kaironomia: On the Will-to-Invent*. Ithaca, N.Y.: Cornell University Press, 1987.

Wilcox, Stanley. "The Scope of Early Rhetorical Instruction." *Harvard Studies in Classical Philology* 53 (1942): 121–55.

_____. "Isocrates' Genera of Prose." *American Journal of Philology* 64 (1943): 427–31.

_____. "Criticisms of Isocrates and His Philosophy." *Transactions and Proceedings of the American Philological Association* 74 (1943): 113–33.

_____. "Isocrates' Fellow Rhetoricians." *American Journal of Philology* 66 (1945): 171–86.

Wilkerson, K. E. "From Hero to Citizen: Persuasion in Early Greece." *Philosophy and Rhetoric* 15, no. 2 (Spring 1972): 104–25.

Windelband, Wilhelm. *A History of Philosophy*. 2 vols. Trans. James H. Tufts. New York: Harper and Row, 1958.

Xenophon. *Memorabilia*. Trans. E. C. Marchant. New York: G. P. Putnam's Sons, 1923.

# Index

Abdera, 24
actual. *See* actuality
actuality, 67–71
Adcock, 48 n. 20
Aeschylus, 42
agonistics. *See* competition(s);
    contest(s)
Alcibiades, 109 n. 28, 111 n. 46
Alcidamas, 27, 63–64, 73 n. 21,
    147 n. 79
Alcmaeon, 144 n. 23
Alexander the Great, 49 n. 40
aliens, 16–17
Allison, 49 n. 35
Amphipolis, 146 n. 51
Anaxagoras, 122
Antigone, 112 n. 55
Antiphon, 24, 26, 42, 48 n. 27, 48 n.
    29, 90, 109 n. 27, 113, 141
Antisthenes, 183 n. 7
Anytus, 80
Apollo, 193
appropriateness. *See prepon,* proper
*aprepes,* 60–63, 134; *see also prepon*
Argos, 138
aristocracy, 12–15
Aristophanes, 19, 22, 42
Aristotle, 4, 9, 13, 28, 32, 38, 43, 45,
    46 n. 7, 47 n. 12, 47 n. 16, 48 n.
    32, 48 n. 34, 49 n. 38, 49 n. 40,
    49 n. 46, 77; on victory, 36; on
    epideictic rhetoric and delivery,
    41, 148 n. 79; his reception of the

sophists, 150–83; compared to
Plato and Isocrates, 150–6;
distinguishing sophists from
philosophers, 153, 161–65;
distinguishing orators from
philosophers, 154; comparing
political science with rhetoric,
154; distinguishing sophists from
dialecticians and eristics, 161–65;
on the beginnings of rhetoric,
156–57; attitude towards the
sophists, 157–60; his portrayal of
the sophists, 161–68
Athena, 120
Athens, 12, 16–17, 24, 51 n. 70,
    51 n. 71, 132, 138, 141, 146 n. 51

Baldry, 50 n. 63, 51 n. 70
Baldwin, 143 n. 2
Barnes, 184 n. 20
Barrett, 108 n. 25
Bayonas, 49 n. 42
Biesecker, 59, 72 n. 16
Blass, 73 n. 21
bricoleur, 25, 28–31
Brown, 73 n. 21
Bryson, 183 n. 7
Bury, 48 n. 20
Butcher, 147 n. 78
Butler, 39–40, 52 n. 73

Cairns, 112 n. 52
Callicles, 26, 28, 49 n. 45, 81, 83, 90,

215